Outstanding Books for the
COLLEGE BOUND

a *yalsa* publication

Outstanding Books for the
COLLEGE BOUND
Titles and Programs for a New Generation

EDITED BY ANGELA CARSTENSEN

AMERICAN LIBRARY ASSOCIATION
CHICAGO   2011

Angela Carstensen is head librarian at Convent of the Sacred Heart, a K–12 independent school for girls in New York City. An active member of YALSA since 2000, she served as the chair of the 2010 YALSA Award for Excellence in Nonfiction for Young Adults committee. She previously served for four years on the Alex Awards committee, and as chair in 2008.

Printed in the United States of America
15 14 13 12 11   5 4 3 2 1

While extensive effort has gone into ensuring the reliability of the information in this book, the publisher makes no warranty, express or implied, with respect to the material contained herein.

ISBNs: 978–0-8389-8570-0 (paper); 978-0-8389-9314-9 (PDF); 978-0-8389-9315-6 (ePub); 978-0-8389-9316-3 (Mobipocket); 978-0-8389-9317-0 (Kindle). For more information on digital formats, visit the ALA Store at www.alastore.ala.org and select eEditions.

Library of Congress Cataloging-in-Publication Data
    Outstanding books for the college bound : titles and programs for a new generation / edited by Angela Carstensen.
        p.   cm.
    "A YALSA publication."
    Includes bibliographical references and index.
    ISBN 978-0-8389-8570-0 (alk. paper)
    1. College students—Books and reading—United States. 2. Youth--Books and reading—United States. 3. Young adults' libraries—United States—Book lists. 4. Young adults' libraries—Activity programs—United States. 5. Best books—United States. I. Carstensen, Angela. II. Young Adult Library Services Association.
    Z1039.C65O9 2011
    028.5'35—dc22
                                                                        2011011853

Cover design by Karen Sheets de Gracia. Cover image © EDHAR/Shutterstock, Inc. Interior design in Liberation Serif and Miso by Casey Bayer.

⊗ This paper meets the requirements of ANSI/NISO Z39.48-1992 (Permanence of Paper).

CONTENTS

INTRODUCTION

ANGELA CARSTENSEN

A NEW, REVISED *Outstanding Books for the College Bound and Lifelong Learners* (OBCB) list is created every five years by a committee comprising public and school librarian members of the Young Adult Library Services Association (YALSA) and college librarian members of the Association of College and Research Libraries (ACRL).

The lists are "primarily intended for students in grades 9–12 who wish to enrich and strengthen their knowledge of various subject areas in both classic and contemporary literature," and the purpose of the list is to "provide reading recommendations to students of all ages who plan to continue their education beyond high school" (as stated in the OBCB Policies, included as an appendix to this volume). The lists also have a long history of appealing to adult lifelong learners, parents, teachers, administrators, and the librarians serving those constituencies.

Current criteria for choosing titles for the lists include readability, cultural and ethnic diversity, balance of viewpoints, variety of formats and genres, and title availability. Recently, the focus has been on a balance between "modern classic titles and those that are newer or speak to current events."

This book is a compilation of the Outstanding Books for the College Bound lists from the past ten years (1999, 2004, 2009), and highlights practical suggestions for using the lists.

Chapter 1 is the first history of the OBCB to be written and published. It demonstrates how the evolution of the OBCB has echoed (and at times contradicted) changes in the American educational system since its beginnings in 1959. This chapter answers the question: Who started the lists and why?

The following four chapters offer practical advice on using the lists with readers in school, public, and college libraries, with a chapter devoted to each, as well as a chapter devoted to lifelong learners. From collection development and readers' advisory to curriculum development and programming, the OBCB lists are relevant for librarians serving teens, young adults, and adult lifelong learners.

Each year, changes were made in the OBCB tradition. In 1999, the title of the lists was changed, adding "and Lifelong Learners" to its name. In 2004, ACRL members were included on the selection committee for the first time. As for the books themselves, a comparison of the 1999 and 2004 lists shows that starting in 2004 the focus shifted from tried-and-true classics to recent literature, or "modern classics."

The year 2004 also ushered in a new set of categories for the lists, created to mirror college curricula. In 1999 the five categories were fiction, nonfiction, biography, drama, and poetry. In 2004 they were changed to humanities, history, literature and language arts, science and technology, and social sciences. In 2009 the categories were updated to arts and humanities, history and cultures, literature and language arts, science and technology, and social sciences.

The introductions to the 2004 and 2009 lists are careful to state that the lists include a combination of fiction, nonfiction, poetry, biography, and drama, creating a conscious bridge to the past.

In the final section of this book, the 1999, 2004, and 2009 lists are combined and re-sorted by genre. It is fortuitous that these three lists incorporate the old and the new, the classic and the modern, creating genre lists with a broad range.

Annotations have been expanded to more adequately express the subject matter and importance of each title. Titles also honored by the YALSA Alex Awards, Best Books for Young Adults (BBYA), and Michael L. Printz Award committees are indicated. All publishers and publication dates are for the first edition, and any titles currently out of print are marked *o.p.*

As the *Outstanding Books for the College Bound and Lifelong Learners* tradition continues to help young students get the most out of their college education, to enhance the educational and cultural experiences of all readers, the tradition can never stop evolving. It will be exciting to witness where the OBCB lists might go from here, to continually reflect the times, the literature, and the librarians dedicated to their creation.

PART I

....

DEVELOPING AND USING THE LISTS

1

....

FORTY YEARS OF OUTSTANDING BOOKS

ORIGIN, HISTORY, AND COMMITTEE PROCESSES

PAULA BREHM-HEEGER

IN 1959 THE *National Education Association Journal* published the first installment of what would become the long-running Outstanding Books for the College Bound and Lifelong Learners lists. While the list was first published in the December 1959 issue of the *NEA Journal* as "Outstanding Fiction for College-Bound Students," it was actually compiled by the Book Selection Committee of the American Library Association's Young Adult Services Division (YASD). The original YASD selection committee was chaired by Marian L. Trahan from the Oakland Public Library and included a total of six members representing public libraries in Boston and Detroit, schools in New York and Connecticut, and one representative from the *ALA Booklist and Subscription Books Bulletin.* Of the many lists that have been produced on a regular and lasting basis by the Young Adult Library Services Association (formerly the Young Adult Services Division), the Outstanding Books for the College Bound list appears to be the only one that was created at the request of an outside group.

By the time the Outstanding Fiction for College-Bound Students list was published in 1959, there had been a long history of collaboration between the NEA and ALA dating back to the turn of the twentieth century. For example, in *Assessment of the Role of School and Public Libraries in Support of Educational Reform,* released by the U.S. Department of Education, it was noted that as early as 1897, the then ALA president John Cotton Dana "urged the National Education Association (NEA) to appoint a committee to study the interrelationships between the two organizations."[1] This report goes on to note that at that time few school libraries existed, and public libraries continued to "assume an educational role for almost forty years, supporting the needs of students and teachers."[2] Additional evidence of collaboration appears in the NEA's *Addresses and Proceedings* documents from the late 1950s. These documents include reports from a joint committee of the National Education Association and the American Library Association, whose function centered on "identifying problems of mutual interest and relationships in the field of library services and education, and of making recommendation for action on these problems to the appropriate units within the two associations."[3]

This committee's existence indicates that the NEA/ALA relationship was active and ongoing in the 1950s. Reports from this joint committee focus on general issues, including advocacy efforts aimed at legislation of interest to both associations and cooperative programs by the NEA at the annual ALA conferences. Both the 1958 and 1959 reports also mention several book selection and book recommendation activities by the ALA youth divisions, including the revision and publication of "Aids in Selection of Materials for Children and Young People" and arrangements for the *NEA Journal* to publish book lists and editorial reviews with the cooperation of YASD. It is worth noting that both the 1958 and 1959 reports indicate interest on the part of the NEA/ALA joint committee in cooperative programs focused on higher education.

This growing interest in higher education by both the NEA and ALA in the late 1950s is not surprising. In 1958, the United States Congress passed the landmark National Defense Education Act, and the number of students attending postsecondary degree–granting institutions had increased during the 1950s. In 1949 the total fall enrollment in degree-granting institutions was just under 2.5 million. By 1959 this figure had increased to more than 3.6 million—a more than one million student increase in a decade.[4] This increase is noteworthy, too, because prior to the passage of the act, financial support by the federal government for higher education had actually declined in the 1950s. This decline coincided with the completion by returning World War II servicemen of their postsecondary education. While the Servicemen's Readjustment Act of 1944 (the GI Bill) supported approximately one million veterans in the pursuit of higher education, this support peaked in 1949. When these GIs began to leave the ranks of college students in the early 1950s, overall federal government support for college attendance likewise decreased.[5]

When the Soviet Union launched their Sputnik satellite in 1957, however, everything changed. Once again, federal support for students seeking higher education began to increase. While the efforts for educational support of the kind provided by the 1958 National Defense Education Act had been gaining ground for several years, "the immediate catalyst for the legislation was the Soviet Union's launch of the Sputnik satellite in 1957, which directly challenged the scientific, technological, and military prowess of the United States."[6] Among its many provisions, the National Defense Education Act made "over the period of four years . . . available nearly a billion dollars for school improvement" and also made it possible for students to take loans for college education at subsidized rates with the intention to "increase the flow of talent into science, mathematics, and foreign language careers."[7]

A review of the articles appearing in the *NEA Journal* from 1958 to 1960 hints at the complex nature of the U.S. educational landscape in late 1950s and provides insight into the reasons the NEA turned to YASD's Book Selection Committee for the creation of the Outstanding Books for the College Bound (OBCB) book lists.

NEA Journal articles suggest increasing concerns about Soviet skills in science and technology. However, many articles also indicate a desire by educators to expand students' knowledge of culture and to support students' creativity in an era when science, math, and technology-related subjects were topping the nation's list of educational priorities.

Several writers in the *NEA Journal*, in fact, express their concern about the negative consequences for students subjected to a standard curriculum with such a specific focus. In his 1959 *NEA Journal* article "Hard Education?" Charles G. Spiegler relates a story about a public librarian desperately attempting to recruit young people for an after-school program taking place at the library focused on the history of jazz. Mr. Spiegler notes that, to his dismay, one after another of the students refused to attend, too focused on their extensive homework to participate. He articulates his concern that "we have begun . . . to harden the once-soft underbelly in our educational system by definite, absolute courses of study, strictly defined, strictly to be adhered to in a well-disciplined age of conformity. And yet, to my mind this isn't hard education at all! In fact, it's the easiest, softest, laziest type of education I know."[8] A similar theme can be found in an April 1959 article by Charles C. Cole Jr. In his article Cole discusses the need to ensure that the minds of new undergraduates are stretched, especially those of gifted and top-performing students. He expresses his concern that the current emphasis on standardized curriculum does not always do enough to hold the attention of students with exceptional abilities.[9]

NEA Journal writers for these years seem acutely aware of the opportunities and challenges presented by the increase in numbers and changing demographics of students seeking a college education. In an October 1958 article Walter Graves discusses these changes in the makeup of the student body, noting that, "For every student in college 50 years ago, there are now 11 jamming our college classrooms."[10] Graves also acknowledges the "greater heterogeneity" of college students.[11] In his October 1959 article Charles Spiegler argues that with millions of young Americans coming to college from various backgrounds, including less-intellectual backgrounds, "dare we, in a democracy, do less than send them back to their cultures somewhat better than we found them?"[12] And a March 1960 article echoes many of these themes by pointing out that the study of different cultures by girls pursuing higher education is "important in developing respect for the values and philosophies of other peoples" and that these college-bound girls are "intelligent, maturing young people who need challenge."[13]

Interestingly, while the ambivalence about the new focus on science and math education and the challenges and opportunities that resulted is obvious in the *NEA Journal*, a review of articles in the *Young Adult Services Division Journal* from the same era does not seem to reflect similar concerns. For example, the December 1959 issue features a "Recent Adult Books for Young People" book list and an article about a conference institute titled "Adults Books for YA Scene," but there is no specific mention of the Soviets, the Cold War, or a growing national focus on the need to improve science, math, and technology skills.

It is in this context, then, that the NEA turned to YASD to create the first OBCB list, and that the list focused, tellingly, on fiction, followed by biography and theater lists in the early 1960s, with no general nonfiction list produced until 1971. Even more telling, it wasn't until 2004—more than forty years after the initial OBCB list—that a science and technology list was even introduced to the OBCB series. Throughout the 1960s, the focus of the lists remained on fiction, biography, and theater. Even when the focus of the lists began to expand in the 1970s and 1980s the specific subject areas remained nonscientific and nontechnical, with topics such as dance, performing arts, poetry, and music—a stark contrast to the focus on science and technology evident in the *NEA Journal* articles of the late 1950s and 1960s.

· EVOLUTION AND CHANGE IN THE 1970S ·

The 1960s witnessed a remarkable increase in the number of people attending degree-granting institutions. By the fall of 1969, approximately eight million people were enrolled in postsecondary institutions—a more than twofold increase from the 3.6 million enrolled in the fall of 1959.[14] In 1965, the Higher Education Act was passed, representing the next major piece of federal legislation supporting higher education. It was also in 1965 that the *NEA Journal* published an Outstanding Books for the College Bound list for the final time. The Outstanding Theater for the College Bound list was featured in the *NEA Journal*'s October 1965 "Bookshelf" section.

By the time the OBCB list was set to be updated in the 1970s, the ownership of the list clearly belonged, then, to the YASD. Any mention of the NEA or the NEA's role in the creation of the list among the committee members selecting the OBCB titles is practically nonexistent in OBCB documents from the 1970s forward. However, it is worth noting that in an August 1971 committee correspondence, the idea is presented that "these lists are used for the most part (at least 90 percent of the 1000s sold) by high school English teachers and librarians in small to medium sized high schools" and that the style of annotations provided for the list should be made in light of what "might be more meaningful to that audience."[15] The NEA may no longer have been involved in the publication of the lists, but teachers and educators remained a primary audience for OBCB.

Prior to 1971 the lists had been produced one at a time and released at periodic but not regular intervals. In 1971 the concept to revise all the lists together was discussed, and the pattern of revising the OBCB list every five years seems to have been established at that time.[16] The 1971 committee began what would evolve into an ongoing discussion on many OBCB committees about what types of books should be included on the list. The available documents from 1971 do not include any official selection criteria. The statement is made that the list is "*not* a 'good read-ing' list" but a "strong survey list" designed to "give a readable, interesting, broad introduction to a field," and it is specifically noted that this list is different from the Best Books list (presumably a reference to the Best Books for Young Adults list).[17]

When the committee charged with producing the 1976 OBCB list began their work in 1974, demand for the OBCB list was strong. Correspondence from YASD president Carol Starr to OBCB committee chair Ruth Smith states that the OBCB lists "were among the most frequent requests the YASD office receives."[18] This popularity was likely a significant factor in the decision to continue to update the lists on a regular basis.

The 1976 committee appears to have been one of the most active OBCB com-mittees. The 1970s were a time of great change and transition for higher education, and it makes sense that the committee working in the middle of this decade would likewise be interested in updating and changing the makeup of the OBCB list. At the beginning of the 1970s, 2,384,000 students in postsecondary degree–granting institutions were age 25 years and older. By 1980 this number had increased to 4,535,000.[19] In 1970, 3,537,000 students entering degree-granting institutions were female. By 1980 this number had risen to 6,223,000. The ethnic makeup of higher education students was changing, too. In 1976, 82.6 percent of students were white and 15.4 percent were minority. By 1980, this had changed to 81.4 percent white and 16.1 percent minority. During the overall 1976–2008 time period, the percentage of Hispanic students rose from 3 percent to 12 percent, the percentage of Asian/Pacific Islander students rose from 2 percent to 7 percent, and the percentage of black students rose from 9 percent to 14 percent.[20]

It was in this historical context that the 1976 OBCB committee began their work. The July 1974 letter inviting committee members to serve on the OBCB Revision Committee included a very basic function statement "to revise the 5 'outstanding' lists published for ALA for young adults for completion in 1975."[21] In a September communication to her committee, Chair Ruth Smith set out basic suggestions for how the work of the committee should be accomplished. In October she offered detailed suggestions of how committee members could locate potential titles for the list. This October communication included a suggestion to consider ways that ALA's Association of College and Research Libraries division publications might be a resource for finding titles for consideration—an important and insightful suggestion on the part of Smith, as in later years ACRL would be asked to take a direct role in the production of the OBCB list.

The question of how to best define an outstanding book is discussed at length in committee correspondence in 1974. Smith attempts to answer the question with assistance from YASD president Carol Starr. This discussion includes one of the few mentions of the NEA's role in the creation of the OBCB by any OBCB committee; Smith relates that Starr informed her, "the ideas originated with the National Education Association for the purpose of providing the college bound with material they 'should have read' when they finish high school."[22] Smith's dissatisfaction with this explanation is clear as she poses the rhetorical question to her committee, "How's that for an ambiguous statement?" Smith does provide some additional detail about the evolving definition of an "outstanding book" by stating in one letter that these are books that should be "important titles which presumably will stand the test of time because they are concerned with fundamentals rather than fads."[23] This ongoing discussion leads Smith to suggest to her committee that they "formulate a set of criteria on which we can agree and submit them to YASD for approval."[24]

The 1976 committee also clearly struggled with another issue that has probably become a familiar conundrum for OBCB committee members over the years: how to effectively gather potential titles. Unlike other YASD/YALSA book lists and awards, titles that can be considered for the OBCB lists were not (and continue not to be) bound by format or publication date. This issue, combined with questions about how best to define *outstanding*, led the 1976 committee to discuss several changes to the list, including format, number of titles, and scope.

Minutes from the 1975 ALA Midwinter Meeting include a series of questions about the lists asked by the committee, such as, "Can we redo them as we see fit?

Why is there no creative writing list? Why is nonfiction except biography and theater all lumped together? Why not a list of 'The Arts'? Why not a list or lists of 150–200 titles of basic books? Can the content of the books determine the number and type of lists?"[25] With no overview or history of the NEA's involvement in the creation of the lists and no historical context for understanding the reasons the subject areas were selected for previous OBCB lists, the 1976 committee suggested significant revisions to OBCB. The 1976 committee would not be the first to consider revising the list's format and topics. Nor would they be the first group to express concern about retaining "Outstanding Books for the College Bound" as the list title.

The 1976 committee provided a plan to overhaul the list, along with specific selection criteria developed for each of what they proposed to be four new lists. They suggested the following statement of purpose for the OBCB committee be officially adopted by the YASD board of directors: "These lists offer the thoughtful student a careful selection of those ageless and contemporary books that encompass the ideas, experience and discoveries which have made significant contributions to human knowledge. Reading these books will promote the self-growth and openness of ideas necessary to develop a creative and evaluative mind."[26]

The changes suggested by the committee were not, however, approved by the YASD board of directors. In a letter to her committee and to YASD president Carol Starr, Smith communicates the rejection of the committee's plans and instructs her committee to "proceed with our assignment by following the original format . . . retain the original five categories and make the additions and deletions which will bring them up to date."[27] While Smith's committee failed to enact changes during their tenure, they did submit a formal committee report at the 1975 annual conference restating their proposed changes and asking that they be enacted before the next release of an OBCB list.[28]

One other noteworthy development during the tenure of the committee that produced the 1976 OBCB list was a January 1975 *Library Journal* article discussing the updating of the OBCB list. This article stated, "Librarians and publishers both will be waiting to see the result of the updating project, which is being carried on at a time when unprecedented heavy pressures for the restriction of the reading of young people are being mounted evidently with the backing of the United States Commissioner of Education Terrel Bell."[29] After the publication of this *Library Journal* article, Ruth Smith received a letter from a concerned mother of a 13-year-old in New Jersey. This mother wrote to express her belief in *not* restricting reading for young people.[30] In response to the letter, the executive director of YASD wrote to the New Jersey mother and assured her that "'hostile pressure' will not affect the revisions of these lists" and that the development of the lists "help librarians who are trying to withstand pressure from adults trying to restrict the reading of teenagers."[31]

· 1980S ·

The work of Ruth Smith and her innovative 1976 committee appears to have prompted a fresh look at the Outstanding Books for the College Bound list. At the 1979 ALA Midwinter Meeting the YASD board authorized the formation of a new committee to begin revising the OBCB list. The function statement for this 1980 committee was "To revise the YASD 'Outstanding Fiction for the College Bound' list. To establish criteria for the selection and procedural guidelines for the list. To examine procedures and make recommendations related to the future production of the entire set of Outstanding lists, including consideration of a name change."[32]

Despite a clear interest in having the committee members revise elements of the list beyond the traditional work of adding and eliminating titles, OBCB committees during the 1980s continued to follow one traditional procedure for creating the list. While the entire list with its separate topic areas was referred to collectively as Outstanding Books for the College Bound, and all titles were released at the same time, selection for the titles in each of the four or five topic areas was accomplished by separate committees, with each committee having a different chairperson. These individual committees had similar but independent selection criteria that they were instructed to "develop carefully and with thought."[33] The individual topic-area lists were given titles that included the topic in the title name such as Outstanding Fiction for the College Bound and Outstanding Biographies for the College Bound. This was the procedure for the 1986 committee, which, like previous committees, had individuals appointed to work on each topic-area list, and each topic area was chaired by an individual with one person acting as the coordinator of the other chairs and committees to ensure that the final list was submitted in the proper format. However, it was during the 1986 committee's tenure that this tradition began to change. That committee made the recommendation "to prepare Outstanding Books for the College Bound as a single work that combines separate lists"—a recommendation that was enthusiastically received by YASD's publishing staff.[34]

This 1986 OBCB committee began their work facing questions that had plagued earlier committees. Communication from the 1986 committee indicates that the number of titles to be included in the overall list, as well as the specific criteria for selection titles, was still up for debate. For example, Mary Ann Paulin, chair of that year's Outstanding Biographies for the College Bound list, asked in one memo, "Are we limited in numbers to the titles that will fit on a trifold, the old format?" and in the same memo wondered "how much emphasis will be given to balancing the lists and to choosing books readable by students."[35] Paulin also suggested a set of specific criteria be used in selecting titles, including "accuracy, objectivity, credibility, believability and literary quality."[36]

A July 1985 letter from OBCB Fiction Committee chair Leslie Edmonds states that while she did speak with YASD executive director Evelyn Shaevel and "other chairs of other committees" about the list and the work of the committee, there remained "many unanswered questions" regarding the format and the topics on which the OBCB list should focus.[37] The ongoing questions about selection criteria are addressed in Edmonds's letters to her committee, and she does recommend that specific criteria such as literary merit, readability, and balance of types of fiction be used.[38]

One additional criterion Edmonds mentions in her communications regarding selection of titles is "titles from 1980 to present need to be added."[39] The inclusion of this statement indicates that the apparent long-running tradition of viewing the OBCB list as an update appears to have continued throughout the 1980s. During this era the OBCB committee continued to be referred to as the Outstanding Books for the College Bound *Revision* Committee.

· 1990S ·

The OBCB committees worked throughout 1990s to expand the kinds of titles and subjects that were included in the OBCB lists. They may have, as Paulin suggested in her 1986 communication, been looking to increase the readability of titles and interest of students in topics on the list. Topics such as film and music appeared. Committee correspondence from this decade focuses heavily on discussions of specific titles and was less concerned with defining what exactly qualifies as an outstanding book. Questions and comments related to criteria still do appear, however, such as a May 1990 comment by one committee member about a title: "I'm not sure it will stand up over time as a book to be read over and over again."[40] Communication from the January 1989 Midwinter Meeting of the Outstanding Nonfiction for the College Bound Committee reinforces that the question of selection criteria was still being discussed as "establish criteria for the list" is the first item on the committee's Midwinter agenda. The idea that the list remains a "revision" of earlier OBCB lists is also evident, as multiple discussions about the "elimination of some titles" and the need to "determine titles to retain from previous list"[41] appear in committee communications from the early 1990s.

The committees of the early 1990s clearly struggled with the "many questions about the ground rules for the compilation of the lists."[42] It is not surprising then that in 1994 the first documented Guidelines for Outstanding Books for the College Bound were established. This signaled an end to much of the confusion and concern about criteria and committee procedure. These guidelines codified the informal procedures which had been used by various OBCB committees for several decades. The guidelines included a clear charge and purpose for the committee and defined the target audience as well as guidelines for title eligibility and committee voting and selection procedures.

· RECENT CHANGES ·

The eve of the twenty-first century brought two significant changes to the OBCB committee and list. First, 1999 is the first year the list was published under its new name, "Outstanding Books for the College Bound and Lifelong Learners." The inclusion of "lifelong learners" in the list name is not surprising, as by fall 2000 nearly six million people older than the age of 25 were enrolled in degree-granting institutions, with 2,749,000 of these students actually being more than 35 years old.[43] This trend in the diversity of students shows no sign of changing as projections for 2012 are that more than seven million students will be more than 25 years old and more than three million will be over the age of 35, making lifelong learners a growing audience for this particular YALSA selection list.[44] The second significant change in 1999 was that, for the first time, the committee included members from ACRL. This experiment in making the OBCB list a joint production of YALSA and ACRL has continued to evolve with the 2004 and 2009 committees. In the 2004

ALA Midwinter Meeting postconference report, OBCB chair Mary Arnold notes that both she and the individual from ACRL acting as the ACRL liaison for the committee believed that future ACRL recruits for the OBCB committee "need more information about the selection committee procedures and time commitment."[45] This issue was addressed by the 2009 committee by having a limited number of ACRL committee members involved. This targeted ACRL involvement allowed the YALSA members, many of whom have experience in selecting nontextbook titles for inclusion on book lists designed for a general audience, the chance to work in a focused manner on gathering input from ACRL without losing focus on the nature of the OBCB list.

The 2004 OBCB committee made a significant change to the list format. This committee abandoned the traditional format, more than four decades old, of using specific topic headings such as biography and fiction in favor of more general, liberal-arts-based topics such as history, science and technology, and literature and languages. Committee reports from 2004 indicate an interest in shifting toward academic categories with "scope and criteria statements based on academic standards."[46] The driving force behind this change to the list was, in the words of 2004 OBCB chair Mary Arnold, "the unique makeup of the committee."[47] According to Arnold, 2004 YALSA president Caryn Sipos was focused on creating a new, meaningful partnership between ACRL and YALSA, and the inclusion of ACRL members on the OBCB committee was part of this focus. When it came to the list format, Arnold reports that "it was the academic librarians who pushed to change the sections to closer resemble college department tracks . . . as an ancillary result, since ACRL members are much more likely to read and recommend nonfiction, we ended up with a heavily nonfiction list as well!"[48] The format change proved to be a success, and the most recent 2009 OBCB list follows this new, updated format.

The latest iteration of the OBCB list demonstrates that this long-running list is one of the most durable, flexible lists offered by YALSA. It has been examined and reinvented by decades of dedicated committee members, and the result of this hard work continues to keep the OBCB in demand and relevant to today's college students and lifelong learners. While they would likely be thrilled to know that individuals seeking postsecondary education of any sort are still using the OBCB, one can't help but wonder what the OBCB founders would think of the changes to the list and the most current version. Would they be surprised? Would they approve of the changes? Or would they simply be happy to learn that students still read and librarians still work diligently to connect these students to just the right resources to help them succeed in college and in life?

· NOTES ·

1. Shirley A. Fitzgibbons, "School and Public Library Relationships: Essential Ingredients in Implementing Educational Reforms and Improving Student Learning," 2000, www.ala.org/ala/mgrps/divs/aasl/aaslpubsandjournals/slmrb/slmrcontents/volume32000/relationships.cfm. Printed with permission from the U.S. Department of Education.
2. Ibid.

3. National Education Association, Joint Committee of the National Education Association and the American Library Association, *Addresses and Proceedings of the Ninety-sixth Annual Meeting Held at Cleveland, Ohio,* 96 (June/July 1958): 338.

4. National Center for Education Statistics, "Table 189: Total fall enrollment in degree-granting institutions by attendance status, sex of student and control of institution: Selected years, 1947 through 2008." *Digest of Education Statistics,* http://nces.ed.gov/programs/digest/d09/tables/dt09_189.asp.

5. "Federal Funds for Higher Education," *Encyclopedia of Education 2002,* Gale U.S. History in Context.

6. Pamela Ebert Lattau, project leader, with Jerome Bracken, Richard Van Atta, Ayeh Bandeh-Ahmadi, Rodolfo de la Cruz, and Kay Sullivan, "The National Defense Education Act of 1958: Selected Outcomes," March 2006, https://www.ida.org/upload/stpi/pdfs/ida-d-3306.pdf.

7. "An NEA Year to Remember: 1958," *NEA Journal* 48, no. 1 (January 1959): 68.

8. Charles G. Spiegler, "Hard Education?" *NEA Journal* 48, no. 7 (October 1959): 39.

9. Charles C. Cole Jr., "Flexible College Curriculums," *NEA Journal* 48, no. 4 (April 1959): 47–48.

10. Walter Graves, "Today's College Student," *NEA Journal* 47, no. 7 (October 1958): 498.

11. Ibid., 498.

12. Spiegler, 39.

13. Ruth Wheeler, "Home Economics for College-Bound Girls," *NEA Journal* 49, no. 3 (March 1960): 19.

14. National Center for Education Statistics, "Table 189."

15. Jane Manthone to Andrea L. Balcken, Aug. 6, 1971.

16. Andrea L. Balcken to Rosemary Young, May 6, 1971.

17. Ibid.

18. Carol Starr to Ruth Smith, Aug. 20, 1974.

19. National Center for Education Statistics, "Table 190: Total fall enrollment in degree-granting institutions, by sex, age, and attendance status: Selected years, 1970 through 2017," *Digest of Education Statstics,* http://nces.ed.gov/programs/digest/d08/tables/dt08_190.asp.

20. National Center for Education Statistics, "Fast Facts: Question: Do you have information on college enrollment?" http://nces.ed.gov/fastfacts/display.asp?id=98.

21. Mary Jane Anderson to Outstanding Books for the College Bound committee members, July 31, 1974.

22. Ruth Smith to Merry Ann Mickelson, Nov. 4, 1974.

23. Ruth Smith to Professor May Benne, Nov. 26, 1974.

24. Smith to Mickelson, Nov. 4, 1974.

25. Marion Hargrove (recorder), Minutes of Outstanding Lists, Revision Committee, ALA Midwinter Meeting, Jan. 20, 1975.

26. Jana Varlejs (recorder), ALA Midwinter Meeting, 1975.

27. Ruth Smith to YASD president and Outstanding Books for the College Bound committee, Jan. 25, 1975.

28. Ruth Smith, Report for Outstanding Lists Revision Committee (ad hoc), June 20, 1975.

29. "Books for the College Bound: Aid in Updating the Lists Asked," *Library Journal* (Jan. 15, 1975): 84.

30. Holly Lucas to Ruth Smith, March 14, 1975.

31. Mary Jane Anderson to Holly Lucas, April 15, 1975.

32. Evelyn Shaevel to Dona Helmer, Feb. 20, 1979.

33. Evelyn Shaevel to Outstanding Books for the College Bound committee chairs, March 26, 1985.

34. Evelyn Shaevel to Herb Bloom, April 24, 1985.

35. Mary Ann Paulin to Outstanding Books for the College Bound committee chairs, [1986].

36. Mary Ann Paulin to Outstanding Biographies for the College Bound committee members, [January 1985].

37. Leslie Edmonds to Outstanding Fiction Committee, July 12, 1985.
38. Ibid.
39. Ibid.
40. Dolores Maminski to Lucy Marx, May 11, 1990.
41. Mary Huebscher to Lucy Marx, Dec. 14, 1989; Outstanding Books for the College Bound: Nonfiction Agenda for Midwinter Meeting, 1990.
42. Elizabeth M. O'Donnell to Susan K. Horiuchi, Dec. 12, 1989.
43. National Center for Education Statistics, "Table 190."
44. Ibid.
45. Mary Arnold, Outstanding Books for the College Bound Postconference Report, Jan. 30, 2004.
46. Mary Arnold, Outstanding Books for the College Bound Conference Report, [2003].
47. Mary Arnold, e-mail to author, Nov. 28, 2010.
48. Ibid.

2

....

OUTSTANDING BOOKS AND PUBLIC LIBRARIES
THE LIST AS MERCHANDISING TOOL

MARY ARNOLD

The fact of knowing how to read is nothing, the
whole point is knowing what to read.
—Jacques Ellul

WHILE THE Outstanding Books for the College Bound and Lifelong Learners list has been a valuable addition to the librarians' toolbox for more than half a century, tools must be used to be effective. Rapid developments in technology offer many new merchandising and marketing variations on the tried and true avenues of booktalking, displays, programs, and readers' advisory. Let's look at ways in which we can capitalize on traditional and innovative library reading connections for college-bound students (and everyone interested in learning and examining new thoughts and ideas) using recent Outstanding Books for the College Bound lists to meet "needs" and create "wants." These outstanding books can help us create an atmosphere that encourages building a community of committed readers eager to share reading responses to new ideas.

YALSA selection lists have long been a staple tool for library collection development, and the annotated OBCB list, updated every five years, is especially useful in highlighting recent titles that selectors may have missed. School librarians mention that the rigorous committee selection process plays a big part in teachers' willingness to adopt subject-related books from the OBCB lists. OBCB plays a unique role in that its usefulness extends to many potential audiences—students, parents, educators, and anyone interested in continued learning and intellectual growth. Readers employ book lists to help them focus interest and choose from the plethora of titles in print, and compilers of book lists hope to influence readers to read specific books. Think of the appeal of Web 2.0 reading websites like Goodreads, Shelfari, and LibraryThing, or the reader-created Listmania book lists on Amazon. Many librarians become reading partners and use these networks as a virtual readers' advisory perch, creating sites like the NEO-RLS Teen Learning Group on Goodreads, where teen librarians from library systems in northeast Ohio share reading suggestions with the world—a great forum to acquaint avid readers with the OBCB tool. Librarians can set up a Goodreads account and form a group with a title that becomes a hub for others to join, then recommend and discuss titles from OBCB lists.

· READERS' ADVISORY ·

Librarians have shared the list with schools that have used it as the basis for summer reading suggestions. Barbara Ruszkowski, librarian at Padua Academy in Delaware, created a summer reading assignment using the 2009 list, which provides a wide variety of reading choices. And as teen librarians well know, that element of choice is all important. Student readers shared reviews of their chosen books that included discussion of readability and interest levels, ease of use, logic of organization, and special features—not unlike the committee considerations for nonfiction titles! Students were also asked to evaluate how reading the book might influence their lives—certainly a prime objective of OBCB committee members as well. Padua teachers particularly recommended titles aimed at adult readers in science, math, and technology, and because the list provides annotations, teachers, students, and parents are easily able to determine the appeal of a book.

There is a growing community of homeschooled students at the high school level, and a variety of online schools, whose families utilize public library resources. Introduce the OBCB lists to parent-educators and administrators for homeschooling associations and virtual academies. Many of these organizations ask to use library meeting space to conduct mandated standardized testing, providing a built-in audience for a quick set of OBCB booktalks to welcome them to the library.

Public librarians are often the first port of call in the college search. While information about college majors, facilities, scholarship opportunities, and the like are crucial, preparing students for the level of reading comprehension that college-level study requires is something we are uniquely prepared to do. Both the 2004 and 2009 lists create reading categories based on college departments of study, so students can get a taste of reading in their chosen area of study and gain a critical understanding of differing viewpoints on issues and ideas. Share the recent OBCB lists with community partners like the Cleveland Scholarship Center (www.cspohio .org), which partners with local county public libraries for events like FAFSA Super Sunday in February. Get lists (and YALSA website links) into the hands of high school guidance counselors and literature and language arts departments. Include a link to the YALSA selection list page from the section of your library's website on the college search process, and highlight one of the annotated titles (don't forget a graphic of the book cover!). Make note of the fact that the books on these lists will also improve vocabulary, which helps those taking the SAT and ACT tests, as well as those writing well-crafted college application essays. Reading a variety of books in various subject areas also introduces students to terms that apply to a particular field of study.

John Briggs, a member of the College Board SAT Reading Development Committee, believes "students need to discover that there are books that our culture has kept as a legacy and these should not be forgotten."[1] The 2004 OBCB committee press release recognized such legacy books by explaining why classics like *To Kill a Mockingbird* were not included on this list. It then pointed to other reading tools of great value in finding those classic titles, particularly fiction, that appear on so many lists of great books and recommended reading, from the National Book Awards and Pulitzer Prizes to the Modern Library Association's 100 Best Novels list.

Many public libraries offer the NoveList Plus database as a readers' advisory tool for customers, and guess what's available through NoveList—the most recent OBCB lists! Show readers how to customize their own college-bound reading by creating folders for annotated titles and how to use the various NoveList custom features to locate additional high-quality reading.

Take books from the list to local schools' college information events to decorate your table or booth, with a copy of the entire list as a bookmark. As you share the many library resources available to aid in the college-application process, throw in a few short book blurbs for the titles you've brought along. Create a scrolling PowerPoint display on a laptop that includes information on the rich resources on the OBCB list, and look for a way to let interested students and parents check out a title right then and there.

Many librarians host book groups in the library or at other community locations, including schools, recreation centers, senior centers, and others. Annotated OBCB lists are a wonderful resource to help book groups to choose titles that may have flown under their radar and can be a new way to host a "Great Books" book group. For many of the OBCB titles, there are ready-made book discussion suggestions on publisher websites, ReadingGroupGuides.com, Litlovers.com, Bookspot.com, and others. The marvel of Skype makes a virtual author visit a possible OBCB-related program that would enhance a book group experience, allowing readers to interact with an author, express their own responses to the book, and ask questions. Or partner with a school librarian for a series of enrichment programs and activities around titles on the OBCB lists that could include Skype interactive author visits.

At Cuyahoga County Public Library (www.cuyahogalibrary.org), a committee of library staff from every age-specific service area highlights under-the-radar titles on the library catalog page. A feature like this on your library's website could easily encompass OBCB categories like social sciences, science and technology, or history and cultures, particularly timed to the college application cycle. Readers could mouse over the book cover for title and author and OBCB list year, click to open the catalog record with full annotation, reserve the book, and check out the cloud tag "OBCB" for additional titles in the library catalog. For some books, readers could choose to listen to a podcast booktalk that gives library staff the chance to "build a buzz" for great college-bound reading. Podcasts can be created and linked to any catalog record, so every OBCB book can get its own commercial! You could even create a hot link from the catalog record and from any auxiliary library teen or college/career web pages to the online list at the YALSA website.

In addition to staff recommendations for OBCB titles, let readers get into the act. "Patron buzz" makes the library interactive and participatory. Web 2.0 applications allow library staff and readers to create categories for readers' advisory by "tagging" OBCB titles by specific category of interest (drama/poetry/biography/history and cultures) or in general ("Great reads if you're college bound" or "Never stop learning and growing").

· BOOKTALKS ·

Booktalking has a proven track record as an effective way to highlight good reading and connect readers with books they may otherwise miss. While school classrooms are a no-brainer for finding a ready student audience, we know there are other audiences to be mined. And you don't necessarily have to start from scratch. That's the great benefit of professional online networks, websites, and a variety of publications that provide the basis of an effective, exciting booktalk for many of the titles on the recent OBCB lists. One such title with a novel multimedia approach that appeals to today's young readers is *Booktalking Bonanza: Ten Ready-to-Use Multimedia Sessions for the Busy Librarian* by Betsy Diamant-Cohen and Selma K. Levi. The techniques for sharing the excitement of a book can be readily adapted to OBCB titles like M. T. Anderson's *Feed*, Sara Gruen's *Water for Elephants*, or Ishmael Beah's *Long Way Gone: Memoirs of a Boy Soldier*. Offer regular booktalk programs at a local senior center, or booktalk a selected OBCB title when you represent the library at your community Chamber of Commerce, school board, or city council meeting.

Online book trailers have become the librarian's best trick for using social media to promote great reading. Libraries have built teen programs around creating these two-minute book commercials and uploading them to YouTube and other media websites. YALSA's Teens and Technology Interest Group program "Lights! Cameras! Booktrailers!" presentation at ALA Annual Conference 2010 showcased a panel of authors and librarians who have successfully used book trailer contests to meld teen interests in reading and technology.[2] Software like Photo Story or Movie Maker allows you to create, add images (from sources like creativecommons.org, Wikimedia.org, or loc.gov, the Library of Congress website), edit, and add special effects. Using flip cameras is fun and easy, as demonstrated on this site, which also includes lots of suggestions for storyboarding techniques and sites for free downloads: http://sites.google.com/site/flipworkshop/home/video-book-trailers/creating-a-book-trailer.

In "Digital Booktalk: Digital Media for Reluctant Readers," Gunter and Kenny emphasize the importance of making meaningful reading connections with our younger digital-native customers. They believe that while story remains the core of both traditional print and digital media, technology is changing and broadening the definition of literacy and how students acquire reading and writing skills. They encourage educators to explore mediated instructional strategies using technologies like the Digital Booktalk web portal to motivate and match readers, especially reluctant or struggling readers, with books.[3]

Ever see digital photo frames used at strategic locations in the library, like at the circ desk, fiction area, teen area, or shelving range for college-related materials? Using Microsoft Publisher or PowerPoint, you can create postcard OBCB book ads as JPEGs and present a slideshow of good reading to catch customers' attention. "Always be selling" doesn't apply only to retail! "Read Me" shelf talkers (use colorful paper and the marvelous annotations created by OBCB members) call attention in the stacks to titles from the list and are a quick and easy merchandising tool.

· SOCIAL NETWORKING ·

Do you blog at your library website? Be sure to blog OBCB titles! Feature a selection of books from the humanities, social sciences, and history and cultures, and be sure instructors at your local high schools, junior colleges, and universities are aware of the uniquely useful arrangement of categories for the 2004 and 2009 lists based on academic disciplines. An added bonus is that these titles are, for the most part, recently published, include a great deal of nonfiction, and tend not to duplicate "classic" reading widely promoted in other recommended reading lists.

   If your library has an institutional presence on social networking sites like Facebook or Twitter, use them to promote OBCB. Your Facebook wall is a great bulletin board for recommending good reading. If you tweet about library programs and activities, promote a different area of OBCB reading each month.

· DISPLAYS ·

OBCB lists lend themselves wonderfully to thematic displays. It's recommended that you re-create the bookstore style of reading abundance with multiple copies of titles and eye-catching realia and props (fall back-to-school displays using OBCB titles might include swaths of colorful artificial leaves, a variety of baskets, perhaps a colorful fall-themed cloth, and, of course, your harvest of good reading).

   Library displays traditionally build around special days or times of year—be sure to include OBCB titles in every display you create. *Chase's Calendar of Events* offers ideas for celebrating enrichment reading every month:

   January—Book Blitz
   February—Library Lover's Month
   March—International Ideas Month
   April—National Poetry Month and National Library Month
   May—Creative Beginnings Month
   June—Bathroom Reading Month
   July—Social Wellness Month
   August—American Adventures Month
   September—Banned Books Week and Library Card Sign-Up Month
   October—Right-Brainer's Rule Month and Go on a Field Trip Month
   November—Inspirational Role Models Month
   December—Spiritual Literacy Month

· PROGRAMMING ·

When librarians plan programs and activities of interest to their local communities, we always include displays about and information on library resources related to the program topic. Try some of the following ideas in your community.

   In conjunction with local college information nights, the library could host a "campus life" panel of college freshmen sharing their real-life experience in a college classroom and dorm, discussing the kinds of supplemental reading that actually appear on a college syllabus, and talking about how reading titles from recommended lists like OBCB can be a practical way to prepare for the rigors of college-level reading. Teen librarians can then offer traditional booktalks, podcasts, and links to online book trailers for titles from the most recent OBCB lists.

What about hosting a program highlighting titles from a particular academic discipline? Invite a professor from a local college to speak on his or her field—an art professor could talk about college art courses while the librarian booktalks Carmen Bernier-Grand's *Frida: Viva la Vida! Long Live Life!* (Marshall Cavendish, 2007). In twenty-six original free-verse poems, the author depicts the thoughts, feelings, and life events of Mexican self-portraitist Frida Kahlo. The poems are accompanied by twenty-four full-color reproductions of Kahlo's paintings.

A sociology professor's discussion could be supplemented by Jared Diamond's *Collapse: How Societies Choose to Fail or Succeed.* What do the lack of Icelandic fisherman, the 2008 Chinese Olympics, and Easter Island tree cutters all have in common? Much more than you might think. *Collapse* explores the political, technological, and ecological decisions that merge in order to sustain or destroy societies.

Promote environmental science with Richard Preston's *The Wild Trees: A Story of Passion and Daring.* Three buddies on spring break climb into a California redwood and discover a new ecosystem atop the trees. Join this group of young scientists in the canopy as they learn safe climbing techniques for the oldest and tallest trees of North America and encounter new species of plants, animals, and love.

The Outstanding Books for the College Bound and Lifelong Learner lists represent one of the most versatile and useful tools public librarians can wield. Make it work for you and the readers you serve.

· NOTES ·

1. Great Schools. "Get Ready for College Reading," www.greatschools.org/students/academic-skills/ready-for-college-reading.gs?content=291&page=all.
2. YALSA Teens and Technology Interest Group. "ALA10: Lights! Camera! Booktrailers!" July 1, 2010, http://yalsa.ala.org/blog/2010/07/01/ala10-lights-camera-booktrailers/.
3. Glenda Gunter and Robert Kenny, "Digital Booktalk: Digital Media for Reluctant Readers," *Contemporary Issues in Technology and Teacher Education* 8 (2008) 84–99, www.citejournal.org/vol8/iss1/currentpractice/article1.cfm.

OUTSTANDING BOOKS IN SCHOOL LIBRARIES

CURRICULUM CONNECTIONS AND READERS' ADVISORY

PRISCILLE DANDO

A COMPREHENSIVE LIST like Outstanding Books for the College Bound and Lifelong Learners is a natural tool for school librarians to use in a variety of ways. The title itself implies an inherent connection to high school and is an efficient avenue to help achieve both the instructional and literary roles of the school library. In her *Booklist* article "Loose Canon," Hazel Rochman poses essential questions: What should be on the shelves in a high school library? What is the appropriate balance between classics, YA literature, and resources to support the curriculum? It is necessary to consider "subject, genre, format and reading level" in collection development to determine the composition that will meet the needs of students.[1] The OBCB list is an excellent tool—with so many titles to choose from, school librarians have a treasure trove at their fingertips to make curriculum connections and excel at readers' advisory.

· WHY FOCUS ON A LIST? ·

The ongoing debate about required reading illustrates the dilemma many teachers face. Although there is an assumption that giving students free choice in titles results in more enthusiasm for reading, teachers have an obligation to ensure that the reading relates to their curriculum and is substantial enough to merit study and analysis. Andrea Cohen's *St. Louis Post-Dispatch* article "Move Over, Gatsby, the High School Reading List Has Expanded" makes the point that the best books included on lists are not there because they fill a niche, but simply because they are "good literature."[2] The shift over the years in the OBCB list creates more of a balance, combining literary quality with teen appeal. In fact, some adults will be surprised to see contemporary best sellers and modern young adult literature (not to mention nonfiction) on this list. Students may also be surprised to see some of their favorite titles such as John Green's *Looking for Alaska* and Jodi Picoult's *Nineteen Minutes* among the recommended reading. The appeal goes hand in hand with literary quality, and with one of the stated criteria being readability, it is likely that students will have an enjoyable experience delving into these titles. Gone is the impression that reading for college-bound students is limited to dusty old classics, and there is a happy medium to be found between lightweight reading and AP texts.

· SUMMER READING ·

Mention a recommended reading list, and one of the first things to come to mind is summer reading requirements. Libby Gorman, in the *Teacher Librarian* article "Purposes behind Summer Reading Lists," conducted an extensive study of summer reading lists. She surveyed librarians regarding why and how they used them. Her findings concluded that lists serve a multitude of educational objectives, including the desire to provide examples of high-quality reading, an outlet for independent study and lifelong learning habits, and challenging reads. She found it surprising that even parents depend on the lists, as they expect their children to read outside of school and especially during the summer whether or not it is required.[3] Certainly, OBCB list excels at all of these objectives, and is an excellent source of summer reading choices for older students. Susan Whittaker, media specialist at The Villages High School in Florida, uses the list to identify titles for summer reading; students complete a variety of assignments based on their reading, including writing "book briefs" and holding online discussions on Moodle (a closed-access course management system). Her juniors and seniors often choose a book from the OBCB list to help complete their independent study in the spring.

· CURRICULUM CONNECTIONS ·

School librarians have always depended on book lists for inspiration in collection development. The current and previous OBCB lists are a critical tool for keeping the collection relevant to students both in what they study and for general knowledge and literature purposes. Because of the lists' multicultural and multigenre nature, every library could benefit from obtaining all titles on the lists. Of course it is convenient that the current list is already categorized by discipline: arts and humanities, history and cultures, literature and language arts, science and technology, and social sciences. The first step in leveraging this organization is to share the lists with faculty. Consider holding an open house and putting the titles on display along with handouts of corresponding online databases or other relevant sources. A teacher workday or one of the days before the school year begins is a prime time to offer coffee and a chance to browse through the displays that relate directly to each teacher's subject area. Teachers may want to check out the books for their own reading, but it is also an opportunity to spark conversation about their courses and what supplemental materials might be appropriate as outside reading.

One of the most valuable uses of the OBCB list is as a resource when a teacher is looking for a book recommendation. Bonnie Prouty, librarian at Lake Braddock Secondary School in Burke, Virginia, turns to the list when a teacher catches her off guard and needs an appealing but substantial read quickly. Her colleague Vicki Emery, media coordinator at Lake Braddock, made a powerful curriculum connection when a teacher approached her for help.

> [The list is a] good source for finding nonfiction books to pair with assigned reading for English classes. For example, an English teacher came in and said that she thought that she would resume assigning *The Grapes of Wrath.* She hadn't assigned it for awhile. I suggested that she pair it with *The Worst Hard Time: The Untold Story of Those Who Survived the Great American Dust Bowl* by Timothy Egan. Egan's book is a National Book Award winner and it comprises first person accounts through interviews and diaries of those who actually lived through the very trying times in the 1930s. I believe that this book also shows how well Steinbeck understood the time and place and was able to develop his characters realistically. Many links and discussion points can be made by comparing the two books.[4]

This experience simply confirmed for the teacher that her school library staff has expertise in literature, resources, and instruction, and she will be even more likely to approach them when she needs recommendations in the future.

· USING THE OBCB LIST AS A TEACHER ·

Teachers are likely to look to the list for ideas on classroom novels or nonfiction works. Whether students have the freedom to choose something from the list that appeals to them, or the teacher determines one work for the whole class to study, there are many books that support the high school curriculum in addition to providing exposure to a topic in preparation for college work. The list is also a boon to teachers organizing literature circles, as it allows students to group themselves by the book they choose to study and discuss. Giving students some selection choice, but ensuring that the choices are meaty enough to sustain discussion, enriches their interpretation of literature. Teachers who use the list to guide student choices will not have to be concerned with the quality of the works. The books on the most recent list that lend themselves to analysis in a particular course are as follows:

SOCIAL STUDIES

Bitterly Divided: The South's Inner Civil War by David Williams
The Book Thief by Marcus Zusak
Collapse: How Societies Choose to Fail or Succeed by Jared Diamond
The Complete Maus: A Survivor's Tale by Art Spiegelman
Damned Lies and Statistics: Untangling Numbers from the Media, Politicians, and Activists by Joel Best
Daniel Half-Human and the Good Nazi by David Chotjewitz

Forgotten Fire: A Novel by Adam Bagdasarian

The Known World by Edward P. Jones

New Found Land: Lewis and Clark's Voyage of Discovery by Allan Wolf

The Night Birds by Thomas Maltman

Pyongyang: A Journey in North Korea by Guy Delisle

The Race Beat: The Press, the Civil Rights Struggle, and the Awakening of a Nation by Gene Roberts and Hank Klibanoff

The Rape of Nanking: The Forgotten Holocaust of World War II by Iris Chang

Shooting under Fire: The World of the War Photographer by Peter Howe

Three Cups of Tea: One Man's Mission to Promote Peace One School at a Time by Greg Mortenson and David Oliver Relin

The Voice That Challenged a Nation: Marian Anderson and the Struggle for Equal Rights by Russell Freedman

A Voyage Long and Strange: Rediscovering the New World by Tony Horwitz

World Religions: The Great Faiths Explored and Explained by John Bowker

The Worst Hard Time: The Untold Story of Those Who Survived the Great American Dust Bowl by Timothy Egan

ENGLISH AND LITERATURE

Caramelo by Sandra Cisneros

Ella Minnow Pea: A Novel in Letters by Mark Dunn

Good Poems edited by Garrison Keillor

Heart to Heart: New Poems Inspired by Twentieth-Century American Art edited by Jan Greenberg

Mister Pip by Lloyd Jones

Rotten English: A Literary Anthology edited by Dohra Ahmad

Shakespeare: The World as Stage by Bill Bryson

Who the Hell Is Pansy O'Hara? The Fascinating Stories behind 50 of the World's Best-Loved Books by Jenny Bond and Chris Sheedy

Your Own, Sylvia: A Verse Portrait of Sylvia Plath by Stephanie Hemphill

SCIENCES

American Earth: Environmental Writing since Thoreau edited by Bill McKibben

The Botany of Desire: A Plant's-Eye View of the World by Michael Pollan

The Genomics Age: How DNA Technology Is Transforming the Way We Live and Who We Are by Gina Smith

Greasy Rider: Two Dudes, One Fry-Oil-Powered Car, and a Cross-Country Search for a Greener Future by Greg Melville

The Green Book: The Everyday Guide to Saving the Planet One Simple Step at a Time by Elizabeth Rogers and Thomas Kostigen

Lost Discoveries: The Ancient Roots of Modern Science—From the Babylonians to the Maya by Dick Teresi

The Race to Save the Lord God Bird by Phillip M. Hoose

A Short History of Nearly Everything by Bill Bryson

*The Weather Makers: How Man Is Changing the Climate and What It Means
for Life on Earth* by Tim Flannery
The Wild Trees: A Story of Passion and Daring by Richard Preston

ELECTIVES

*The Annotated Mona Lisa: A Crash Course in Art History from Prehistoric to
Post-Modern* by Carol Strickland
Dressed: A Century of Hollywood Costume Design by Deborah Nadoolman
Landis
Frida: Viva la Vida! Long Live Life! by Carmen Bernier-Grand
*My Start-Up Life: What a (Very) Young CEO Learned on His Journey through
Silicon Valley* by Ben Casnocha
Naked Economics: Undressing the Dismal Science by Charles Wheelan
Our Movie Heritage by Tom McGreevey and Joanne Yeck
Photography: An Illustrated History by Martin Sandler

Teachers know their students best, and in advanced classes or even when an individual student is a more mature reader, the list is a great place to identify supplementary reading. Cohen describes the advantage that students who read challenging books have over others on standardized tests. The vocabulary and reading comprehension skills required on such tests is more easily honed when students regularly read high-quality texts. Several studies support her assertions. Richard Anderson et al., in their 1985 report from the U.S. Department of Education, *Becoming a Nation of Readers*, make several recommendations, one of which is to ensure opportunities for independent reading. The report states that "children's reading should include classic and modern works of fiction and nonfiction that represent the core of our national heritage."[5] Stephen Krashen's *Knowledge Quest* article, "Anything but Reading," may provide the most convincing evidence of the potential the OBCB list has for improving performance. The article synthesizes a number of studies, all of which conclude that students who are high achievers in reading read more than their counterparts. "Self-selected, voluntary reading" has a direct relationship to improving literacy, and while some adults lament a lack of motivation among students to read, Krashen notes that the most successful motivator is providing access to "interesting, comprehensible reading material," the very criteria for inclusion on the OBCB list.[6] The value of supplementary reading is not only proven for those who are high-achieving readers. Steve Metz notes in "Closing the Gap with Summer Reading," published in *The Science Teacher,* that more than a decade of research at Johns Hopkins concluded that "two-thirds of the achievement gap between lower- and higher-income youth can be attributed to unequal access to summer learning opportunities." Based on that information, Metz believes that recreational summer reading is a must for everyone.[7]

· DISPLAYS AND MARKETING ·

Once the titles are available in the collection, the OBCB list becomes a tremendous resource for readers' advisory. Thomas Kaun of the Bessie Chin Library at Redwood

High School in Larkspur, California, has a quick tip. He recommends keeping copies of the list at the circulation desk. Students frequently pick up the list, and parents see it and take a copy themselves during back-to-school nights, open houses, and tours of the building. If the list is too bulky to keep at the desk, it would be easy to create jazzy bookmarks by discipline. Susan Whittaker takes it one step further by linking to the list on her school's website and promoting it in her library's newsletter to parents. Because it is such a broad list, there is something to appeal to everyone.

The OBCB list is a natural for displays. During the fall college application season, intersperse the titles with other books and resources for college readiness. Books on applying to and selecting a college, study guides, and choosing a major are complemented nicely by copies of the list and its books. In the spring, seniors might be interested in reading books like those on the list that are intended to help prepare students for encountering unfamiliar experiences, points of view, and challenges.

· BOOKTALKS ·

Booktalks are a classic promotional tool for a reason—students tend to read what librarians take the time to spotlight, probably because librarians' enthusiasm for the titles shines through. When an advanced class has a free-choice independent reading assignment, booktalking from the list pays off with suggestions of out-of-the-ordinary titles. Books on the most recent list with a natural hook for booktalks include these:

American Shaolin: Flying Kicks, Buddhist Monks, and the Legend of Iron Crotch: An Odyssey in the New China by Matthew Polly

Another Day in the Frontal Lobe: A Brain Surgeon Exposes Life on the Inside by Katrina Firlik

Beautiful Boy: A Father's Journey through His Son's Addiction by David Sheff

Born Standing Up: A Comic's Life by Steve Martin

Eagle Blue: A Team, a Tribe, and a High School Basketball Season in Arctic Alaska by Michael D'Orso

From Clueless to Class Act: Manners for the Modern Man by Jodi R. R. Smith

John Lennon: All I Want Is the Truth by Elizabeth Partridge

Killed Cartoons: Casualties from the War on Free Expression edited by David Wallis

The Magical Life of Long Tack Sam by Anne Marie Fleming

The Radioactive Boy Scout: The True Story of a Boy and His Backyard Nuclear Reactor by Ken Silverstein

A Rare Breed of Love: The True Story of Baby and the Mission She Inspired to Help Dogs Everywhere by Jana Kohl

Rosencrantz and Guildenstern Are Dead by Tom Stoppard

Sold by Patricia McCormick

Someday This Pain Will Be Useful to You by Peter Cameron

Stiff: The Curious Lives of Human Cadavers by Mary Roach

Sunrise over Fallujah by Walter Dean Myers

The Taste of Sweet: Our Complicated Love Affair with Our Favorite Treats by Joanne Chen

Tweak: Growing Up on Methamphetamines by Nic Sheff

What Is the What: The Autobiography of Valentino Achak Deng; A Novel by
     Dave Eggers

Wheelchair Warrior: Gangs, Disability, and Basketball by Melvin Juette and
     Ronald J. Berger

*The Year of Living Biblically: One Man's Humble Quest to Follow the Bible as
     Literally as Possible* by A. J. Jacobs

It is clear that booktalk ideas are available for virtually every class when examining the list by discipline. Extend this idea by providing students the opportunity
to create podcasts promoting the books that can be shared with a wide audience.
Collaborating on podcasts with an English teacher can satisfy several objectives.
From the teacher's point of view, writing for a specific audience and crafting an
engaging style are skills that are suited for an oral presentation, and required by the
podcast recording. It is an opportunity to incorporate technology in an authentic
manner, and is an entertaining assessment of a student's understanding of the book.
The librarian can assist with the technology and give pointers for what makes a
good book review. Creating book trailers through video production or Microsoft's
Photo Story program fulfills similar objectives. An added bonus to these projects
is the end result of a pool of student-created advertisements for reading the OBCB
list available online to the student body at large.

· BOOK GROUPS ·

The most successful book group discussions revolve around titles that are substantial enough to spark a reaction or contain a compelling conflict. A quick review of
the list reveals several books that have proven to be popular with adult book clubs.

The Devil in the White City by Erik Larson

The Glass Castle by Jeannette Walls

The Kite Runner by Khaled Hosseini

The Known World by Edward P. Jones

A Lesson before Dying by Ernest Gaines

A Long Way Gone by Ishmael Beah

The Pillars of the Earth by Ken Follett

The Red Tent by Anita Diamant

The Road by Cormac McCarthy

Three Cups of Tea by Greg Mortenson and David Oliver Relin

The Tipping Point by Malcolm Gladwell

Tuesdays with Morrie by Mitch Albom

Water for Elephants by Sara Gruen

Other excellent book club choices include:

The Absolutely True Diary of a Part-Time Indian by Sherman Alexie

The Book Thief by Marcus Zusak

The Complete Maus: A Survivor's Tale by Art Spiegelman

The Complete Persepolis by Marjane Satrapi

The Curious Incident of the Dog in the Night-Time by Mark Haddon
Eagle Blue by Michael D'Orso
Extremely Loud and Incredibly Close by Jonathan Safran Foer
Feed by M. T. Anderson
Little Brother by Cory Doctorow
Never Let Me Go by Kazuo Ishiguro
The Secret Life of Bees by Sue Monk Kidd

· THE BOTTOM LINE ·

The Outstanding Books for the College Bound and Lifelong Learners list does not make the claim that all educated people have read these books. Rather, it is a modern collection of titles representing different points of view that provide insight into our world. Students seeking a challenge and who are curious about any number of topics will find something to enjoy and learn from on this list. Savvy school librarians will understand the value of these collected titles and strive to incorporate them into their programs.

· NOTES ·

1. Hazel Rochman, "Loose Canon," *Booklist,* Sept. 1, 1996, 114.
2. Andrea Cohen, "Move Over, Gatsby, the High School Reading List Has Expanded," *St. Louis Post-Dispatch,* March 26, 2003.
3. Libby Gorman, "Purposes behind Summer Reading Lists," *Teacher Librarian* 37, no. 5 (June 2010): 52.
4. Interview with the author, Sept. 1, 2010.
5. Richard C. Anderson et al., *Becoming a Nation of Readers: The Report of the Commission on Reading,* ERIC (ED253865).
6. Stephen Krashen, "Anything but Reading," *Knowledge Quest* 37, no. 5 (May–June 2009): 18.
7. Steve Metz, "Closing the Gap with Summer Reading," *Science Teacher* 76, no. 5 (Summer 2009): 8.

OUTSTANDING BOOKS IN AN ACADEMIC SETTING

JUDITH WALKER

IMAGINE IT'S A beautiful fall day during the first week of the semester on a university campus. New freshmen, transfer students, and returning upperclassmen are scurrying between classes. There in the quad are some folks hawking the services of the library as the masses rush by. It's the Week of Welcome, a time when all the departments and services across campus vie for the attention of students, to let them know they are there to support students in their academic endeavors. The library's theme is A Personal Librarian for Every Student. One librarian approaches a couple of students looking at the display and offers them some "smart pills" (Skittles) courtesy of the library. She begins to tell them about the library when one of the students says, "We're both math majors and don't really need the library."

The undaunted librarian reminds them many of the most famous mathematicians were lovers of literature and there is a very strong correlation between mathematics, literature, and language. Then she asks them if they have read any good math books lately. This puzzles them. They indicate they both like to read, but the only math books they are familiar with are their textbooks.

"You mean to tell me you haven't read *Super Crunchers, Numerati,* or the *Story of Phi* yet?" asks the librarian, who then launches into a brief booktalk about the three titles.[1] By the time the students move on to their next class, they have learned about a number of other titles as well as the services the library has to offer them.

Does this sound like a pipe dream? Well, it's not. This exchange actually occurred, and I was the librarian. Although I am the education librarian at a sprawling campus of more than 25,000 students, I was able to engage these two math students with some literary gems because I was one of three representatives from the Association of College and Research Libraries (ACRL) on the Outstanding Books for the College Bound committee sponsored by the Young Adult Library Services Association (YALSA), which selected the titles for the list published in 2009. Prior to this appointment I was familiar with the list but had not really paid much attention to it. I did recommend it periodically to high school librarians and tried to make sure we had most of the titles, but it was not a high priority. After all, the mission of an academic library is to support the university's curriculum, not to purchase recreational reading material.

After serving on the committee I have an entirely different approach to the list, and that's not just because I spent two years reading books, discussing them, and then agonizing over which ones should go on the list. True, I invested a lot of time and energy in the process. But what I realized was that these books could have a positive impact on college students and become an integral part of the university curriculum. I have a background as a school librarian and have taught courses on integrating children's literature (fiction and nonfiction) across the curriculum. While working with these books it dawned on me that the same principles I used in those circumstances apply to trade books in the college curriculum.

Over the past few decades there have been numerous reports about the decline in reading among college students. Among the most recent are two by the National Endowment for the Arts: "Reading at Risk" and "To Read or Not to Read."[2] However, there hasn't been much research into why exactly this is occurring. A small study by Jolliffe and Harl at the University of Arkansas tried to determine if indeed their students were reading less and why. Their findings indicated students were actually very engaged with their own reading but not with reading related to their classes. For them, course-related reading was uninspiring and dull.[3] A study by Jensen and Moore of the use of trade books in a freshman biology course came to a similar conclusion. In short, students see their textbooks as very expensive volumes of facts that do not relate to their real life.[4] This should sound familiar; K–12 students and teachers have been making this same complaint for decades now. So one possible conclusion is it's not the students but the textbooks that are causing the decline. And that's where the Outstanding Books for the College Bound titles can support the university curriculum so effectively. The rest of this chapter will discuss some ways I have used the list with my students and faculty, and also will propose other ways the list might be used in an academic setting. Since I was on the subcommittee to choose the titles for the 2009 science and technology section of the list, I will tend to use those titles as examples, but most of what I will suggest can be applied to any of the titles.

First and foremost, I encourage academic librarians to read as many titles on the list as possible, especially those in their specialty area. It is difficult to get anyone else (faculty or students) interested in using the list if you aren't familiar with the books. Although the list is targeted to high school students, most of the titles would fit into the category I call "adult books for young adults." Many of the titles may have already found their way onto college and university library shelves through traditional collection development channels. When reviewing the titles from earlier lists, I discovered that our institution had approximately 65 percent of the titles—

with most of them in our general collection, not our children's/young adult collection. It's also a good possibility you have read many of the titles already.

As the education librarian, I work closely with the faculty, teaching methods classes. During my sessions with the middle and secondary science teachers, we have had discussions about what science books the students are reading and how they can encourage their middle and high school students to read books other than the textbooks. I start off booktalking several titles from the list. Two of my favorites (because of their enticing titles) are *Stiff: The Curious Lives of Human Cadavers* and *Dr. Tatiana's Sex Advice to All Creation: The Definitive Guide to the Evolutionary Biology of Sex*. *Stiff* includes a great deal of information on anatomy as well as historical background. It's not for the squeamish, though. The "Dear Abby" format of *Dr. Tatiana's Sex Advice* makes reading the book entertaining as well as informative. I also like to booktalk *The Wild Trees: A Story of Passion and Daring* because it follows some pretty ordinary people on a quest to find the tallest redwood trees, and on the way they discover an entirely new and unknown ecosystem. It proves you don't have to be genius to be a good scientist. After I've booktalked a few titles, the students usually begin to share titles they have discovered. The discussion has gotten pretty animated at times.

Because our college of education stresses inquiry-based learning, students and teachers are not married to the textbook. That allows more opportunities to incorporate trade books into the curriculum. Several faculty members require students to read trade books in addition to their texts. I have made a concentrated effort to make those faculty members aware of the titles on the OBCB list. A number of them are using it as a supplementary reading list for their courses.

Another course where I highlight the OBCB titles is the reading in the content areas course for middle and secondary preservice teachers. These students are familiar with some middle-grade titles like Louis Sachar's *Holes* and Lois Lowry's *Number the Stars* because they had to read them when they were in middle and high school. But they don't have a clue about where to find books to incorporate into the content areas they plan to teach. The OBCB list is the perfect place to start since it doesn't have an overwhelming number of titles and is organized by broad content areas.

Moving away from my immediate subject area, OBCB titles can be very useful in other undergraduate courses. Many of our general education courses are interdisciplinary courses such as Arts and Society; Global and Intercultural Connections; Literature and Culture; Science, Technology, and Society; and Issues in Health and Quality of Life. These courses are designed to encourage critical thinking skills and help students understand the complex issues in our society. Titles such as *The Annotated Mona Lisa: A Crash Course in Art History from Prehistoric to Post-Modern* and *This Land Was Made for You and Me: The Life and Songs of Woody Guthrie* would certainly make the arts come alive. Jared Diamond's *Collapse: How Societies Choose to Fail or Succeed* will provide more information and insight into today's world than any dry textbook. And to really understand how science and politics interact, students can try Bill Bryson's *A Short History of Nearly Everything*, although it's not nearly as short as the title suggests.

One could go on and on with great suggestions from the OBCB list, but picking the books is easy. Getting faculty to incorporate these books into their curriculum is the tricky part. Because general education courses are more or less experimental in nature—meaning the faculty are encouraged to use more nontraditional methods of teaching these courses—they are ideal for integrating the OBCB titles, but meeting with all the diverse faculty has been a monumental endeavor. Working together, several other librarians and I have made some inroads into the classes. As more faculty become aware of the list, its use should begin to take hold.

What holds true for the general education courses is also true for the First-Year Experience courses, also known as freshman learning communities at some institutions. We have found that since many of these sections are designed to help students develop positive learning strategies, the faculty teaching these courses are more open to incorporating new activities. Another avenue still to be explored is the common reading experience, which is the college or university equivalent to One Book, One Community reading campaigns used to unite cities across the country. For example, all incoming freshmen are assigned to read a particular book, in order to create common ground before they arrive on campus in the fall. Many of the OBCB titles would be excellent choices, and in fact several of them have already been used purely by accident.

There are two additional ways to promote the OBCB titles that are worth discussing. Both are borrowed from other areas of librarianship: literature circles and readers' advisory. Both of these ideas have great potential.

Howrey and Rachelson of DeVry University–South Florida discussed a project they helped create based on the literature circle concept. Small groups of students, faculty, and librarians come together to discuss in depth a popular title, such as *Tuesdays with Morrie*. Participation is voluntary, although some faculty bestow extra credit for attendance. Students are expected to read the book so they can discuss it; however, the program also incorporates other formats, such as audio and video. It includes speaker events, where the students can discuss the title personally with the author. In addition to the face-to-face discussions, students are encouraged to participate in an online discussion via the program's blog (http://readdevry .blogspot.com).[5]

This program draws on the best practices of First-Year Experience courses, freshman learning communities, and the common reading experience. It is a collaborative effort between the library and the college of liberal arts and sciences. Many of the titles used over the past six years of the project are titles from the OBCB list. A top-down program like this would take a lot of planning and coordination, to say the least. But once the faculty buys into it, the program could have a tremendous impact on student reading and critical thinking skills.

In the past many college and university libraries included some type of readers' advisory service. Institutions created browsing collections of popular books for recreational reading. Today, most mid-sized and large college and university libraries have moved away from this service in favor of acquiring only scholarly material. Our library still maintains a small browsing collection, which is donated by our local newspaper after they have printed reviews of the books. But the idea of readers' advisory is not dead. It has just been transformed. Or perhaps resurrected would be a better metaphor—resurrected in cyberspace. Many academic librarians are using a variety of digital tools to create annotated bibliographies for specific or interdisciplinary subject areas. Some are being attached to course content; others are appearing in blogs or as news items on home pages. Considering the students now entering our institutions are digital natives, this may be the best way to spread the word about OBCB titles. We could even set up virtual book clubs where students could comment on and discuss the titles in depth.

I have presented just a few ways that the OBCB titles could be used within the academic setting. Like most every other service academic librarians provide to students and faculty, it needs to be promoted. Displays, newsletters, blogs, RSS feeds, Twitter, and so on are all well and good. But the truth is the most effective way to promote these titles is face-to-face. Talk to faculty about the list. Booktalk the titles whenever and wherever possible. Smaller institutions will have the advantage because of their more closely knit community, but if you can get folks reading the books, the OBCB list will sell itself.

· NOTES ·

1.   Ian Ayres, *Super Crunchers* (Bantam, 2007), OBCB 2009; Stephen Baker, *The Numerati* (Houghton Mifflin, 2008); Mario Livio, *The Golden Ratio: The Story of Phi* (Broadway Books, 2002), OBCB 2004.

2.   National Endowment for the Arts, "Reading at Risk: A Survey of Literary Reading in America," Washington, DC: National Endowment for the Arts, 2004; ibid., "To Read or Not To Read: A Question of National Consequence," Washington, DC: National Endowment for the Arts, 2007.

3.   David A. Jolliffe and Allison Harl, "Texts of Our Institutional Lives: Studying the 'Reading Transition' from High School to College—What Are Our Students Reading and Why?" *College English* 70, no. 6 (2008): 599–617. See also Jude D. Gallik, "Do They Read for Pleasure? Recreational Reading Habits of College Students," *Journal of Adolescent and Adult Literacy* 42, no. 6 (1999): 480–88.

4.   Murray Jensen and Randy Moore, "Reading Trade Books in a Freshman Biology Course," *American Biology Teacher* 70, no. 4 (2008): 206–7, 209–10.

5.   Mary M. Howrey and Esther S. Rachelson, "Toward a 'Lifetime of Literacies': Library Reading Circles for College Students," August 2009. Miramar, Fla.: DeVry University South Florida. www.eric.ed.gov/contentdelivery/servlet/ERICServlet?accno=ED506075.

5

....

OUTSTANDING BOOKS FOR NONTRADITIONAL STUDENTS AND LIFELONG LEARNERS

PENNY JOHNSON

ARE WE NOT all potentially college bound?

The term *college bound* creates images of eager teenagers, filling their last years in high school with academically challenging classes such as AP English, physics, and calculus. College campuses are presumably for young adults, newly independent, focusing on sports, parties, and professors. But many high school graduates do not go directly to college. Financial, academic, or personal reasons often send young adults into the workforce or after other pursuits. Millions of teens may never step foot on a college campus, although many do finally enroll in a college program, and the number of latecomers is rising.

Indeed, according to the National Center for Education Statistics, an agency of the U.S. Department of Education, the traditional college student is not typical. Fully three-quarters of all enrolled postsecondary students do not fit the description of "young single adult."[1] Adults beyond the 18–22 age bracket are returning to college to retrain for a new career, to enhance a current job situation, or to fulfill a lifetime goal. *College bound*, then, is really a term that can describe any adult in America.

Thus a collection of lists with the title *Outstanding Books for the College Bound* is quite useful for anyone at any age. Like keeping fresh batteries in a smoke alarm, choosing to read books from these lists keeps minds energized and ready for whatever circumstances may arise.

Libraries can effectively use these titles for adult collections and programs as well as for teen audiences. For example, consider inviting the public to a seminar on educational opportunities for nontraditional students. Emphasize the usefulness of the OBCB book lists to attendees who are considering a return to formal schooling.

Another seminar designed to teach study skills to nontraditional students would also be useful to patrons. Use books from the OBCB lists to demonstrate techniques for effective learning.

· OUTSTANDING BOOKS FOR THOSE UNBOUND BY COLLEGE ·

Of course, all education is fundamentally self-education. Professors and formal curricula may guide us, but we are ultimately responsible for our own education. Thomas Carlyle stated, "[What we become] depends on what we read, after all manner of professors have done their best for us. The true university of these days is a collection of books."[2]

Whether we have left our college days behind or still dream of donning a cap and gown, we have a lifetime of opportunities to educate ourselves unbound by college curricula and requirements. Seeking those opportunities is imperative. Futurist Alvin Toffler observes, "The illiterate of the twenty-first century will not be those who cannot read and write, but those who cannot learn, unlearn, and relearn."[3]

Librarians and library staff should be the foremost role models in their community for self-education. A continual process of learning, unlearning, and relearning is imperative for those who profess to be the "information gurus" that a library career implies. While considering how to encourage others to pursue a lifetime of learning, library specialists should also examine their own education plans.

What is one of the best ways to foster lifelong learning? As with any worthwhile project, finding the best-quality tools. Time and energy are finite resources. For those who choose to invest that time and energy in self-education, *Outstanding Books for the College Bound* offers a convenient way to identify titles worthy of attention.

Recognizing lifelong learning as a satisfying, and indeed necessary, pursuit, those unbound by college can find many meaningful ways to organize and pursue their self-appointed education. OBCB book lists can provide road maps and guides through the journey. Consider these reading action plans for both librarians and their patrons.

· BE YOUR OWN COLLEGE ADVISEMENT CENTER ·

Formal college programs provide a plan that includes a list of required courses. College curricula usually include general education requirements along with requirements in a student's major field to ensure a well-rounded education. For instance, the University of Wisconsin requires every student to take courses in natural science, social science, and humanities, literature, and art. As students enrolled in their own Lifelong Learner University (Go LLU!), readers can use OBCB book lists to create and fulfill their own curriculum requirements. Using any university's plan as a template, readers can choose books that match the same requirements. For example, following the UW plan, readers could choose a book from the science and technology list, the social sciences list, and the arts and humanities list. Then choose a "major" and read several books from one list, such as history.

Libraries can build on this model by sponsoring a Lifelong Learner University book group, where participants create their "curriculum" together using the OBCB book lists. This type of program can help re-create some of the social aspects of on-campus life as readers meet to discuss each book.

· SOMETHING OLD, SOMETHING NEW, SOMETHING RANDOM, SOMETHING TRUE ·

Sally Ashmore of Omaha, Nebraska, has a reading plan for her lifelong learning program based on the phrase "something old, something new, something random, something true." She reads one book matching each criterion, and then begins again. She considers the OBCB book lists a valuable tool for locating high-quality books as she reads through the cycle. Sally especially appreciates the nonfiction listings. Readers not associated with libraries or academia often find it difficult to identify outstanding nonfiction books. These book lists highlight great titles that otherwise might go unnoticed by readers.

Libraries might print book lists arranged according to the "something old, something new, something random, something true" cycle, thus offering a new way for patrons to pursue a reading plan.

Another library collection display idea is to create "book bundles" featuring OBCB books. A book bundle, as described in an article in the June 2010 issue of *VOYA*, is a set of three or four books packaged with a rubber band and a tag.[4] Each bundle has a specific theme. The OBCB book lists provide several theme ideas, or bundles could be created using the "something old, something new" pattern or the "college advisement center" theme.

· GOING DEEP, GOING WIDE ·

College students and those unbound by college face the same dilemma when choosing how to spend their leisure reading time. Does one spend those precious few hours reading a book in his or her field, or outside that field? An education, be it formal or self-administered, that provides both depth and breadth produces a well-rounded individual who can contribute in many venues. These lists of outstanding books allow a reader to go deep or go wide, or to choose both directions at once.

Amy, a newly graduated microbiologist, is eager to read all the books on the science and technology list to deepen her knowledge and expertise in her field. Vicki, a busy graduate student, feels she barely has time to eat or sleep. Any extracurricular reading she chooses must scream "research efficient." She appreciates the history list that points her in the direction of excellent books in her field that meet her criteria for possible future use.

On the other hand, Roger seeks to expand his horizons beyond his everyday pursuits. After spending a full workday concentrating on technology, he prefers to read a book from the OBCB arts and humanities list or history and cultures list. He finds going wide with his reading choices gives him a much-needed break from job-related stress.

A library could consider providing an online blog or forum for readers who are "going deep" in a particular genre or subject. Allow them to share insights as they read all of the books on one list.

Dedicate an area of library shelves to OBCB books. Arrange the books according to OBCB subject rather than traditional Dewey or Library of Congress designation, thus allowing those who are seeking deep or wide reading experiences to easily locate relevant titles.

· FEEDING THE CREATIVE MIND ·

The accepted definition of creativity is the production of something original and useful. To be creative requires generating many unique ideas and then combining those ideas into the best result. Avid reader Jarkko Laine recognizes reading as excellent fuel for the creative mind. In a guest column posted to *Design Pepper Blog* on Feb. 5, 2008, he states, "I read all the time. It helps me learn new things, become a better writer, entertain myself. But most importantly, reading feeds my creativity."[5]

Creative readers expect the books they read to be informative and mind-expanding, yet entertaining. Reading is not a drudgery to add to an already overloaded schedule. One of the dangers of neatly organized and annotated book lists such as OBCB is the implication that a reader should start at the top of a list and toil through it. Thus reading these books joins the same category as eating vegetables or getting a flu shot. That does not sound like an effective formula for feeding the creative mind.

To create a storm in the mind and generate new creative ideas, reading needs to be fun, lively, and, yes, sometimes unorganized. To eliminate reading drudgery, one might open up this outstanding collection of book lists and point. This method for choosing a book may lead to a subject or author that enlightens in a completely unexpected, unintended way. Entrepreneur Burke Hedges writes, "Reading, like no other medium, can transform your life in a flash, and you never know which book, at which time in your life, might be the one that rocks your world and inspires you to grow in ways you never thought possible."[6]

A library might encourage patrons to feed their creativity with a "reading grab bag." Write the titles of OBCB books on individual slips of paper. Place the slips in a grab bag or box. Invite patrons to pull a slip from the box to determine his or her next book. (Libraries will need a system to assure all the books in the grab bag have immediate availability to avoid disappointed readers!)

· FINDING THE TIME ·

While browsing through these lists of outstanding books, Natalie's excitement grew as she contemplated reading from this diverse collection. And then reality sank in. As a busy young mother, how would she ever find the time to enjoy them?

In this fast-paced world, we can easily consider sitting down with a good book a luxury that is impossible to afford. The college unbound look with envy at those who enjoy a spring break or a summer vacation when plenty of free time allows reading to take center stage. When juggling work, family, and social obligations, how does one find the time to read?

Libraries should be the leading advocates for finding that reading time. Treat readers like VIPs with comfortable reading accommodations and special quiet nooks. Lead the fight to eliminate the attitude that sitting down with a good book is a luxury most do not have the time to enjoy.

One idea is to provide a graffiti wall in the library featuring pictures of OBCB books. A large whiteboard or chalkboard, a bulletin board, or simply a stretch of white butcher paper can be used. Allow patrons to write ideas on the wall with colorful markers or chalk about how they find time to read.

To jump-start the process, library staff might consider adding the following ideas to the graffiti wall:

> For a designated time daily or weekly, turn off all of the
>   screens—TV, computer monitor, iPod, and phone. (Okay,
>   so the Kindle doesn't count!)
> Read out loud with a partner
> Go to sleep later or wake up earlier
> Read during lunch breaks and coffee breaks
> Take a bath (and a book) instead of a shower
> Always carry a book to take advantage of unexpected moments
> Keep a book in the bathroom
> Designate family reading time each week
> Listen to audiobooks on the road, while doing housework or
>   yard work, or while exercising
> Talk to others about books and reading
> Give yourself permission to stop everything and read

In addition, libraries can spotlight reading with special programs celebrating National Poetry Month, Teen Read Week™, International Children's Book Day, and other observances. Celebrate books!

Sponsor a public workshop on time management, with the speaker emphasizing tips on how to schedule reading time into a busy adult life.

Stephen R. Covey says, "The key is not to prioritize what is on your schedule, but to schedule your priorities."[7] Avid readers use many techniques to find time for reading despite overcrowded day planners. Libraries should help patrons discover those techniques so they can explore the outstanding books on these lists.

· SHINING AN ADDITIONAL SPOTLIGHT ON OBCB TITLES ·

The library is an important symbol of self-education. Libraries should actively identify high-quality materials for the lifelong learner. With OBCB book lists as a tool, librarians can provide specific opportunities for the college unbound to find, appreciate, and share outstanding books. Consider these additional ideas for spotlighting titles:

- Feature the OBCB book lists on the library website. Create a link from each title to the library catalog. Remember to include e-books and audiobooks.
- Create a special spine label designating books that appear on the OBCB lists.
- Take the opportunity to emphasize the origin and purposes of the OBCB lists. Through printed and online resources, answer these spoken or unspo-

ken questions patrons may have about the lists: Why are these particular titles considered outstanding? Who determined what titles were chosen? How are these titles relevant to my life and my situation?

- Create a community journal, both online and on paper. As patrons read a book from one of the OBCB lists, encourage them to write a review and add it to the journal.

A frequently quoted maxim, attributed to former basketball coach John Wooden, observes: "Five years from now, you're the same person except for the people you've met and the books you've read."[8] By using these power lists of outstanding books, the college bound as well as those unbound by college can add depth and breadth and creativity to their reading experiences. The lists in *Outstanding Books for the College Bound* are a cornucopia for those seeking a lifetime of self-education. Whatever plan a reader uses to feast upon these books, the mind and soul will be well fed. May every librarian seek to be an inviting maître d'!

· NOTES ·

1. National Center for Education Statistics, "Special Analysis 2002: Nontraditional Undergraduates," http://nces.ed.gov/programs/coe/2002/analyses/nontraditional/index.asp.
2. Thomas Carlyle, *On Heroes and Hero Worship and Heroics in History* (Public Domain Books, 2006, Kindle edition).
3. Alvin Toffler in "Toffler Quotes," www.alvintoffler.net/?fa=galleryquotes.
4. Gigi Yang and Erica Segraves, "Book Bundles: Readers Advisory in a Package," *VOYA* 33, no. 2 (June 2010): 132–34.
5. Jarkko Laine, "Seven Tips for Creative Reading," *Design Pepper Blog*, Feb. 5, 2008, http://designpepper.com/blog/post/seven-tips-for-creative-reading.
6. Burke Hedges, *Read and Grow Rich: How the Hidden Power of Reading Can Make You Richer in All Areas of Your Life* (Tampa: INTI, 1999), 22.
7. Stephen R. Covey, *The 7 Habits of Highly Effective People* (New York: Rosetta Books, 2009, Kindle edition).
8. Goodreads.com, "John Wooden Quotes," www.goodreads.com/author/quotes/23041.John_Wooden.

PART II

....

THE ANNOTATIONS

REVISED AND EXPANDED BY ANGELA CARSTENSEN

6

....

OUTSTANDING BOOKS FOR THE COLLEGE BOUND AND LIFELONG LEARNERS, 1999

THE 1999 OBCB list follows the traditional genre categories in use (with minor variations) since the inception of OBCB in 1959: fiction, nonfiction, biography, drama, and poetry. The charge for the OBCB committee, taken from the policies and procedures document, is "To prepare a revised and updated edition of the Outstanding Books for the College Bound booklists every five years." The 1999 list is very much a revision of the 1994 list. They share many titles and the traditional emphasis on the humanities. The 1999 list is noteworthy for its extended poetry list.

· FICTION ·

Agee, James. *A Death in the Family*. McDowell Oblensky, 1957. OBCB 1999.
   The enchanted childhood summer of 1915 becomes a baffling experience for six-year-old Rufus Follet when his father dies suddenly in a car accident. This autobiographical novel about family and loss encompasses life before the accident and surrounding the funeral.

Allison, Dorothy. *Bastard out of Carolina*. Dutton, 1992. OBCB 1999, 2004, 2009.
   Bone confronts illegitimacy, poverty, the troubled marriage of her mother and stepfather, and the stigma of being considered "white trash" as she comes of age in South Carolina. Despite the fact that she lives among a large extended and protective family, Bone's stepfather, Daddy Glen, becomes increasingly abusive; her mother is either unable or unwilling to protect her; and Bone herself is too young or too embarrassed to reveal what is happening to her.

Alvarez, Julia. *In the Time of Butterflies.* Algonquin, 1994. OBCB 1999, 2004.

The four Mirabel sisters were called the Mariposas, or butterflies. Alvarez brings these historical figures to life by having the sisters tell their own story, beginning in childhood, through involvement with the resistance, culminating in murder and martyrdom. Their courage helped to liberate the Dominican Republic from Trujillo's dictatorship.

Anaya, Rudolfo. *Bless Me, Ultima.* Warner, 1972. OBCB 1999.

In rural New Mexico shortly after World War II, Ultima, a wise old mystic, helps Antonio, a young Hispanic boy, resolve personal dilemmas caused by the differing backgrounds and aspirations of his parents and society. Elements of magical realism combine with themes of religious, cultural, and social conflict.

Atwood, Margaret. *The Handmaid's Tale.* Houghton Mifflin Harcourt, 1986. OBCB 1999.

In Gilead, a Christian fundamentalist dystopia, fertile lower-class women serve as birth-mothers for the upper class. Offred chronicles her life in the new Republic, beginning with her training at the Rachel and Leah Center, then as handmaid to the Commander and his wife, all the while dealing with memories of the husband and child that are lost to her.

Butler, Octavia. *Parable of the Sower.* Four Walls Eight Windows, 1993. OBCB 1999.

Lauren Olamina begins her story in 2024, at the age of 15, living outside Los Angeles in a gated community that barely protects its inhabitants from the crime and poverty outside. Lauren, who suffers from a hereditary trait called hyperempathy that causes her to feel others' pain physically, survives the destruction of the enclave and journeys north along the dangerous highways of 21st-century California in search of safety.

Card, Orson Scott. *Ender's Game.* Tor, 1985. OBCB 1999.

In a world decimated by alien attacks, the government trains young geniuses like Ender Wiggin in military strategy with increasingly complex computer games. Ender is only six years old when he is identified by the government as their best hope against the alien "buggers" and sent to Battle School.

Chopin, Kate. *The Awakening.* H. S. Stone & Co., 1899. OBCB 1999.

Edna Pontellier, an unhappy wife and mother, discovers new qualities in herself when she visits Grand Isle, a resort for the Creole elite of New Orleans. Her restlessness increases when she meets and falls in love with Robert Lebrun at the resort. When he leaves her abruptly she never fully recovers, eventually leaving her family and refusing to follow convention.

Cisneros, Sandra. *The House on Mango Street.* Vintage, 1991. OBCB 1999.

In short, poetic stories, Esperanza describes life in a low-income, predominantly Hispanic neighborhood in Chicago. As Esperanza comes of age, she is torn between tradition and discovering life outside her neighborhood and culture.

Dostoyevsky, Fyodor. *Crime and Punishment.* J. M. Dent, 1866. OBCB 1999.

A sensitive intellectual is driven by poverty to believe himself exempt from moral law. Rodion Raskolnikov, a poor student, kills two people. Dostoyevsky examines life in 19th-century Russia, the nature of good and evil, and the psychology of a murderer in this quintessential Russian novel.

Ellison, Ralph. *Invisible Man.* Random House, 1952. OBCB 1999.

A young African American seeking identity during his high school and college days, and later in New York's Harlem, relates his terrifying experiences. He begins in the South of the 1920s and ends in Harlem with the realization that he is invisible to the white world.

Emecheta, Buchi. *The Bride Price.* G. Braziller, 1976. OBCB 1999.

Aku-nna, a very young Nigerian (Ibo) girl, and Chike, her teacher, fall in love despite tribal custom forbidding their romance. After Aku-nna's father dies unexpectedly, her uncle expects her to bring a generous bride price when she marries. But she meets Chike, who will not allow anyone else to have her, and her uncle will not accept their relationship. A tribal curse dooms Aku-nna to die in childbirth.

Faulkner, William. *The Bear.* Vintage, 1931. OBCB 1999.

Ike McCaslin's hunting trips for the legendary bear, Old Ben, are played out against opposing ideas of corruption and innocence. Ike's story is told in past and present narratives, laying out the hunting trips in which he participated from ages 10 to 16, in the late 1870s and early 1880s, ending with a final glimpse of the Mississippi woods in the present, about to fall to a lumber company.

Frazier, Charles. *Cold Mountain.* Atlantic Monthly Press, 1997. OBCB 1999.

Inman, a wounded Civil War soldier, escapes the hospital to endure the elements, The Guard, and his own weakness and infirmity in a journey, an odyssey, to return to his sweetheart, Ada. Meanwhile, Ada is fighting her own battle to survive while farming the mountainous North Carolina terrain.

Gaines, Ernest. *A Lesson before Dying.* Knopf, 1993. OBCB 1999, 2009.

In 1940s Louisiana, Jefferson, a young black man, faces the electric chair for murder. When his attorney states, "I would just as soon put a hog in the electric chair as this," his grandmother persuades disillusioned teacher Grant Wiggins to visit Jefferson in the penitentiary and help him gain a sense of dignity and self-esteem before his execution.

Gardner, John. *Grendel.* Knopf, 1971. OBCB 1999.

In a unique interpretation of the Beowulf legend, the monster Grendel relates his struggle to understand the ugliness in himself and mankind in the brutal world of 14th-century Denmark. Grendel's love of words illuminates the importance of language as an interpreter of the truth of events, and the power of art as alternative to violence.

Gibbons, Kaye. *Ellen Foster.* Algonquin, 1987. OBCB 1999.

Casting an unflinching yet humorous eye on her situation, 11-year-old Ellen tells the story of surviving her mother's death, an abusive father, and uncaring relatives to find a loving home and a new mama. In this coming-of-age southern novel, Ellen also learns that skin color does not determine character.

Heller, Joseph. *Catch-22.* Simon & Schuster, 1961. OBCB 1999.

In this satirical novel, Captain Yossarian confronts the hypocrisy and absurdity of war and bureaucracy as he frantically attempts to outwit the army and survive. A Mediterranean island is home base for the soldiers, where they escape the horrors of World War II Europe.

Hemingway, Ernest. *A Farewell to Arms.* Scribner, 1929. OBCB 1999.

World War I is the setting for this love story of an English nurse and a wounded American ambulance officer. They meet in Italy. After Frederic is wounded, Catherine visits him in the hospital, and they fall in love. When Frederic is ordered back to the front he sees that the Italian army has lost its optimism and decides to desert, taking Catherine with him to Switzerland where their story meets a tragic end.

Hesse, Hermann. *Siddhartha.* New Directions, 1951. OBCB 1999.

Emerging from a kaleidoscope of experiences and tasted pleasures, Siddhartha transcends to a state of peace and mystic holiness in this strangely simple story. Drawing on Eastern religions, particularly Buddhism and Hinduism, Siddhartha journeys toward self-knowledge.

Huxley, Aldous. *Brave New World.* Chatto & Windus, 1932. OBCB 1999.

In a chilling vision of the future, babies are produced in bottles and exist in a mechanized world without soul. Individuality is not allowed by the state; stability is everything. A revolt ensues when John the Savage is introduced into this controlled society, having grown up outside, an exception with his own thoughts and feelings.

Keneally, Thomas. *Schindler's List.* Simon & Schuster, 1982. OBCB 1999.

Oskar Schindler, a rich German factory owner, risks his life and spends his personal fortune to save Jews listed as his workers during World War II. This "documentary novel" takes the form of a series of stories based on the memories of Schindler himself, the Jews who were saved, and other witnesses to the Holocaust.

King, Laurie R. *The Beekeeper's Apprentice; or, On the Segregation of the Queen.* St. Martin's, 1994. OBCB 1999.

In 1915, retired Sherlock Holmes meets his intellectual match in 15-year-old orphan Mary Russell, who collaborates with him to investigate the kidnapping of an American senator's daughter. Mary continues to work with Holmes whenever she is on holiday from Oxford University, even while their lives are threatened by a master criminal.

Kosinski, Jerzy. *The Painted Bird.* Houghton Mifflin, 1965. OBCB 1999.

An abandoned dark-haired child wanders alone through isolated villages of Eastern Europe in World War II, struggling to survive. He witnesses evil and savagery, tormented by the peasants he encounters.

Lee, Harper. *To Kill a Mockingbird.* Lippincott, 1960. OBCB 1999.

Scout, a young girl, tells of life in a small Alabama town in the 1930s, and how she and her brother, Jem, learn to fight prejudice by watching their father's defense in court of an African American man falsely accused of raping a white woman.

LeGuin, Ursula. *The Left Hand of Darkness.* Walker, 1969. OBCB 1999.

First envoy to the technologically primitive world of Gethen (Winter), Genly Ai is sent to persuade the planet to join Ekumen, an organization of planets promoting cooperation and harmony. Ai deals with a hostile climate; a suspicious, bickering government; and his own conventional sexual mores. The inhabitants of Gethen are androgynous until specific periods when they are able to choose between being male and female; thus anyone can have children, equalizing the genders.

Malamud, Bernard. *The Fixer.* Farrar, Straus, and Giroux, 1966. OBCB 1999.

Victim of a vicious anti-Semitic conspiracy, Yakov Bok is in a Russian prison for years, waiting for a trial, with only his indomitable will to sustain him through solitary confinement. Based on the true, infamous case of a man falsely imprisoned for murder in 1911–13 Kiev.

Markandaya, Kamala. *Nectar in a Sieve.* J. Day Co., 1954. OBCB 1999.

Natural disasters, arranged marriage, and industrialization of her village are the challenges educated Rukmani must face as the bride of a peasant farmer in southern India in the early 1950s.

Mason, Bobbi Ann. *In Country.* Harper & Row, 1985. OBCB 1999.

After her father is killed in the Vietnam War, teenager Samantha Hughes lives with her uncle Emmett, whom she suspects suffers from the effects of Agent Orange. In struggling to understand the war and her father, Sam hangs out with a group of veterans, reads her father's letters and diary, and travels with her uncle from their Kentucky hometown to Washington, D.C., to visit the Vietnam War Memorial.

McCullers, Carson. *The Member of the Wedding.* Houghton Mifflin, 1946. OBCB 1999.

Twelve-year-old tomboy Frankie Adams is determined to be the third party on her brother's honeymoon, despite all advice. The day before the wedding she walks around town, meets a soldier, visits her father at work, and returns home for a talk with their housekeeper, Berenice, and her young, ill cousin, John Henry. Set in the South during World War II.

McKinley, Robin. *Beauty.* Harper & Row, 1978. OBCB 1999.

Ironically, Beauty's sisters are the ones who grow up to be lovely, while she must be content with intelligence. The family is forced to abandon their comfortable life in the city and move to a country house on the edge of a dense forest. When their father plucks the wrong rose, Beauty saves his life by offering herself to the Beast. Love is the key to unlocking a curse and transforming the Beast into a man in this romantic, traditional retelling.

Mori, Kyoko. *Shizuko's Daughter.* Henry Holt, 1993. OBCB 1999.

In the years following her mother's suicide, Japanese teenager Yuki develops the inner strength to cope with her distant father, her resentful stepmother, and her haunting, painful memories. Yuki's relationship with her grandmother helps, as do her artistic abilities and independent nature.

Morrison, Toni. *Beloved.* Knopf, 1987. OBCB 1999.

Preferring death over slavery for her children, Sethe murders her infant daughter who later mysteriously returns and almost destroys the lives of her mother and sister. In post–Civil War Ohio, Sethe recounts the horrors of life as a slave on Sweet Home Farm and her escape, offering some explanation for the tragedy that followed.

O'Brien, Tim. *The Things They Carried: A Work of Fiction.* Houghton Mifflin, 1990. OBCB 1999.

Interrelated short stories follow Tim O'Brien's platoon of American soldiers through a variety of personal and military encounters during the Vietnam War.

O'Connor, Flannery. *Everything That Rises Must Converge.* Farrar, Straus, and Giroux, 1965. OBCB 1999.

A collection of nine short stories about misfits in small southern towns that force the reader to confront hypocrisy, prejudice and complacency.

Potok, Chaim. *The Chosen.* Simon & Schuster, 1967. OBCB 1999.

A baseball injury brings two Jewish boys together in World War II–era Brooklyn. Both are sons of religious fathers. Danny's father is a Hasidic rabbi who expects Danny to follow in his footsteps. Reuven's father is Orthodox, and a Hebrew scholar. When they enter college, both boys study to be rabbis, one by choice, the other out of obligation.

Power, Susan. *The Grass Dancer.* Putnam, 1994. OBCB 1999.

Ending in the 1980s with the love story of Charlene Thunder and grass dancer Harley Wind Soldier, this multigenerational tale of a Sioux family is told in the voices of the living and the dead, reaching back to 1864. Power weaves magic, visions, and the spirit world into everyday life.

Shaara, Michael. *The Killer Angels.* McKay, 1974. OBCB 1999.

Officers and foot soldiers from both the Union and Confederacy approach and then fight the bloody Battle of Gettysburg. The battle is presented from the points of view of several important participants, providing a revealing portrayal of the turning point in the Civil War.

Steinbeck, John. *The Grapes of Wrath.* Viking, 1939. OBCB 1999.

An Oklahoma farmer and his family leave the Dust Bowl during the Great Depression to go to the promised land of California. The Joads endure a difficult journey only to encounter the hard life of migrant workers.

Uchida, Yoshiko. *Picture Bride.* Northland, 1987. OBCB 1999.

In the early 1900s, Hana Omiya journeys from her small village in Japan to the promised land of America to marry a man she has never met. Taro is older and less well-off than she expected, but they marry and raise a family, facing racial prejudice and financial struggle, but supported by close friendships. They lose everything when World War II arrives and they are sent to a relocation camp with only a few suitcases.

Watson, Larry. *Montana 1948.* Milkweed, 1993. OBCB 1999.

The summer he is 12, David watches as his family and small town are shattered by scandal and tragedy. His father is the sheriff. His uncle Frank is a war hero and the town doctor. When a young Sioux woman refuses to be treated by Frank, she reveals his reputation for raping Native American women.

Wright, Richard. *Native Son.* Harper, 1940. OBCB 1999.

For Bigger Thomas, an African American man accused of a crime in the white man's world, there could be no extenuating circumstances, no explanations—only death. A young man in 1930s Chicago, Thomas commits two murders. His behavior is presented as inevitable due to the racist and unjust world in which he lives.

Yolen, Jane. *Briar Rose.* Tom Doherty, 1992. OBCB 1999.

Disturbed by her grandmother Gemma's unique version of "Sleeping Beauty," Rebecca seeks the truth behind the fairy tale. It leads her to Poland during the Holocaust, and the extermination of homosexuals in the concentration camps.

· NONFICTION ·

Alvarez, Walter. *T. Rex and the Crater of Doom.* Princeton University Press, 1997. OBCB 1999.

Geologist Alvarez presents the development of the impact theory of dinosaur extinction as the adventure/mystery it was. Alvarez was one of the four scientists who proposed the theory, which was initially ridiculed by the scientific community. They proved it using geology and the discovery of the impact crater in the Yucatan Peninsula.

Aronson, Marc. *Art Attack: A Short Cultural History of the Avant-Garde.* Clarion, 1998. OBCB 1999.

Discover everything you ever wanted to know about bohemians, hipsters, and the development of the world's most radical art. In this social history of art in the 20th century, the visual is accompanied by the musical and literary, from Stravinsky and Nijinsky to Warhol to rock and roll. Generous black-and-white illustrations are presented beside film and music recommendations, inviting readers to make this book a multimedia experience.

Asinof, Eliot. *Eight Men Out: The Black Sox and the 1919 World Series.* Holt, Rinehart, and Winston, 1963. OBCB 1999.

It's all here: the players, the scandal, the shame, and the damage the 1919 World Series caused America's national pastime. The scandal went far beyond the players to the owners, politicians, and gamblers. Asinof delves into the 1921 trial that made the players the scapegoats for everyone involved and re-creates the post–World War I time period in American history.

Atkin, S. Beth. *Voices from the Streets: Young Former Gang Members Tell Their Stories.* Little, Brown, 1996. OBCB 1999. o.p. (BBYA)

Gang members from all races and backgrounds describe why they joined, and why—and how—they left. Their first-person narratives are filled with street language and harsh events, made more positive by the fact that these young people are reconstructing their lives after leaving gang life. Black-and-white photographs of the subjects are included.

Bernstein, Leonard. *The Joy of Music.* Simon & Schuster, 1959. OBCB 1999.

Bernstein describes all aspects of classical music in a passionate, accessible narrative, even while admitting the impossibility of fully explaining organized sound with words. Bernstein addresses Beethoven, jazz and musical theater, opera, and the American symphony, always focusing on the music itself.

Blackstone, Harry, Jr. *The Blackstone Book of Magic and Illusion.* Newmarket Press, 1985. OBCB 1999, 2004.

The classic of legerdemain describes the rich history of modern magic from ancient times to the present, including vaudeville, Broadway, Vegas, and television. Illustrated with black-and-white photographs, Blackstone's book reveals the secrets and psychology behind popular magic tricks and effects. The foreword is by Ray Bradbury.

Blais, Madeleine. *In These Girls, Hope Is a Muscle.* Atlantic Monthly Press, 1995. OBCB 1999. (BBYA)

Learn about the year of heart, sweat, and muscle that transformed the Amherst Lady Hurricanes basketball team into state champions. Blais follows this high school basketball team through its 1992–93 season, covering the lives of the individual players, how they developed into a winning team, and the small town that united behind them.

Bodanis, David. *The Secret Family: Twenty-four Hours Inside the Mysterious World of Our Minds and Bodies.* Simon & Schuster, 1997. OBCB 1999. o.p. (Alex Award)

The unseen world around us and within our bodies is shown in vivid detail as we follow a typical family through their day. Photography and text combine to awe and disgust the reader. Bodanis reveals everything from the ingredients in baby food, to the germs exchanged during a first kiss, to the disturbing effects of antibiotics.

Boorstin, Jon. *Making Movies Work: Thinking like a Filmmaker.* Silman-James Press, 1996. OBCB 1999.

Both novice and expert can enjoy this behind-the-scenes look at the art of filmmaking. Boorstin posits that movies must work on three levels: voyeur, vicarious, and visceral. Successful films make the audience feel, and Boorstin writes about the craft necessary to create that success.

Brown, Dee. *Bury My Heart at Wounded Knee: An Indian History of the American West.* Holt, Rinehart, and Winston, 1970. OBCB 1999.

There's another side of America's western expansion: the one seen through Native American eyes. Brown tells how American Indians lost their land to white settlers from 1860 to 1890, tracing history from the Long Walk to Wounded Knee, and the brutal results of resistance.

Brumberg, Joan Jacobs. *The Body Project: An Intimate History of American Girls.* Random House, 1997. OBCB 1999.

The historical evolution of body perception has turned the value system of American girls inside out. Brumberg traces physical enhancements through the 19th and 20th centuries, from clothing and makeup to piercings and diets. She also covers cultural changes that have affected menstruation, hygiene, and sexuality. Generous illustrations and primary-source research augment the text.

Carson, Rachel. *Silent Spring.* Houghton Mifflin, 1962. OBCB 1999.

This landmark book gave birth to the environmental movement and is still chillingly relevant today. Carson writes about pesticides and other chemicals, and the way in which they are poisoning the natural world and making their way into our food sources.

Chang, Iris. *The Rape of Nanking: The Forgotten Holocaust of World War II.* Basic Books, 1997. OBCB 1999, 2009.

Barely a postscript in official Japanese history, the horrific torture and murder of hundreds of thousands of Chinese citizens took place over the course of just seven weeks. The Japanese army invaded Nanking in December 1937 and proceeded to slaughter over 300,000 soldiers and civilians. Chang analyzes the continued Japanese denial of responsibility, then turns to the story of a German businessman who persuaded Hitler to put a stop to the killing.

Clark, Kenneth. *Civilisation: A Personal View.* Harper & Row, 1969. OBCB 1999. o.p.

Clark explores history through the works, impulses, and beliefs of the great creative individuals of Western civilization. This book is the companion to an acclaimed BBC television series in which Clark illuminated European and American cultural history from the fall of the Roman Empire to the present.

Cooke, Mervyn. *The Chronicle of Jazz.* Abbeville Press, 1998. OBCB 1999. o.p.

Cooke provides a comprehensive guide to this uniquely American musical form. This is a chronological, year-by-year history of jazz from the turn of the century to the early 1990s, including discographies, biographies, and photographs, which takes into account the roots of the form as well as its interaction with other musical styles.

Copland, Aaron. *What to Listen For in Music.* McGraw-Hill, 1939. OBCB 1999.

The composer provides a basic introduction to the mysteries of musical composition and music appreciation. Copland takes the reader through the fundamentals (rhythm, melody, harmony, tone color), then introduces texture, classical forms (sonata, fugal, variation, etc.) and contexts, such as opera and film.

Cumming, Robert. *Annotated Art.* Dorling Kindersley, 1995. OBCB 1999. o.p.

Art masterpieces from the 14th century to the present are made understandable through the exploration of some of the world's greatest paintings. Each painting is briefly interpreted from a variety of angles: technique, subject matter, time period, artist, and symbolism.

Day, David. *The Search for King Arthur.* Facts on File, 1995. OBCB 1999. o.p.

Discover through magnificent illustrations and romantic retellings what is fact and what is legend about this fifth-century hero, Artorius Dux Bellorum. Incorporating literature, art, religion, and politics, Day places Arthur, as well as related people and events, in context.

Diamond, Jared. *Guns, Germs, and Steel: The Fates of Human Societies.* Norton, 1997. OBCB 1999, 2004.

Why do some societies become rich and powerful while others remain poor and powerless? Diamond, an evolutionary biologist, contends that three elements—guns, germs, and steel—determined the course of history. The rise of human civilizations is explained in terms of geography, ecology, and the development of agriculture.

Dorris, Michael. *The Broken Cord.* Harper & Row, 1989. OBCB 1999.

Dorris, part Native American, was 26 and single when he decided to adopt a child. He knew that Adam was small for his age, and behind his peers developmentally. However, the persistent physical and emotional problems of his adopted son baffled him until he learned the condition had a name: Fetal Alcohol Syndrome.

Du Bois, W. E. B. *The Souls of Black Folk: Essays and Sketches.* A. C. McClurg, 1903. OBCB 1999.

Educator Du Bois describes the lives and history of African American farmers, including the career of Booker T. Washington. In this collection of 14 essays, Du Bois illuminates the injustices of being an African American at the turn of the 20th century, and declares race to be the 20th century's most important issue.

Due, Linnea. *Joining the Tribe: Growing Up Gay and Lesbian in the '90s.* Anchor Books, 1995. OBCB 1999.

Being young and gay in America means surviving cruelty, abuse, and isolation, as these individual stories of courage from teens around the country attest. There are also tales of support from family, friends, and communities. Due provides context and commentary while allowing the teens to tell their own stories.

Edelman, Marion Wright. *The Measure of Our Success: A Letter to My Children and Yours.* Beacon Press, 1992. OBCB 1999.

A child advocate shares her thoughts on values, raising families, service, and the future of our country. Edelman founded the Children's Defense Fund, is a civil rights attorney, and raised three sons. Here she shares 25 Lessons for Life and a letter to her sons.

Epictetus and Sharon Lebell. *The Art of Living: The Classic Manual on Virtue, Happiness, and Effectiveness.* HarperCollins, 1995. OBCB 1999.

A modern interpretation of the Stoic philosopher (Epictetus was born in 55 A.D.) answers the timeless questions of how to be a good person and live a good life. Lebell updates his advice, which is based on knowing the difference between what we can and cannot control and responding to life accordingly.

Faludi, Susan. *Backlash: The Undeclared War against American Women.* Crown, 1991. OBCB 1999.

This unflinching analysis examines the current status of American women and gender equality. Faludi posits that the achievements of feminism unleashed a backlash against women in the 1980s and finds evidence in TV, film, advertising, fashion, politics, and popular psychology. A model of passionate writing and meticulous research.

Finn, David. *How to Look at Sculpture: Text and Photographs.* Harry N. Abrams, 1989. OBCB 1999. o.p.

To understand sculpture, you have to know what to look for. Finn teaches the reader how to fully experience and appreciate sculpture: the importance of viewing from multiple angles, placement of the sculpture, light, touch, texture, form, and materials. The author includes examples from a variety of time periods and cultures, and his photographs are especially elucidating.

Ford, Michael Thomas. *The Voices of AIDS: Twelve Unforgettable People Talk about How AIDS Has Changed Their Lives.* Morrow Junior Books, 1995. OBCB 1999. o.p. (BBYA)

Individuals whose AIDS experiences have been catalysts for making a difference share their poignant and personal stories. All twelve, both men and women, are active in the fight against AIDS, and for AIDS education. Informational sections alternate with the interviews.

Fouts, Roger. *Next of Kin: What Chimpanzees Have Taught Me about Who We Are.* Morrow, 1997. OBCB 1999.

Describing his career of communicating with chimpanzees, Fouts explains evolutionary, genetic, and emotional bonds with our next of kin. In particular, Fouts relates his experiences with the chimpanzees in his American Sign Language program, including his groundbreaking work on Project Washoe.

Freedman, Samuel G. *Small Victories: The Real World of a Teacher, Her Students, and Their High School.* Harper & Row, 1989. OBCB 1999.

How does New York's Seward Park, an overcrowded, underfunded inner-city high school, send 92 percent of its graduates to college? Freedman follows one English teacher, Jessica Siegel, through the 1987–88 school year, alternating her experience with chapters about other members of the school community.

Fremon, Celeste. *Father Greg and the Homeboys: The Extraordinary Journey of Father Greg Boyle and His Work with the Latino Gangs of East L.A.* Hyperion, 1995. OBCB 1999. o.p. (BBYA)

Conscience, parent, motivator, drill sergeant: Father Greg was all this and more to the gangbangers who called his barrio parish community home. Boyle worked to find jobs and schooling for the kids in his neighborhood, helping them to change their lives. Fremon intersperses first-person narratives from several of the boys.

Garfunkel, Trudy. *On Wings of Joy: The Story of Ballet from the 16th Century to Today.* Little, Brown, 1994. OBCB 1999, 2004.

Immerse yourself in the world of ballet, from its earliest choreography to the life of a modern ballerina. Garfunkel provides entertaining, comprehensive coverage of the history of ballet, as well as the lives of the great dancers, choreographers, and composers involved.

Goldberg, Vicki. *The Power of Photographs: How Photography Changed Our Lives.* Abbeville Press, 1991. OBCB 1999.

Photographers and photographs evolve, rather than springing forth fully formed. The history of the photograph is traced from the daguerreotype to the present, and specific, famous photographs are reproduced and studied for their influence on larger events such as the Vietnam War and the civil rights movement.

Gombrich, E. H. *The Story of Art.* Phaidon, 1995 (original: Phaidon, 1950). OBCB 1999.

Everything from cave paintings to the experimental art of today is covered, in words and pictures, in one of the most famous and popular art books ever published. This 16th edition has enhanced and expanded illustrations, improved captions, and a new index.

Gould, Stephen Jay. *The Mismeasure of Man.* Norton, 1981. OBCB 1999.

Gould's history of the attempt to quantify intelligence could be called the "misuse of science." He demonstrates that those who insisted on finding ways to measure intelligence throughout history did so in order to maintain their own position as the most worthy, in particular white European men.

Green, Bill. *Water, Ice, and Stone: Science and Memory on the Antarctic Lakes.* Harmony Books, 1995. OBCB 1999.

A chemist investigates Antarctica's ice-covered lakes and discovers beauty and poetry. This is an account of fieldwork in Antarctica that illuminates the process of scientific research, while delivering an adventure story and a personal reflection on what motivates us to explore our world.

Hafner, Katie, and Matthew Lyon. *Where Wizards Stay Up Late: The Origins of the Internet.* Simon & Schuster, 1996. OBCB 1999.

The origins of the world's first computer network are explained, with tales of the motivations, breakthroughs, and personalities that created it. It began with ARPANET, a network created in the 1960s to link research laboratory computers across the country. The authors profile the men, agencies, and universities that made the Internet possible, substantiated by extensive interviews.

Hamilton, Edith. *Mythology.* Little, Brown, 1942. OBCB 1999.

Gods and heroes, their clashes and adventures, come alive in this splendid retelling of the Greek, Roman, and Norse myths.

Hawking, Stephen. *A Brief History of Time: From the Big Bang to Black Holes.* Bantam, 1988. OBCB 1999.

Cosmology becomes understandable as the author discusses the origin, evolution, and fate of our universe. Hawking addresses cutting-edge questions about gravity, black holes, time, and the Big Bang in a manner accessible to the lay reader.

Hersch, Patricia. *A Tribe Apart: A Journey into the Heart of American Adolescence.* Fawcett Columbine, 1998. OBCB 1999.

An intimate three-year journey through contemporary adolescence with eight "typical" teens in Reston, Virginia, reveals a separate culture spawned not from personal choice, but rather from adult alienation and abandonment. Hersch concludes that teenagers want and need more guidance and attention.

Hersey, John. *Hiroshima.* Knopf, 1946. OBCB 1999.

Six Hiroshima survivors reflect on the aftermath of the first atomic bomb. Hersey begins with what each person was doing when the bomb was dropped, then follows them through the aftermath.

Holy Bible: New Revised Standard Version. Collins, 1973. OBCB 1999.

Biblical scholars revise text and modernize terms to bring one version of the Bible up-to-date.

Hubbell, Sue. *A Country Year: Living the Questions.* Random House, 1986. OBCB 1999.

A former wife and librarian observes her natural surroundings during a year spent as a beekeeper on a beautiful Ozark farm. Most of the short chapters are essays about a particular plant or animal and include a small sketch. Hubbell's writing is shaped by the seasons of honey production and her own constantly inquiring mind.

Humes, Edward. *No Matter How Loud I Shout: A Year in the Life of Juvenile Court.* Simon & Schuster, 1996. OBCB 1999.

Humes paints a tragic and heartbreaking portrait of the chaos characterizing America's juvenile justice system where, as one inmate writes, "my screams have no voice, no matter how loud I shout." Humes spent 1994 studying the system in Los Angeles, following the cases of seven young people and some of the adults trying to work effectively within it.

Jonas, Gerald. *Dancing: The Pleasure, Power, and Art of Movement.* Harry N. Abrams, 1992. OBCB 1999.

This international survey explores dance as social, cultural, and religious expression. This illustrated volume was created as the companion to a 1983 television series which brought together experts from across the field. *Dancing* spans the world, including both

Western and non-Western, traditional and modern, and points out similarities in the way dance is used in various societies.

Jones, K. Maurice. *Say It Loud! The Story of Rap Music.* Millbrook Press, 1994. OBCB 1999. o.p.

From a village in West Africa to a street in Brooklyn to MTV, rappers make the Scene. Jones traces rap music from its birth thousands of years ago, to its dissemination via the slave trade, through its effects on young people today. The inclusion of quotes, lyrics, and photographs, as well as careful documentation, create a complete study of a popular culture.

Junger, Sebastian. *The Perfect Storm: A True Story of Men against the Sea.* Norton, 1997. OBCB 1999. (Alex Award)

Haunting premonitions didn't save seven fisherman from the ferocious and deadly power of the sea. Junger interviewed survivors, Coast Guard rescue swimmers, and family members to create an adventure narrative about the doomed swordfish boat and crew that perished in October 1991 off the coast of Nova Scotia.

Karnos, David D., and Robert G. Shoemaker, eds. *Falling in Love with Wisdom: American Philosophers Talk about Their Calling.* Oxford University Press, 1993. OBCB 1999.

Contemporary philosophers share their contemplations and epiphanies. Sixty-two short essays by today's teachers of philosophy reveal different paths to the discipline, and a passion for the study of meaning.

Kendall, Elizabeth. *Where She Danced.* Knopf, 1979. OBCB 1999. o.p.

The contributions of major innovators and the conditions of their times are the basis for this history of modern American dance. Kendall studies the ancestors of modern art dance in America, from spectacle-extravaganzas to the revival of ballet as an art form, Ruth St. Denis, Martha Graham, musical theater, and Hollywood.

Kerner, Mary. *Barefoot to Balanchine: How to Watch Dance.* Anchor Books, 1990. OBCB 1999. o.p.

Understand dance by reading about its history, choreography, and backstage action. Kerner teaches readers to evaluate dance by outlining the elements (basic steps, techniques, and types of movement), and what to watch for in a performance.

Kolb, Rocky. *Blind Watchers of the Sky: The People and Ideas That Shaped Our View of the Universe.* Addison-Wesley, 1996. OBCB 1999.

Kolb delivers a witty and lively history of astronomy and cosmology over the last 400 years. He emphasizes the process of discovery as a disorganized human struggle, presenting major leaps of understanding in a humorous manner.

Kotlowitz, Alex. *The Other Side of the River: A Story of Two Towns, a Death, and America's Dilemma.* Nan A. Talese, 1998. OBCB 1999.

Geographically, only a river separates two closely neighboring towns, but the murder mystery surrounding the death of a young black man exposes a deeply rooted racial divide. Eric McGinnis's body was found in that Michigan river in 1991. On one side predominantly white St. Joseph, on the other poverty-ridden predominantly African American Benton Harbor.

Kozol, Jonathan. *Savage Inequalities: Children in America's Schools.* Crown, 1991. OBCB 1999.

Kozol's stinging indictment of America's public school system advocates an equal distribution of per pupil funding to right the gross inequities in our current system. Visiting schools around the country, he found tracking that separates minority children into secondary tiers. Teachers and students speak for themselves, revealing appalling conditions and racial segregation.

Krakauer, John. *Into Thin Air: A Personal Account of the Mount Everest Disaster.* Villard, 1997. OBCB 1999. (Alex Award, BBYA)

His dream expedition to Everest became a nightmare when human error and a sudden storm combined to claim the lives of some of the world's best mountain climbers. Krakauer went to Nepal in 1996 to report on the commercialization of climbing to the peak, and came away with a tragic narrative of survivor's guilt, questions about the presence of amateur climbers in such a setting, and the responsibilities of the relationship between guides and clients.

McCloud, Scott. *Understanding Comics: The Invisible Art.* Kitchen Sink Press, 1993. OBCB 1999.

A comic book asks and answers the question of whether or not comics are a literary form. McCloud tells the history of using pictures to tell stories and explains how comics are created and how they should be read.

McPhee, John. *In Suspect Terrain.* Farrar, Straus, and Giroux, 1982. OBCB 1999.

Traveling along I-80 from New York City to Chicago with geologist Anita Harris, McPhee describes the geologic features that reveal the history of the Appalachians. Harris does not accept all of the elements of plate tectonic theory and glacial geology as they stand; this work reveals the questions still being studied and the land that provides the evidence.

Murray, Albert. *Stomping the Blues.* McGraw-Hill, 1976. OBCB 1999.

An aficionado gives the lowdown on what the blues are, what they are not, and their origins. Murray also finds the connections between blues and both art music and popular music today.

Occhiogrosso, Peter. *The Joy of Sects: A Spirited Guide to the World's Religious Traditions.* Doubleday, 1994. OBCB 1999.

This lively, easy-to-understand guidebook to world religions is for everyone from the faithful believer to the curious doubter. Contains chapters on Hinduism, Buddhism, Taoism, Judaism, Christianity, Islam, and New Age religions.

O'Gorman, James F. *ABC of Architecture.* University of Pennsylvania Press, 1998. OBCB 1999.

Function, structure, and beauty are the interdependent basics—the ABC—of architecture. Writing for the beginner, O'Gorman provides a concise introduction to both the history and theory of the topic.

Paulos, John Allen. *Innumeracy: Mathematical Illiteracy and Its Consequences.* Hill and Wang, 1988. OBCB 1999.

Paulos illustrates the importance of understanding (and the consequences of misunderstanding) mathematical concepts in everyday life. Entertaining anecdotes balance diatribe proving innumeracy equal in significance to illiteracy in modern society.

Penn, W. S., ed. *The Telling of the World: Native American Stories and Art.* Stewart, Tabori, & Chang, 1996. OBCB 1999. o.p.

Traditional and contemporary legends, stories, and art from many North American tribes explain our world. The book is organized according to the life cycle, from birth through adolescence, marriage, family, old age, death, and renewal. Tales are inventively paired with contemporary art.

Petroski, Henry. *Invention by Design: How Engineers Get from Thought to Thing.* Harvard University Press, 1996. OBCB 1999.

Using examples from paper clips to monumental bridges, Petroski shows how engineers work. A series of case studies is presented, enhanced by illustrations and quotes from patent applications. Petroski shows how technical failures are resolved and inventions are made economically affordable.

Pipher, Mary. *Reviving Ophelia: Saving the Selves of Adolescent Girls.* Putnam, 1994. OBCB 1999.

Pipher looks at societal "girl poisoning" and the emotional and psychological havoc it wreaks on the lives of young women. She uses case histories, anecdotal evidence, and research findings, as well as her own work as a psychotherapist, to demonstrate the difficulties and dangers faced by teenage girls in today's world.

Regis, Ed. *Virus Ground Zero: Stalking the Killer Viruses with the Centers for Disease Control.* Pocket Books, 1996. OBCB 1999.

The history of the CDC is told through the handling of the 1995 Ebola outbreak in Zaire. Regis presents the CDC as a heroic institution, successfully combating infectious disease since its creation in the 1940s.

Rybczynski, Witold. *The Most Beautiful House in the World.* Viking, 1989. OBCB 1999.

The author's dream of building a boat evolves into the expansion of a boathouse into a full-scale home, a process he uses to explain complex architectural ideas. Rybczynski meditates on the meaning of a house and the nature of an architect's work.

Sheehan, Neil. *A Bright Shining Lie: John Paul Vann and America in Vietnam.* Random House, 1988. OBCB 1999.

A soldier exposes the corruption undermining the American war effort in Vietnam. Lt. Col. John Paul Vann was an army field adviser who became disillusioned with the way the war was being fought and run. He shared his pessimism with the press in Saigon, including Sheehan. Several years of research resulted in this blend of biography, history, and Sheehan's own memories of the conflict.

Sherman, Robert, and Philip Seldon. *The Complete Idiot's Guide to Classical Music.* Alpha Books, 1997. OBCB 1999. o.p.

This practical guide will help the reader to understand and enjoy classical music. The authors cover all the basics, including a history of classical music, composers, performers, instrumental and vocal music including opera, identifying the sound of particular instruments, concert hall etiquette, starting a listening collection, and even buying a sound system.

Simon, David, and Edward Burns. *The Corner: A Year in the Life of an Inner-City Neighborhood.* Broadway Books, 1997. OBCB 1999.

Crack owns this corner and infects the lives of all those within reach. Simon and Burns (creators of the HBO series *The Wire*) follow the McCullough family for a year, exposing life on the drug-filled streets of Baltimore.

Singh, Simon. *Fermat's Enigma: The Epic Quest to Solve the World's Greatest Mathematical Problem.* Walker, 1997. OBCB 1999.

A Princeton professor pursues a lifelong dream of solving a 350-year-old mathematical puzzle. Singh follows the story of Andrew Wiles, who worked in solitude for seven years before presenting a solution for Fermat's theorem in 1993, while tracing the failed attempts that preceded his.

Sobel, Dava. *Longitude: The True Story of a Lone Genius Who Solved the Greatest Scientific Problem of His Time.* Walker, 1995. OBCB 1999, 2004.

The little-known story behind the greatest innovation in navigational science: an 18th-century version of the GPS. The English government created a contest with an incredibly generous cash prize for the person who could devise a way to determine east-west position while at sea. The popular option was astronomy, but clockmaker John Harrison's chronometer eventually proved the solution to the problem.

Spiegelman, Art. *The Complete Maus: A Survivor's Tale.* Knopf/Pantheon, 1996. OBCB 1999, 2009.

The author portrays his parents' experiences during the Holocaust, their time at Auschwitz, survival, and years in the United States in this seminal graphic novel. Spiegelman also reveals his own struggle to come to terms with the past, the success of *Maus: A Survivor's Tale*, and the effects of his choice to represent the Nazis as cats and the Jews as mice.

Strickland, Carol. *The Annotated Mona Lisa: A Crash Course in Art History from Prehistoric to Post-Modern.* Andrews McMeel, 2007. OBCB 1999, 2009.

In an accessible format, this unique work provides a basic working knowledge of art and art history through short essays, sidebars, and photographs. Strickland covers it all, from cave paintings to digital media.

Stringer, Christopher, and Robin McKie. *African Exodus: The Origins of Modern Humanity.* Henry Holt, 1997. OBCB 1999. o.p.

The authors support the theory of a single origin of modern humanity with paleoanthropological, archaeological, and DNA evidence. They show that all modern-day humans are of one race, which originated in Africa less than 100,000 years ago. The many complexities surrounding human evolution are elucidated, using numerous illustrations for clarification.

Thomas, Lewis. *The Lives of a Cell: Notes of a Biology Watcher.* Viking, 1974. OBCB 1999.

Twenty-nine short essays offer an optimistic scientist's view of a wide variety of subjects.

Watson, James D. *The Double Helix: A Personal Account of the Discovery and Structure of DNA.* Atheneum, 1968. OBCB 1999.

The author re-creates the excitement of co-discovering the structure of DNA with Francis Crick and winning the Nobel Prize as a result. Watson demonstrates to the nonscientist how the scientific method works, and shares his experiences, warts and all.

Williams, Juan. *Eyes on the Prize: America's Civil Rights Years, 1954–1965.* Viking, 1987. OBCB 1999.

From *Brown v. Board of Education* to the Voting Rights Act, Williams outlines the social and political gains of African Americans, detailing the events of the civil rights movement. Photographs and words by participants are interspersed.

Yolen, Jane, ed. *Favorite Folktales from Around the World.* Pantheon, 1986. OBCB 1999.

This collection of international folktales provides an understanding of the roots of diverse cultures. The tales are grouped by theme, and each section is introduced by Yolen, who emphasizes connections to a tradition of oral storytelling around the world. One hundred and sixty tales from over 40 cultures are included, both classics and lesser-known stories.

· BIOGRAPHY ·

ISABEL ALLENDE

Allende, Isabel. *Paula.* HarperCollins, 1995. OBCB 1999.

At the bedside of her dying daughter, Allende spins tales of childhood, of ancestors, and of becoming a novelist. In this memoir she tells of her childhood in Chile, her uncle Salvador's reign as president of Chile and his violent death, and the family's flight to Venezuela. Allende writes of her own mother, her grandmother, her marriages, and occasionally touches on fantasy.

AMERICAN SERVICE PERSONNEL

Edelman, Bernard, ed. *Dear America: Letters Home from Vietnam.* Norton, 1985. OBCB 1999.

Letters from those who made it back and from those who did not return provide a glimpse into the lives of the men and women who served during the Vietnam War.

MAYA ANGELOU

Angelou, Maya. *I Know Why the Caged Bird Sings.* Random House, 1970. OBCB 1999.

In the first of her five autobiographies, the African American writer, poet, and actress traces her coming of age in 1930s and '40s America. After their parents separate, Marguerite (Maya) and her brother (ages 3 and 4) are shuttled between living with their grandmother in rural Arkansas, and their mother in St. Louis and later San Francisco. Maya endures rape at a young age, a later unwanted pregnancy, and the loss of her brother to the merchant marines.

RUSSELL BAKER

Baker, Russell. *Growing Up.* Congdon & Weed, 1982. OBCB 1999.

A columnist with a sense of humor takes a gentle look at his childhood in Virginia, New Jersey, and Baltimore during the Depression. Baker intersperses stories of his mother's and father's lives before his birth with those of his own youth, enlistment in the Navy, meeting his future wife, and becoming a *Baltimore Sun* reporter in 1950.

MARIE CURIE

Curie, Eve. *Madam Curie: A Biography.* Doubleday, 1937. OBCB 1999.

In sharing personal papers and her own memories, a daughter pays tribute to her unique and generous mother, a scientific genius. Eve Curie emphasizes her mother's achievements: her work on radioactivity, her discovery of radium and polonium, and winning the Nobel Prize twice, in physics and chemistry.

FREDERICK DOUGLASS

Douglass, Frederick. *Narrative of the Life of Frederick Douglass, an American Slave, Written by Himself.* Anti-Slavery Office, 1845. OBCB 1999.

Former slave and famed abolitionist Frederick Douglass describes the horrors of his enslavement and eventual escape. Born into slavery, Douglass escaped in 1838 at the age of 20 and moved to Massachusetts, where he began his abolitionist activities.

RICHARD FEYNMAN

Feynman, Richard P., as told to Ralph Leighton. *Surely You're Joking, Mr. Feynman: Adventures of a Curious Character.* Norton, 1985. OBCB 1999.

This Nobel Prize–winning physicist was also a bongo drummer, a practical joker, and a loving husband. His autobiography is a series of anecdotes based on conversations with Ralph Leighton during drumming sessions.

ANNE FRANK

Frank, Anne. *Anne Frank: The Diary of a Young Girl.* Doubleday, 1952. OBCB 1999. (BBYA)

In 1942 Amsterdam, Anne and her sister and parents went into hiding in an attempt to escape deportment to a concentration camp. Through the diary she kept, 13-year-old Anne Frank put a human face on the Holocaust experience.

JOHN HOCKENBERRY

Hockenberry, John. *Moving Violations: War Zones, Wheelchairs, and Declarations of Independence.* Hyperion, 1995. OBCB 1999. (BBYA)

Journalist Hockenberry is fearless and funny as he relates the personal and professional experiences he encounters from his wheelchair. He shares how he was left a paraplegic after a car accident at age 19, then tells of his rehab, marriage, and being an NPR correspondent in the Middle East.

STONEWALL JACKSON

Robertson, James I. *Stonewall Jackson: The Man, the Soldier, the Legend.* Macmillan, 1997. OBCB 1999.

Both the genius and the failings of the confederate Civil War general are chronicled in this meticulous account, which emphasizes Jackson's religious faith and military career.

JI-LI JIANG

Jiang, Ji-li. *Red Scarf Girl: A Memoir of the Cultural Revolution.* HarperCollins, 1997. OBCB 1999. (BBYA)

A young Chinese girl must make difficult choices when the government urges her to repudiate her ancestors and inform on her own parents. Jiang was 12 in 1966, when the Cultural Revolution began. Her family suffered because Jiang's grandfather was once a landlord. Over time Jiang transforms from a follower to a young adult who questions those in power.

MARY KARR

Karr, Mary. *The Liars' Club: A Memoir.* Viking, 1995. OBCB 1999.

Growing up in "a family of liars and drunks" is never easy, and yet, despite alcoholism, rape, and other dark secrets, the author makes childhood in an east Texas refinery town sound as funny as it was painful.

HELEN KELLER

Keller, Helen. *The Story of My Life.* Grosset & Dunlap, 1902. OBCB 1999.

Overcoming deafness and blindness to become an outstanding citizen, Helen Keller embodies courage, passion, and perseverance. Keller writes about the illness that left her disabled; learning to express herself, to read and write and speak; her relationship with her teacher, Annie Sullivan; and life through her second year at Radcliffe.

YELENA KHANGA

Khanga, Yelena, and Susan Jacoby. *Soul to Soul: A Black Russian American Family, 1865–1992.* Norton, 1992. OBCB 1999. o.p.

A young Russian journalist of African American and Jewish heritage analyzes and compares attitudes on race, religion, and sexism in Russia and America. After growing up in white, anti-America Soviet Union, Khanga worked at *Moscow News* and then in Boston at the *Christian Science Monitor.* In America she tracked down her relatives and had strong reactions to the racism she encountered.

JAMAICA KINCAID

Kincaid, Jamaica. *My Brother.* Farrar, Straus, and Giroux, 1997. OBCB 1999.

The author returns to the Caribbean island of her birth to help care for her younger brother who is dying of AIDS. She never knew him well because she left for the United States when she was 16 and he was only 3. Caring for her brother during his last year, Kincaid also faces up to her difficult relationship with their mother.

MERIWETHER LEWIS

Ambrose, Stephen E. *Undaunted Courage: Meriwether Lewis, Thomas Jefferson, and the Opening of the American West.* Simon & Schuster, 1996. OBCB 1999.

Lewis and Clark brave the wilds of North America in a vivid account of exploration and adventure. This biography of Meriwether Lewis relies on the journals of both Lewis and Clark, as well as the author's own travels along their route. Lewis lived in the White House as secretary to Thomas Jefferson for two years, and was hand-picked for the expedition. Following the years of exploration, Lewis suffered from depression and took his own life.

MARK MATHABANE

Mathabane, Mark. *Kaffir Boy: The True Story of a Black Youth's Coming of Age in Apartheid South Africa.* Macmillan, 1986. OBCB 1999.

Growing up under the brutalities of apartheid South Africa, Mathabane describes the growing unrest in his country. Mathabane was born outside Johannesburg, the son of desperately poor parents. His mother sacrificed to send him to school where he excelled, eventually escaping to America on a tennis scholarship.

JAMES MCBRIDE AND RUTH MCBRIDE-JORDAN

McBride, James. *The Color of Water: A Black Man's Tribute to His White Mother.* Riverhead, 1996. OBCB 1999.

McBride's father, a black Harlem musician, and his mother, the daughter of an Orthodox Jewish rabbi, married in 1942. The author blends his own story with that of his white mother, who battled poverty and racism to raise 12 children in Queens.

FRANK MCCOURT

McCourt, Frank. *Angela's Ashes: A Memoir.* Scribner, 1996. OBCB 1999.

Illness, hunger, alcoholism, and death plagued McCourt's childhood in Ireland, but some-how he survived with his spirit and humor intact. His father drank what little money the family had, his mother was reduced to begging for assistance, and he lost three siblings to sickness. As a teenager, McCourt learned to be ashamed of poverty and discovered Shakespeare and the Irish Catholic Church.

VED MEHTA

Mehta, Ved. *Sound-Shadows of the New World.* Norton, 1985. OBCB 1999.

Leaving his home, family, country, and culture behind, a blind Indian 15-year-old boy travels to Arkansas in 1949 to attend a special school where he is challenged by handi-cap, loneliness, poor preparation, and culture shock. He learns to walk without a cane, using the school's system of sounds and shadows, and eventually leaves for college in California.

ANN MOODY

Moody, Ann. *Coming of Age in Mississippi.* Dial Press, 1968. OBCB 1999.

One of the first brave young African American students to participate in a lunch counter sit-in, Moody becomes a heroine of the civil rights movement. Moody grew up in the rural South in the 1940s and '50s; Emmett Till's lynching took place one week before she began high school. An excellent student, she won a basketball scholarship to college, and began to join in demonstrations and sit-ins.

PAT MORA

Mora, Pat. *House of Houses.* Beacon Press, 1997. OBCB 1999.

With magic and imagination, author Pat Mora weaves the voices of her ancestors into her own personal account of growing up in a Mexican American family in El Paso, Texas. The story begins with a visit to the cemetery, where all of her relatives come alive. Songs, recipes, and stories enliven this account in 12 chapters, one for each month of a year in the family's life.

LUIS RODRIGUEZ

Rodriguez, Luis. *Always Running: La Vida Loca, Gang Days in L.A.* Curbstone Press, 1993. OBCB 1999.

Hoping to dissuade his son from the life, Rodriguez tells the story of his youth in a Los Angeles gang in the 1960s and '70s. Rodriguez found a way out through poetry and education, and recounts his experiences as a Chicano activist.

RICHARD RODRIGUEZ

Rodriguez, Richard. *Hunger of Memory: The Education of Richard Rodriguez; An Autobiography.* D. R. Godine, 1982. OBCB 1999.

Rodriguez is the son of Mexican immigrants whose journey through the educational system convinced him that family, culture, and language must be left behind to succeed in mainstream America. *Hunger of Memory* was controversial upon publication due to the author's criticism of affirmative action; Rodriguez did not believe he should be considered a minority, thanks to his education.

TSAR NICHOLAS ROMANOV AND TSARINA ALEXANDRA

Massie, Robert K. *Nicholas and Alexandra.* Atheneum, 1967. OBCB 1999.

On the brink of revolution, the last tsar of Russia and his family become victims of their own mismanagement and personal problems. While the royal family is Massie's focus, he presents a clear picture of Russia as a whole during the time period.

ELEANOR ROOSEVELT

Cook, Blanche Wiesen. *Eleanor Roosevelt: Vol. 1, 1884–1933.* Viking, 1992. OBCB 1999.

Born into a privileged world, Eleanor Roosevelt became a champion of the underprivileged and a fighter for human rights. After a difficult childhood, Eleanor was orphaned at age 12 and taken in by relatives, fell in love with and married her cousin, then found an agenda of her own, supporting the rights of women, children, and workers.

HARRY S. TRUMAN

McCullough, David G. *Truman.* Simon & Schuster, 1992. OBCB 1999.

This notable president earned America's respect by helping to end World War II and reshape the world for postwar peace. McCullough evaluates Truman's presidency and praises him for being an ordinary American with solid values. The controversies of his presidency included dropping the atomic bomb, sending troops into the Korean War, establishing the CIA, and desegregating the armed forces.

TOBIAS WOLFF

Wolff, Tobias. *This Boy's Life: A Memoir.* Atlantic Monthly Press, 1989. OBCB 1999.

In and out of trouble in his youth, this charter member of the "Bad Boys' Club" survives boyhood in this coming-of-age memoir. After his parents divorce when he is 10, Wolff moves with his mother from Florida to the Pacific Northwest to avoid a violent boyfriend. When she remarries, he must deal with an abusive stepfather until escaping to a boarding school back east.

RICHARD WRIGHT

Wright, Richard. *Black Boy: A Record of Childhood and Youth.* Harper, 1945. OBCB 1999.

Wright writes his autobiography as a novel, recalling his pre–World War II youth in the Jim Crow South, when racial and personal obstacles seemed insurmountable.

MALCOLM X

Malcolm X with the assistance of Alex Haley. *The Autobiography of Malcolm X.* Grove Press, 1965. OBCB 1999.

A great and controversial Black Muslim figure relates his transformation from street hustler to religious and national leader. Malcolm Little moved to Michigan after his father was killed by white supremacists. He spent years in foster homes, then as a drug dealer and pimp in New York and Boston. While in prison, he converted and joined the Nation of Islam, changed his name, and quickly became a leader in the organization. He later left the Nation of Islam, but continued as an activist until his assassination in 1965.

· DRAMA ·

Albee, Edward. *Three Tall Women.* Dramatists Play Service, 1994. OBCB 1999.
A frustrated 92-year-old reveals three arduous and painful stages of her life, embodied by three versions of the same woman (one in her 20s, one at 52, and one at 92). She remembers the fun of childhood, her marriage, and her biggest regret, that she and her gay son are estranged.

Beckett, Samuel. *Waiting for Godot.* Grove Press, 1954. OBCB 1999.
Two tramps wait eternally for the elusive Godot in this first success of the Theater of the Absurd. Estagon and Vladimir (Gogo and Didi) consider various activities and conversations to pass the time as they spend two days waiting along the side of a road.

Bernstein, Leonard, Arthur Laurents, and Stephen Sondheim. *West Side Story.* Random House, 1958. OBCB 1999.
The "American" Jets and Puerto Rican Sharks, rival gangs on the west side of New York City, battle it out in song and dance as Tony and Maria fall in love in this musical based on Shakespeare's *Romeo and Juliet.*

Christie, Agatha. *Mousetrap.* Samuel French, 1954. OBCB 1999.
A group of guests are stranded at an inn by a snowstorm. The next day, a police sergeant arrives to tell them that a woman was murdered in London, and that her murderer is likely among their group.

Coward, Noel. *Blithe Spirit.* Doubleday, Doran, 1941. OBCB 1999.
A drawing-room farce in which a novelist's second marriage is disturbed by the ghost of his first wife.

Fugard, Athol. *"Master Harold" . . . and the Boys.* Knopf, 1982. OBCB 1999.
This one-act play takes place in a tea room in Port Elizabeth, South Africa, in 1950. Hally, a precocious white teenager and son of the tea room owner, lashes out at two older black friends who are substitute figures for his alcoholic father, who is returning home from the hospital later that day.

Hansberry, Lorraine. *A Raisin in the Sun.* Random House, 1959. OBCB 1999.
The sudden appearance of money tears a 1950s African American family apart. Mama uses most of the money to buy a house for the family, which is in a white neighborhood, promising difficulties with the neighbors.

Hellman, Lillian. *The Little Foxes.* Random House, 1939. OBCB 1999.
Members of the greedy and treacherous Hubbard family compete with each other for control of the mill that will bring them riches in the post–Civil War South. In a play resembling a Greek tragedy, Regina and her two brothers wish to borrow money from Regina's ill husband in order to invest in the cotton mill. When he refuses, the depth of Regina's hatred is revealed.

Ibsen, Henrik. *A Doll's House.* Joshua James Press, 1879. OBCB 1999.
In this 19th-century Scandinavian play, Nora, one of feminism's great heroines, steps off her pedestal and encounters the real world. When her lawyer husband repudiates her innocent actions out of concern for his own reputation, Nora sees her life clearly for the first time and leaves her family behind.

Ionesco, Eugene. *Rhinoceros.* Grove Press, 1959. OBCB 1999.
The subject is conformity; the treatment is comedy and terror. As everyone in his town turns into a rhinoceros, Berenger rejects his former alienation, alcohol abuse, and laziness to become a man willing to resist conformity, even if he is the only one left.

Kushner, Tony. *Angels in America: A Gay Fantasia on National Themes. Pt. 1, Millennium Approaches (1992); Pt. 2, Perestroika (1993).* Theatre Communications Group. OBCB 1999.

Kushner chronicles AIDS in America during the Reagan era, through the lives of two couples. God has abandoned heaven, gay men are hiding their homosexuality and dying in secret, greed and corruption, political speeches, magical realism . . . all come together in a fantasia of life and death.

Larson, Jonathan. *Rent.* Morrow, 1996. OBCB 1999.

This award-winning musical depicts life, death, passion, drug addiction, and loyalty among AIDS-stricken artists in New York's East Village. Loosely based on Giacomo Puccini's 19th-century opera, *La Bohème.*

Miller, Arthur. *Death of a Salesman.* Viking, 1949. OBCB 1999.

After years on the road as a traveling salesman, Willy Loman faces his failure as husband, father, and human being. His sons are unsuccessful (one has even been in jail) and disdainful of their father. The only solution he can see is suicide.

O'Neill, Eugene. *Long Day's Journey into Night.* Yale University Press, 1956. OBCB 1999.

This painful autobiographical play set in 1912 Connecticut reveals the illusions and delusions of the Tyrone family. James is a miserly retired actor; his wife Mary is addicted to morphine and on the brink of madness. Their older son is an alcoholic; the younger is consumptive. As the day turns to night, the father and sons drink and share resentments and blame.

Sartre, Jean Paul. *No Exit.* Knopf, 1946. OBCB 1999.

In this existential drama, three people are trapped in a drawing room together, an experience which constitutes their punishment in hell.

Shakespeare, William. *King Lear.* 1605. OBCB 1999.

King Lear decides to divide his kingdom among his daughters, according to how well they express their love for him. The one daughter who sincerely loves him refuses to make a speech, and is disinherited. When the other two fail to support him, Lear goes mad. Political deception and romantic jealousy cause tragic ends for all.

Shaw, George Bernard. *Pygmalion.* Dodd, Mead, 1914. OBCB 1999.

Professor Higgins bets a friend he can turn common Eliza Doolittle into a duchess.

Stoppard, Tom. *Rosencrantz and Guildenstern Are Dead.* Grove Press, 1967. OBCB 1999, 2009.

Two bit players from Shakespeare's *Hamlet* are thrust into a terrifying and surreal new situation. Involved in court intrigue beyond their control, Rosencrantz and Guildenstern find themselves trapped in a futile, fatal situation. This witty, existential play addresses individual freedom, fate, and luck.

Uhry, Alfred. *Driving Miss Daisy.* Theatre Communications Group, 1988. OBCB 1999.

At the beginning of the play, 72-year-old Daisy crashes her car backing out of her garage. Her son hires a black chauffeur, Hoke. Over the next 25 years, Hoke and Daisy develop a deep and abiding friendship, even as they fight to maintain their dignity as they age. Daisy needs to keep control over her life, while Hoke gently resists her attempts to boss him around.

Vogel, Paula. *How I Learned to Drive.* Theatre Communications Group, 1998. OBCB 1999.

The friendship between Li'l Bit and her uncle Peck turns toward alcohol and seduction over the course of Li'l's adolescence. The play takes place in 1960s Maryland, a mix of flashback, monologue, and voice-over.

Wilde, Oscar. *The Importance of Being Earnest.* Joshua James Press, 1895. OBCB 1999.

Can a baby, abandoned at Victoria Station, grow up to find love, romance, identity, and the importance of being earnest? In this satirical play, two couples create and endure much identity confusion before living happily ever after.

Wilder, Thornton. *Our Town.* Coward McCann, 1938. OBCB 1999.

Love and death in a typical American small town are seen through the eyes of the Stage Manager. Neighbors George and Emily happily court and marry. When Emily dies in childbirth she is given the chance to experience one day over again.

Williams, Tennessee. *The Glass Menagerie.* Random House, 1945. OBCB 1999.

A brother is haunted by the memory of his teenage sister, who took refuge from the world in her collection of glass animal figurines. Amanda encourages her son Tom to bring home suitors to meet his painfully shy sister. When this does not work out as planned, they have a terrible fight and Tom leaves home for good.

Wilson, August. *Fences: A Play.* New American Library, 1986. OBCB 1999.

Troy, a garbageman and ex-convict, recalls his career as a Negro League baseball star. He admits to his wife, Rose, that he has fathered a child with another woman. When the other woman dies in childbirth, Troy and Rose take responsibility for the baby, even as their grown son leaves home for good. *Fences* is the second in Wilson's Century Cycle depicting 20th-century African American life.

· POETRY ·

Blum, Joshua, et al., eds. *The United States of Poetry.* Harry N. Abrams, 1996. OBCB 1999. (BBYA)

Contemporary poems enhanced by outstanding photographs and other illustrations highlight poets ranging from Nobel laureates to rappers. The poems are organized by theme, to reflect the premise that poetry reflects American culture, so the works of former presidents, Beats, and cowboys exist side by side in this attractive volume.

Carlson, Lori M., ed. *Cool Salsa: Bilingual Poems on Growing Up Latino in the United States.* Henry Holt, 1994. OBCB 1999.

Party times, hard times, memories, and dreams come to life in these English, Spanish, and Spanglish poems. The collection mixes traditional and street poetry, famous and lesser-known poets. Each poem is presented in its original language and in translation. For the poems mixing both languages, a glossary of translations is included.

Ciardi, John, and Miller Williams. *How Does a Poem Mean?* Houghton Mifflin, 1960. OBCB 1999. o.p.

A poet and a critic discuss the value and nature of poetry, using selections from six centuries of American and English poems. A poem is more than its subject matter; it is about form, imagery, rhythm, sound.

Dickinson, Emily. *Dickinson: Poems.* Everyman's Library Pocket Poets. Everyman's Library, 1993. OBCB 1999.

A compact collection of the best known works of an eminent American poet proves that good things do come in small packages.

Dunning, Stephen, Edward Lueders, Naomi Shihab, Deith Gilyard, and Demetrice Q. Worldy, comps. *Reflections on a Gift of Watermelon Pickle . . . and Other Modern Verse.* Scott Foresman, 1995. OBCB 1999.

Photographs complement or illustrate 114 poems chosen for their appeal to young people. The poems range from sharp and biting to easygoing and optimistic; poets from the recognized to the relatively unknown.

Giddings, Robert. *The War Poets.* Orion Books, 1988. OBCB 1999. o.p.

The work of a variety of World War I poets, many of whom died in the conflict, is reinforced with biographical notes and a brief history of "the war to end all wars." Illustrated with paintings and photographs, poetry of Rupert Brooke, Robert Graves, Wilfred Owen, Siegfried Sassoon, and more is included.

Gillan, Maria Mazziotti, and Jennifer Gillan, eds. *Unsettling America: An Anthology of Contemporary Multicultural Poetry.* Penguin, 1994. OBCB 1999.

This poetry feast challenges stereotypes about who or what is American. Poems by Louise Erdrich, Lucille Clifton, Sherman Alexie, Pat Mora, Sonia Sanchez, and Lawrence Ferlinghetti, among many, many others, are divided into thematic sections: "Uprooting," "Performing," "Naming," "Negotiating," and "Re-envisioning."

Gordon, Ruth, ed. *Pierced by a Ray of Sun: Poems about the Times We Feel Alone.* HarperCollins, 1995. OBCB 1999. o.p. (BBYA)

Poets from around the world and across time reflect on solitude and loneliness. The poems in this collection chosen for young readers reflect both hope and despair.

Heaney, Seamus, and Ted Hughes, eds. *The Rattle Bag.* Faber and Faber, 1982. OBCB 1999.

This hefty compilation includes poems from the oral tradition. The two editors, famous poets themselves, simply present their favorite poetry arranged alphabetically, in hopes that each poem will communicate on its own terms.

Homer. *Odyssey.* Translated by Robert Fagles. Viking, 1996. OBCB 1999.

Smell the salt air and experience Odysseus's temptations as the ancient world and his journey come alive again through this fresh poetic translation.

Miller, E. Ethelbert, ed. *In Search of Color Everywhere: A Collection of African-American Poetry.* Stewart, Tabori, & Chang, 1994. OBCB 1999. o.p. (BBYA)

From spirituals to rap to classic works by famous poets, this presentation delights the senses. Recent and past poetry, by the renowned and the up-and-coming, unite in an anthology with range.

Neil, Philip, ed. *Singing America.* Viking, 1995. OBCB 1999. o.p.

Experience American poetic heritage through dramatic black-and-white drawings that illustrate a wealth of poetry from Walt Whitman to spirituals, songs of the Sioux, the national anthem, and Woody Guthrie.

Niatum, Duane, ed. *Harper's Anthology of 20th Century Native American Poetry.* Harper & Row, 1988. OBCB 1999.

The century's best Native American poets capture their cultural heritage through powerful poetry. Niatum has gathered work by 36 poets from 30 different tribes. The collection ends with a brief biography of each poet.

Nye, Naomi Shihab, sel. *The Tree Is Older Than You Are: A Bilingual Gathering of Poems and Stories from Mexico with Paintings by Mexican Artists.* Simon & Schuster Books for Young Readers, 1995. OBCB 1999. (BBYA)

Modern and ancient Mexican poetry, prose, and paintings from all regions come alive in this lavish anthology. English translations are laid out next to the original folktales, stories, and poems.

Nye, Naomi Shihab, and Paul B. Janeczko, eds. *I Feel a Little Jumpy around You: A Book of Her Poems and His Poems Collected in Pairs.* Simon & Schuster Books for Young Readers, 1996. OBCB 1999. (BBYA)

In this anthology of thought-provoking modern poems, male and female writers view life from gender perspectives. The grouping of nearly 200 poems in pairs by topic reveals as many similarities as differences.

Oliver, Mary. *New and Selected Poems.* Beacon Press, 1992. OBCB 1999.

The Pulitzer Prize–winning poet presents a smorgasbord of her poems, composed and published over the last three decades, about life, death, and humanity's relationship to the natural world.

Rosenberg, Liz, ed. *Earth-Shattering Poems.* Henry Holt, 1998. OBCB 1999. o.p.

Poets from around the world and through the centuries, encompassing many different cultures, express the emotional intensity of life's experiences. The poems are presented in chronological order, beginning with Sappho.

Rubin, Robert Alden, ed. *Poetry Out Loud.* Algonquin, 1993. OBCB 1999.

Poems from the world's greatest poets, including raps, ballads, and other lyrics, are annotated and followed by suggestions for reading aloud.

Smith, Philip, ed. *100 Best-Loved Poems.* Dover, 1995. OBCB 1999.

Shakespeare, English and American ballads, and the classics most of us remember and love are part of the treasure found in this collection of traditional poetry.

Stallworthy, Jon, ed. *A Book of Love Poetry.* Oxford University Press, 1986. OBCB 1999.

You can experience love throughout the ages, as expressed in the past 2,000 years of poetry from around the world. The poems are arranged thematically in sections such as "Declarations," "Persuasions," and "Desolations."

OUTSTANDING BOOKS FOR THE COLLEGE BOUND AND LIFELONG LEARNERS, 2004

THE 2004 LIST is organized into five academic disciplines: humanities, history, literature and language arts, science and technology, and social sciences, and it includes fiction, nonfiction, poetry, biography, and drama. The committee selected works using a variety of criteria: readability, cultural and ethnic diversity, balance of view points, and variety of genres and title availability, with a focus on titles published within the previous five years.

· HUMANITIES ·

Adler, Sabine. *Lovers in Art.* Prestel USA, 2002. OBCB 2004.
  Romance and art are natural companions in this gorgeous book that spans five centuries of Western European art. Subjects range from biblical to mythological, from wedding portraits to the first flush of attraction, from peasants to royalty. An introductory essay on love and marriage through the ages is followed by full-page reproductions accompanied by facing pages of text.

Belloli, Andrea P. *Exploring World Art.* Getty Publications, 1999. OBCB 2004.
  Divided into chapters titled "Time and Space," "Other Worlds," "Daily Life," "History and Myth," and "The World of Nature," Belloli's book gives young readers a fresh look at Western European art in a global context and introduces the ways in which artists of different times and cultures express universal themes. Readers learn to connect art to their daily lives and to the world around them.

Bissinger, H. G. *Friday Night Lights: A Town, a Team, and a Dream.* Perseus Books, 1990. OBCB 2004.

In Odessa, Texas, high school football games regularly attract as many as 10,000 fans. Football is more than a recreational interest, it is the town's passion. Bissinger, an investigative journalist, moved his family to Odessa in order to follow the 1988–89 season. He portrays individual team members and townspeople, exploring racial attitudes and favoritism shown to the athletes, representing both the flaws and the attraction of the football craze in Texas.

Blackstone, Harry, Jr. *The Blackstone Book of Magic and Illusion.* Newmarket Press, 1985. OBCB 1999, 2004.

The classic of legerdemain describes the rich history of modern magic from ancient times to the present, including vaudeville, Broadway, Vegas, and television. Illustrated with black-and-white photographs, the book reveals the secrets and psychology behind popular magic tricks and effects. The foreword is by Ray Bradbury.

Brassaï. *Brassaï: Letters to My Parents.* University of Chicago Press, 1997. OBCB 2004.

European photographer Brassaï (1899–1984) details his life's experiences in letters home, describing both his own development as an artist and the fascinating world of Paris from 1920 to 1940. Brassaï was interested in the lowlife of the city as well as the highlife, and he was friends with many important writers and artists. Illustrated with several of his photographs.

Card, Orson Scott. *Sarah.* Forge, 2001. OBCB 2004.

The character of Sarah, Abraham's beloved wife, illuminates this rendering of a pivotal story from the Old Testament. Sarah and her sister, Qira (Card's creation), contrasts of wisdom and selfishness, narrate the story. Set in Egypt and the Sinai Peninsula, this is the first in Card's Women of Genesis series.

Chevalier, Tracy. *Girl with a Pearl Earring.* Dutton, 1999. OBCB 2004. (Alex Award, BBYA)

Sixteen-year-old Griet tells the story of her time as a maid in the busy 17th-century household of Delft painter Johannes Vermeer. Griet has an artistic eye and eventually becomes assistant and muse to the famous artist. But she is confined by the class system of her time. This fictional imagining of a mystery of the art world—Who was the girl in that famous painting?—brings Vermeer's world to life.

Corio, David, and Vivian Goldman. *The Black Chord.* Universe Books, 1999. OBCB 2004. o.p.

The often-painful evolution of African American music is explored with a funky text by Vivian Goldman and lively, original photographs by David Corio. The modern sounds of jazz, reggae, hip-hop, rap, and more are traced to their influences from around the world.

Coulton, Larry. *Counting Coup: A True Story of Basketball and Honor on the Little Big Horn.* Warner, 2000. OBCB 2004. (Alex Award, BBYA)

Working through racism, alcoholism, and domestic violence, the players on Hardin High School's girls' basketball team struggle to win in life as well as on the court. Coulton spent 15 months on the Crow reservation in Montana. His narrative follows one player in particular, Sharon LaForge, whose on-the-court successes are balanced by personal struggles.

Crutcher, Chris. *Whale Talk.* Greenwillow, 2001. OBCB 2004. (BBYA)

What does a guy do when he has all the talents to be a star athlete, but hates his high school athletic program? T.J. Jones is black, Japanese, and white in a town with little diversity, and he hates injustice. He is inspired by a favorite teacher to form a swim team in a school without a pool in order to win a varsity letter jacket for its members, in particular a mentally challenged boy abused for wearing his dead brother's jacket.

Franck, Frederick, ed. *What Does It Mean to Be Human? Reverence for Life Reaffirmed by Responses from Around the World.* St. Martin's, 2000. OBCB 2004.

Thought-provoking essays on one of the most essential questions one can ask. Social activists, artists, and spiritual leaders reflect on being human in a changing society. Contributors range from Wilma Mankiller to James Earl Jones, Joan Chittister to Cornel West, Jimmy Carter to the Dalai Lama. Franck gathered the essays in reaction to an increasing contempt for life reflected in modern war, poverty, and human trafficking.

Garfunkel, Trudy. *On Wings of Joy: The Story of Ballet from the 16th Century to Today.* Little, Brown, 1994. OBCB 1999, 2004.

Immerse yourself in the world of ballet, from its earliest choreography to the life of a modern ballerina. Garfunkel provides entertaining, comprehensive coverage of the history of ballet, as well as the lives of the great dancers, choreographers, and composers involved.

Goldberg, Myla. *Bee Season.* Doubleday, 2000. OBCB 2004.

Eliza's extraordinary gift for spelling leads her to understand the sounds of the alphabet in a way that echoes the teachings of the mystical Kabbalah. Before discovering her talent, nine-year-old Eliza was quite ordinary, nearly overlooked by her scholarly father and lawyer mother in favor of their talented son. Now family dynamics shift and every member undergoes a change, not always for the better.

Greenberg, Jan, ed. *Heart to Heart: New Poems Inspired by Twentieth-Century American Art.* Harry N. Abrams, 2001. OBCB 2004, 2009. (BBYA, Printz Honor)

Can a painting speak? This collection of lyrical responses to famous American works of art will make you a believer. Large, colorful reproductions are paired with the poems they inspired in writers such as Jane Yolen, Ron Koertge, and Marvin Bell. Brief biographies of the contributors round out a lively collection.

Hedges, Chris. *War Is a Force That Gives Us Meaning.* Public Affairs, 2002. OBCB 2004.

A Pulitzer Prize–winning author presents a passionate, thought-provoking look at war through the ages, and exposes the myths of the culture of combat. Hedges covered conflicts in the Middle East, the Balkans, Africa, and South America. He uses these experiences, sharing harrowing eyewitness accounts, to consider questions such as: What makes war attractive? What is its effect on societies? On culture?

Howe, Peter. *Shooting under Fire: The World of the War Photographer.* Artisan, 2002. OBCB 2004, 2009.

Ten leading combat photographers share their experiences of horror, humor, bravery, and daring while reporting from Vietnam, Haiti, Chechnya, El Salvador, Sarajevo, and Afghanistan. Over 150 black-and-white and color photographs provide a powerful and moving look at war and those who risk everything to document it.

King, Ross. *Brunelleschi's Dome: How a Renaissance Genius Reinvented Architecture.* Walker, 2000. OBCB 2004.

In this vivid re-creation of the political and artistic milieu of 15th-century Florence, the audacious and secretive Filippo Brunelleschi achieves the impossible and makes possible modern building. Details of daily life during the period intermingle with the feats of engineering accomplished in order to complete the cathedral of Santa Maria del Fiore.

Light, Alan, ed. *The Vibe History of Hip Hop.* Three Rivers Press, 1999. OBCB 2004.

The editors of *Vibe* magazine look at the music, dance, and fashion that have evolved into hip-hop culture. From the sound that began in 1970s New York City, to the first recording to hit the charts, through commercial success and predictions for the future, this generously illustrated history covers it all.

Livingstone, Lili Cockerville. *American Indian Ballerinas.* University of Oklahoma Press, 1999. OBCB 2004.

Four Native American women from Oklahoma share the struggles and triumphs of their dance careers and personal lives in stories that inspire with courage and beauty. All born in the 1920s and '30s, Maria Tallchief, Rosella Hightower, Marjorie Tallchief, and Yvonne Chouteau each achieved international fame. The author, a former dancer herself, interviewed her subjects extensively in order to achieve this unique addition to the history of dance in the 20th century.

McGreevey, Tom, and Joanne Yeck. *Our Movie Heritage.* Rutgers University Press, 1997. OBCB 2004, 2009.

This work provides over one hundred beautiful pictures of top stars, directors, and others in the film industry, but the focus is on film preservation and the race against time to salvage what is left of the large number of films that are currently deteriorating in our nation's vaults, theaters, and private collections. Film, and its reflection on American culture, is in peril: 90 percent of silent films, and 50 percent of feature films made before 1950, have vanished.

Perry, John. *Encyclopedia of Acting Techniques: Illustrated Instruction, Examples, and Advice for Improving Acting Techniques and Stage Presence—from Tragedy to Comedy, Epic to Farce.* Quarto, 1997. OBCB 2004.

The actor's life—see how it's done by the pros in this extravagantly color illustrated primer on dramatic performance. Contains step-by step advice for improving technique and stage presence in all genres and styles, including preparing the text and role, the rehearsal process, and even makeup basics.

Sandler, Martin. *Photography: An Illustrated History.* Oxford University Press, 2002. OBCB 2004, 2009.

This work looks at photography as it evolved from daguerreotypes in the 1800s to the respected art form that it is today. Numerous compelling black-and-white and color photographs document technological developments, the contributions of pioneers in the field, as well as the impact photography has had upon all aspects of society.

Smith, Huston. *Illustrated World Religions: A Guide to Our Wisdom Traditions.* Harper, 1995. OBCB 2004.

The interconnectivity of the world's great religious movements, with their parallel and disparate beliefs, is lyrically explored. The author intersperses his own text with excerpts from the sacred texts and important images from each religion in this introduction to

Hinduism, Buddhism, Confucianism, Taoism, Islam, Judaism, Christianity, and the primal religions. This edition places the emphasis on religious art.

Vreeland, Susan. *The Passion of Artemisia.* Viking, 2002. OBCB 2004.

This eloquent rendering of the story of Italian painter Artemisia Gentileschi (1593–1653) evokes appreciation of both her magnificent art and her struggles to succeed as an artist. Raped by an assistant in her father's painting studio in Rome, Artemisia tells the story of the trial, an unhappy marriage, and her professional successes—winning the patronage of the Medici family and being elected to the Accademia dell-Arte.

· HISTORY ·

Alexander, Caroline. *The Endurance: Shackleton's Legendary Antarctic Expedition.* Knopf, 1998. OBCB 2004. (Alex Award, BBYA)

It's man against nature at the dawn of World War I, as the lure of the last unclaimed land on earth dazzles with its beauty and danger in this adventure of discovery and survival. Alexander weaves together excerpts from crew members' journals and 170 photographs by expedition photographer Frank Hurley, lending an intimacy and immediacy to the everyday lives of the explorers and the landscape.

Aronson, Marc. *Witch Hunt: Mysteries of the Salem Witch Trials.* Simon & Schuster, 2003. OBCB 2004.

Revisit a time of nightmare, fear, hysteria—beyond *The Crucible*, sift through the myths, half-truths, and misinformation to make up your own mind about what really happened in Salem Village and why. Aronson persuades readers to think for themselves about various theories, while using plentiful primary-source quotes to clarify the events.

Berg, A. Scott. *Lindbergh.* Putnam, 1998. OBCB 2004.

Daring, mysterious, and one of the 20th century's first superstars—who was the man behind the myth and how did his historic flight across the Atlantic remake the world? This is the Pulitzer Prize–winning, definitive biography of a controversial, tragic, and heroic man, one of the first to be hounded by the modern media.

Danticat, Edwidge. *The Farming of Bones.* Soho Press, 1998. OBCB 2004.

Set in the Dominican Republic during the Trujillo dictatorship, this is a Caribbean holocaust story. During a time when nationalist madness and ethnic hatred turn island neighbors into executioners, Haitian immigrants Amabelle and Sebastien hold on to love, to dignity—and struggle to survive.

Ellis, Joseph E. *Founding Brothers: The Revolutionary Generation.* Knopf, 2000. OBCB 2004.

What seems like a foregone conclusion was anything but—six dramatic vignettes reveal the men behind the events of the most decisive decade in American history. This Pulitzer Prize winner covers the Burr/Hamilton rivalry, negotiations for the location of the capital, the future of slavery, Washington's farewell address, John and Abigail Adams during his presidency, and the correspondence between Adams and Jefferson late in their lives.

Frank, Mitch. *Understanding September 11: Answering Questions about the Attacks on America.* Penguin, 2002. OBCB 2004.

These events are burned into images we can never forget—but after the pain of September 11 we ask why and learn about the historical, religious, and cultural issues that led to the attacks. After recounting the events of the day, Frank objectively explains relevant concepts to young readers, including Islam, the Taliban, al Qaeda, and the West's interests in the Middle East.

Geras, Adele. *Troy.* Scholastic, 2001. OBCB 2004. (BBYA)

A city under siege, epic battles and heroes, powerful supernatural forces—it's the story of the Trojan War seen through the eyes of its women in one of our oldest stories of the cruelty of war. The perspectives of four teenagers close to the main players are primary (especially their tangled infatuations), while gods and goddesses occasionally share visions and prophecies. Gossiping servants provide the chorus.

Glancy, Diane. *Stone Heart: A Novel of Sacajawea.* Overlook Press, 2003. OBCB 2004.

You are there on the epic journey of Lewis and Clark that opened the West to the call of manifest destiny. Sacajawea narrates through fictional diary entries revealing her mystical experience of the journey. Glancy intersperses the explorers' actual journal entries, which present a very different interpretation of events. Contrasts disclose an inherent clash of cultures in a vast new land.

Hansen, Drew D. *The Dream: Martin Luther King Jr. and the Speech That Inspired a Nation.* HarperCollins, 2003. OBCB 2004.

This great humanitarian and leader did indeed have a dream, and it has resonated through the years to expand all of our hopes for a future built on tolerance. Hansen analyses the speech itself, discusses its theological and intellectual roots, and compares the speech as written with the speech as delivered. He also examines the period before and after 1963 in order to study why the speech had such an impact.

Harper, Kenn. *Give Me My Father's Body: The Life of Minik, the New York Eskimo.* Steerforth Press, 2000. OBCB 2004.

Imagine the horror as Minik visits the Museum of Natural History and learns the true fate of his father. In 1897, explorer Robert Peary returned to New York City from Greenland with six Eskimos. Minik was only a child at the time, and when his father died almost immediately upon their arrival, Peary abandoned him. This is Minik's story, which focuses on his efforts to recover his father's body from the museum and give him a traditional burial.

Lanier, Shannon. *Jefferson's Children: The Story of One American Family.* Random House, 2000. OBCB 2004. (BBYA)

Thomas Jefferson fathered two families—one black, one white. Lanier, a descendant of Jefferson and Sally Hemings, traveled the country with photographer Jane Feldman talking with and photographing other descendants of Thomas Jefferson. This is a story (in the format of a photo album) about family, a story about identity, a story about secrets revealed and history made complete.

Least Heat-Moon, William. *Columbus in the Americas.* Wiley, 2002. OBCB 2004.

Was he a visionary and daring explorer, or a ruthless conquistador with dreams of riches and glory? Discover the truth behind the myth of a man whose impact still resonates through the continents he stumbled across. Using Columbus's own logbooks and other firsthand accounts, this book emphasizes the way Columbus treated the Native Americans he encountered, and covers all of his journeys to the New World.

Marrin, Albert. *Terror of the Spanish Main: Sir Henry Morgan and His Buccaneers.* Dutton, 1999. OBCB 2004.

What lies behind the dark and romantic image of the pirate, and what is the legacy of this brutal and bloody time? Sir Henry Morgan was knighted by King Charles II of England for plundering Spanish ships and colonies. Marrin's detailed use of primary sources creates a striking portrait for young readers of life at sea and on land during the 17th century.

McCullough, David G. *John Adams.* Simon & Schuster, 2001. OBCB 2004.

He was a man of his times who transcended his times, and one of the least understood of the Founding Fathers. Adams was happy as a Massachusetts lawyer before participating in the First Continental Congress; the rest is lively and well-recorded history thanks to the letters between John and his wife Abigail.

Poets of World War II. Library of America, 2003. OBCB 2004.

They have been called the Greatest Generation, and in their own voices they reveal the true price of their call to arms. Edited by Harvey Shapiro, whose own work is included.

Rogasky, Barbara. *Smoke and Ashes: The Story of the Holocaust.* Holiday House, 2002 (revised, expanded edition). OBCB 2004. o.p.

Some of history's darkest days are examined in this even-handed yet moving look at the horror and humanity of the Holocaust and its aftermath. Quotes and photographs effectively draw young readers into the causes, events, and resistance movements.

Sagas of Icelanders: A Selection. Penguin, 2001. OBCB 2004.

Nordic epics open up a world of wonder and power, a Viking world of heroic adventure and discovery at the turn of the first millennium. This collection includes the Vinland Sagas, which tell the story of Leif Eriksson's voyage to North America.

Starkey, David. *Six Wives: The Queens of Henry VIII.* HarperCollins, 2003. OBCB 2004.

How one man's matrimonial woes elevated a very disparate group of women to temporary positions of power, changed the way a nation was ruled, and shook the foundations of the Catholic Church. Emphasizing Catherine of Aragon and Anne Boleyn, the author aims to set the record straight, separating legend and fact.

Tuchman, Barbara. *A Distant Mirror: The Calamitous 14th Century.* Knopf, 1978 (reissue). OBCB 2004.

Castles and crusades, plague and famine, the glittering excitement of new ideas and discoveries, and the agony and displacement of war—the 14th century was a time not unlike our own in its rhythms and dimension. In order to ground her study of the period, Tuchman follows the life of one nobleman, French knight Enguerrand de Coucy VII (1340–1397), who married a daughter of the King of England.

Ung, Loung. *First They Killed My Father: A Daughter of Cambodia Remembers.* HarperCollins, 2001. OBCB 2004, 2009. (BBYA)

The perils of life under the brutal Pol Pot regime change a young woman's life forever, as she and her family find themselves fugitives of war, without even their names to remind them of what they lost. Ung tells her story in the present tense, taking the reader from her ideal childhood in the cosmopolitan city of Phnom Penh to work camps and training as a child soldier, through the loss of her parents and her eventual escape to Thailand and the United States.

Von Drehle, David. *Triangle: The Fire That Changed America.* Atlantic Monthly Press, 2003. OBCB 2004.

Beyond the terror, destruction, and loss of life, this event changed the landscape of our cities and the lives of working people everywhere. On March 25, 1911, in New York City, 146 people, most teenagers or women in their early 20s, were killed in a fire in the Triangle Shirtwaist factory. Von Drehle recounts the events with an emphasis on the people involved, social justice, and labor history.

War Letters: Extraordinary Correspondence from American Wars. Scribner, 2001. OBCB 2004.

The Legacy Project preserves the voices of soldiers and statesmen who lived through violent times that changed the course of nations. Listen to their stories in their words— they will inform and inspire you. Each letter is given context by editor Andrew Carroll. They include letters written during the Civil War, both world wars, Korea, the Cold War, Vietnam, the Persian Gulf War, Bosnia, and Somalia.

Watson, Peter. *The Modern Mind: An Intellectual History of the 20th Century.* HarperCollins, 2001. OBCB 2004.

It was a time of marvelous optimism and belief in the perfectibility of man through science and new ideas. Explore the thoughts of the major players from Freud to Einstein, and events from Kitty Hawk to the distant reaches of the universe. Watson leaves the wars and politics to others, and concentrates on the scientific, artistic, technological, literary, and medical.

Weatherford, Jack. *Indian Givers: How the Indians of the Americas Transformed the World.* Crown, 1988. OBCB 2004.

Discover how profoundly the native peoples of North and South America influenced what we eat, how we trade, and our system of government. European and world history are shown to have been influenced by American silver and gold as well as native foods such as the potato.

Winchester, Simon. *Krakatoa: The Day the World Exploded; August 27, 1883.* HarperCollins, 2003. OBCB 2004.

When the earth's most dangerous volcano exploded off the coast of Java, hundred-foot waves flung ships inland, a rain of hot ash made temperatures plummet, the shock wave traveled around the world seven times, and 40,000 people died. The aftermath of this disaster saw the rise of radical Islam, civil unrest, and a legacy of anti-Western militancy that continues today.

· LITERATURE AND LANGUAGE ARTS ·

Abelove, Joan. *Go and Come Back.* Puffin, 2000. OBCB 2004. (BBYA)

In a story of mutual culture shock, Alicia, a young Isabo girl in a remote area of Peru, is just as fascinated by the American anthropologists, Joanna and Margarita, as they are with the ways of her people. The arrival of the New Yorkers in the Amazon jungle results in many misunderstandings until Alicia saves and adopts an unwanted baby, and gets to know the visitors better.

Allison, Dorothy. *Bastard out of Carolina.* Dutton, 1992. OBCB 1999, 2004, 2009.

Bone confronts illegitimacy, poverty, the troubled marriage of her mother and stepfather, and the stigma of being considered "white trash" as she comes of age in South Carolina. Despite the fact that she lives among a large extended and protective family, Bone's stepfather, Daddy Glen, becomes increasingly abusive; her mother is either unable or unwilling to protect her; and Bone herself is too young or too embarrassed to reveal what is happening to her.

Alvarez, Julia. *In the Time of Butterflies.* Algonquin, 1994. OBCB 1999, 2004.

The four Mirabel sisters were called the Mariposas, or butterflies. Alvarez brings these historical figures to life by having the sisters tell their own story, beginning in childhood, through involvement with the resistance, culminating in murder and martyrdom. Their courage helped to liberate the Dominican Republic from Trujillo's dictatorship.

Anderson, Laurie Halse. *Speak.* Farrar, Straus, and Giroux, 1999. OBCB 2004. (BBYA, Printz Honor)

Calling the police to a party is a tough choice, but what made Melinda call is the devastating secret that keeps her locked in silence. Ostracized by her former friends, Melinda tells the story of her 9th-grade year, during which she feels completely isolated and depressed. Slowly, her inner strength and experiences in art class help her to reach out and to heal.

Anderson, M. T. *Feed.* Candlewick, 2002. OBCB 2004, 2009. (BBYA)

In this society your brain cyberfeed provides an endless stream of information, entertainment, and advertising. When Violet's feed is disrupted, she's cast adrift, and everyone is forced to examine the power of the feed in his or her life.

Bagdasarian, Adam. *Forgotten Fire: A Novel.* Random House, 2000. OBCB 2004, 2009. (BBYA)

"Who will remember the Armenians?" Hitler asked, referencing the Armenian genocide as his inspiration for the final solution. This brutal hidden chapter of history is seen through the eyes of 12-year-old survivor Vahan Kendarian, whose world was shattered within a matter of days.

Chambers, Aidan. *Postcards from No Man's Land.* Dutton, 2002. OBCB 2004. (BBYA, Printz Winner)

At 17, Jacob has gone to Amsterdam to explore his life. His quest strangely parallels discoveries about his grandfather's life there during World War II. While in Amsterdam, Jacob meets an older Dutch woman, Geertrui, whose own teenage story intersects with Jacob's search.

Cisneros, Sandra. *Caramelo.* Knopf, 2002. OBCB 2004, 2009.

LaLa Reyes learns the stories of her Awful Grandmother and weaves them into a colorful history of her 20th-century Mexican family, taking the reader from Mexico City to Chicago to San Antonio. The "caramelo," a striped shawl begun by her great-grandmother, symbolizes their traditions.

Foster, Thomas. *How to Read Literature like a Professor: A Lively and Entertaining Guide to Reading between the Lines.* HarperCollins, 2003. OBCB 2004.

All authors leave clues to lead readers deeper into the inner meanings of their writings. Learn how to follow literary breadcrumbs in any story with this practical and entertaining guide. Foster covers a wide range of symbols and narrative devices such as journeys, mythology, fairy tales, politics, violence, Shakespearean and biblical references, and more.

Frank, E. R. *Life Is Funny.* DK, 2000. OBCB 2004.

Growing up in New York can be agonizing, humorous, and always a challenge for the Brooklyn teens who tell their stories in rich hip-hop language. Pregnancy, abuse, love, beauty, alcoholism, intolerance, cutting, anger, friendship, and family mix together in this intense multicultural, multiracial tour de force.

Freymann-Weyr, Garret. *My Heartbeat.* Houghton Mifflin, 2002. OBCB 2004. (BBYA, Printz Honor)

Ellen loves her older brother, Link, and has a crush on his best friend, James. When she turns 14 and starts high school, Ellen begins to suspect a special relationship between them, even as she becomes closer to James.

Kaplow, Robert. *Me and Orson Welles.* MacAdam/Cage, 2003. OBCB 2004.

What would it be like to spend a week with the great Orson Welles, even sleeping in his pajamas? Richard Samuels, a budding teenage actor, gets the opportunity to see what life on stage, and backstage, is really like on Broadway in 1937 when he wins a small part in young Welles's debut production of *Julius Caesar* at the Mercury Theater. Richard falls in and out of love more than once in this charming, romantic coming-of-age novel.

Kingsolver, Barbara. *The Bean Trees.* Harper & Row, 1988. OBCB 2004.

In Kingsolver's debut novel, Taylor Greer leaves Kentucky after high school and heads west to find a new life. When a Native American baby is abandoned in her car, she learns that responsibilities and independence are not mutually exclusive in this story of family and community.

Lamott, Anne. *Bird by Bird: Some Instructions on Writing and Life.* Anchor Books, 1995. OBCB 2004.

Advice to the fledgling writer: "Just take it bird by bird." A gentle, anecdotal guide for beginning authors about both the writing process and the writer's life.

Mah, Adeline. *Chinese Cinderella: The True Story of an Unwanted Daughter.* Delacorte, 1999. OBCB 2004. (BBYA)

Wu Mei, also called Adeline, is the Fifth Younger Sister of her family, and the one who bears the blame for all their bad fortune. Wu Mei is cruelly mistreated by her new stepmother and neglected by her father. She is saved by her academic achievements and eventually becomes a doctor and a writer in this inspirational tale of survival in 1940s China.

Myers, Walter Dean. *Monster.* HarperCollins, 1999. OBCB 2004. (BBYA, Printz Winner)

Sixteen-year-old Steve Harmon is accused of being an accomplice to murder in the shooting of a Harlem convenience store owner. He creates a screenplay of his wrenching experiences at the crime scene, in jail, and on trial. Is Steve guilty, or was he simply in the wrong place at the wrong time?

Nye, Naomi Shihab. *Nineteen Varieties of Gazelle: Poems of the Middle East.* HarperCollins/Greenwillow, 2002. OBCB 2004. (BBYA)

Another world, another culture—poems that personalize the conflicts and people, deepening understanding of the impact of September 11. Many of the poems deal with being an Arab American in the United States, with peace, and with war.

O'Connor, Patricia. *Woe Is I: The Grammarphobe's Guide to Better English in Plain English.* Putnam, 1996. OBCB 2004.

When there's something important to say, how you say it counts. O'Connor makes pronouns, antecedents, and more grammar-ology fun and painless for both novices and experts, including many examples.

Pullman, Philip. *The Golden Compass.* Knopf, 1996. OBCB 2004. (BBYA)

Lyra Belacqua, a young girl living in an alternate Oxford, and her animal daemon, Pantalaimon, save her uncle from an assassination attempt, then set out to find her kidnapped playmate and uncover a sinister plot involving disappearing children and mysterious Dust. Lyra travels far north where she must use her special powers to thwart evil and redeem the world.

Reynolds, Sheri. *A Gracious Plenty.* Harmony Books, 1997. OBCB 2004.

What happens to us when we die? Finch Nobles was only four when she pulled a pot of boiling water down on herself, resulting in horrible scars. Now she is a recluse, a cemetery keeper in a small southern town who can talk to the dead, helping them examine what keeps them tied to the earth and resolve their tragedies.

Sapphire. *Push.* Knopf, 1996. OBCB 2004.

Precious Jones had her father's baby at 12 and now, at 16, she is pregnant by him again. She is also physically and verbally abused by her mother. But an alternative school, a dedicated teacher, and classmates who understand help her fight back. She is a survivor, telling her own story.

Satrapi, Marjane. *Persepolis.* Pantheon, 2003. OBCB 2004. (Alex Award, BBYA)

Marjane Satrapi grew up in revolutionary Iran, experiencing the overthrow of the Shah and the establishment of a new regime that abolished personal freedoms, especially for women. Her own family is affected as a beloved uncle is put to death for rebelling against the government. Satrapi uses dramatic black-and-white illustrations to tell her story.

Sebold, Alice. *Lucky: A Memoir.* Scribner, 1999. OBCB 2004, 2009.

"You save yourself or you remain unsaved." With these words, Sebold recounts the brutal rape that she was "lucky" to survive as a college freshman. Tragedy and hope combine as she makes her way through a survivor's maze of emotions, and the arrest and trial of her attacker.

Shakur, Tupac. *A Rose That Grew from Concrete.* Simon & Schuster, 1999. OBCB 2004.

Written when Tupac was 19 and not yet a star, these poems bring emotion, power, and passion to the experience of becoming yourself. Each piece is written in his own hand, complete with corrections and occasional drawings and ideographs, and illustrated with black-and-white photographs.

Smith, Anna Deveare. *Fires in the Mirror: Crown Heights and Other Identities.* Dramatists Play Service, 1999. OBCB 2004.

A dramatic look at the Crown Heights riots and race in the United States through the voices of 23 fascinating and unique characters, based on interviews with real people.

· SCIENCE AND TECHNOLOGY ·

Bradshaw, Gillian. *The Sand-Reckoner.* Forge, 2000. OBCB 2004. (Alex Award)

A youthful Archimedes comes into his own as a mathematician, an engineer, and a fascinating human being in this engaging novel. After spending a few years studying in Alexandria, the center of intellectual life, Archimedes returns home to Syracuse to find his father dying, his country at war with Rome, and a woman who shares his interests. Still a very young man, Archimedes must take responsibility for his family and make difficult choices.

Brown, David. *Inventing Modern America: From the Microwave to the Mouse.* MIT Press, 2001. OBCB 2004.

Whose idea was it? Brown enthusiastically reveals the human stories and faces behind American scientific and technological innovations and achievements from the computer mouse to the pacemaker. Full-color photographs and diagrams enhance the stories of thirty-five 20th-century innovators.

Bryson, Bill. *A Short History of Nearly Everything.* Broadway Books, 2003. OBCB 2004, 2009.

A renowned travel writer brings complex scientific concepts to life by describing how the universe and life as we know it came to be. Bryson focuses his distinctive humor and intelligence on every topic from the Big Bang to Darwin's trip on the *Beagle* to the fate of the dodo, how we know what we know, and the people who figured it out.

Enzensberger, Hans. *The Number Devil: A Mathematical Adventure.* Henry Holt, 1998. OBCB 2004.

A boy who hates math in school dreams of a devil who guides him through a colorful, Alice in Wonderland–like world of mathematical concepts. In the course of 12 dreams, the sly devil tricks and challenges the boy into having fun with math through conversations about everyday phenomena.

Fagan, Brian. *The Little Ice Age: How Climate Made History, 1300–1850.* Basic Books, 2000. OBCB 2004.

Fagan provides a fascinating look at how climate change influenced the course of the last thousand years of Western history. He highlights climate's impact on the Viking discovery of North America, the Industrial and French Revolutions, and the Irish potato famine. Although modern warming trends are addressed, Fagan does not make a political argument for policy change.

Feynman, Richard. *What Do You Care What Other People Think? Further Adventures of a Curious Character.* Norton, 1998. OBCB 2004.

Quirky, hilarious, and fascinating essays from one of the 20th century's greatest physicists cover everything from his early childhood to his work on the atomic bomb. Several essays address his time on the Rogers Commission, which investigated the Challenger explosion.

Flannery, Sarah, with David Flannery. *In Code: A Mathematical Journey.* Workman Publishing, 2001. OBCB 2004. o.p.

One teenager's discoveries in the science of cryptography dramatically impact the modern world. In this mixture of memoir and mathematical puzzle book, Sarah shares her love of her family, her love of a good challenge, the experience of winning the 1999 Ireland's Young Scientist of the Year and European Young Scientist of the Year awards at the age of 16, and how she dealt with the resulting media attention.

Hawking, Stephen. *The Universe in a Nutshell.* Bantam, 2001. OBCB 2004.

The physics guru illuminates startling new theories about our world in a lavishly illustrated sequel to *A Brief History of Time.* The inclusion of graphics and an entertaining writing style help nonscientists understand concepts like black holes, M-theory, relativity, dimensions, and time.

Horvitz, Leslie A. *Eureka! Scientific Breakthroughs That Changed the World.* Wiley, 2002. OBCB 2004.

Horvitz explores the dramatic events and thought processes of 12 great minds that led to profound scientific discoveries, including television, theories of gravity and evolution, the periodic table, and the double helix. The author examines the impact of these discoveries on the way we live, think, and view the world around us.

Hoyt, Erich, and Ted Schultz, eds. *Insect Lives: Stories of Mystery and Romance from a Hidden World.* Wiley, 1999. OBCB 2004.

Hoyt and Schultz compiled a diverse collection of brief essays and illustrations that entice readers to explore the fascinating and mysterious world of insects. Each of the 10 chapters is arranged around a theme such as metamorphosis, architecture, social insects, or mating and reproduction.

Judson, Olivia. *Dr. Tatiana's Sex Advice to All Creation: The Definitive Guide to the Evolutionary Biology of Sex.* Metropolitan Books, 2002. OBCB 2004.

A "Dear Abby"–style science column that answers the who, what, when, where, why, and how of a fascinating variety of sexual activity for all creatures great and small. In an understanding, conversational tone, Dr. Tatiana answers letters from insects, reptiles, mammals, and more, revealing surprising details of animal mating habits and reproductive biology.

Krauss, Lawrence. *Atom: An Odyssey from the Big Bang to Life on the Earth . . . and Beyond.* Little, Brown, 2001. OBCB 2004.

Follow a single oxygen atom on a fantastic voyage from the beginning of the universe to far into the future. The history of the cosmos is revealed, including the evolution of stars, the production of chemical elements, the creation of our own solar system, and life on other planets.

Lambrecht, Bill. *Dinner at the New Gene Café: How Genetic Engineering Is Changing What We Eat, How We Live, and the Global Politics of Food.* St. Martin's, 2001. OBCB 2004.

Lambrecht traces the scientific and political controversies surrounding the use of genetically modified organisms and the food we eat. Sharing firsthand interviews from all sides of the debate, this is an unbiased report including corporate, government, activist, and farmer viewpoints from around the world.

Livio, Mario. *The Golden Ratio: The Story of Phi, the World's Most Astonishing Number.* Broadway Books, 2002. OBCB 2004.

A captivating journey through art and architecture, botany and biology, physics and mathematics. This ratio, 1.6180339887 . . . impacts so many facets of our lives that it has fascinated us through the ages. From the stories of those obsessed with phi to debunking common myths, this is a generously illustrated volume about the irrational number discovered by Euclid over 2,000 years ago.

Nash, Madeline. *El Niño: Unlocking the Secrets of the Master Weather-Maker.* Warner, 2002. OBCB 2004.

Hard work and chance led to the discovery of El Niño and La Niña, powerful climatic systems that we still struggle to understand. Nash examines those who discovered and researched the phenomenon, as well as those affected by its destructiveness around the world—not only hurricanes, but also drought and disease.

Nolen, Stephanie. *Promised the Moon: The Untold Story of the First Women in the Space Race.* Four Walls Eight Windows, 2002. OBCB 2004.

This is the story of Dr. Randy Lovelace and Jerri Cobb and the other female pilots tested for their abilities to become NASA astronauts during the 1960s, the early days of the space race. This compelling history of women in aviation reveals why, despite passing the grueling physical and mental exams, they never went to the moon.

Porter, Roy. *Madness: A Brief History.* Oxford University Press, 2002. OBCB 2004.

What is meant when we say "madness"? Examine the wide range of possibilities, from witches to electric shock therapy to Prozac. Porter addresses the causes and treatments of mental illness in every period of history, from the ancient to the modern, including madness as possession, asylums, its intersection with creative genius, shock therapy, and controversial drug treatments.

Preston, Richard. *The Demon in the Freezer: A True Story.* Random House, 2002. OBCB 2004.

A striking portrait of smallpox makes readers uncomfortably aware that it could rise again as a biological weapon of mass destruction. Beginning with the October 2001 anthrax attack on the Hart Senate Office Building, Preston proceeds through the history of smallpox and the World Health Organization's work to eradicate it, giving the tale the pacing and graphic description of a thriller.

Rigden, John S. *Hydrogen: The Essential Element.* Harvard University Press, 2002. OBCB 2004.

A fascinating history is revealed in this probe of a simple scientific giant, the hydrogen atom. Rigden tells the stories of the many scientists absorbed in the study of hydrogen since its discovery in the 18th century. The history of hydrogen is also the history of modern physics.

Roach, Mary. *Stiff: The Curious Lives of Human Cadavers.* Norton, 2003. OBCB 2004, 2009. (Alex Award, BBYA)

Discover the amazing life-after-death adventures of human bodies in this examination of how medical and research scientists use cadavers to make our lives better. In an engaging, humorous style, Roach takes the reader along on her investigations into the varied fates of cadavers. She also examines the ways in which remains are disposed of in different cultures.

Sobel, Dava. *Longitude: The True Story of a Lone Genius Who Solved the Greatest Scientific Problem of His Time.* Walker, 1995. OBCB 1999, 2004.

The little-known story behind the greatest innovation in navigational science: an 18th-century version of the GPS. The English government created a contest with an incredibly generous cash prize for the person who could devise a way to determine east-west position while at sea. The popular option was astronomy, but clockmaker John Harrison's chronometer eventually proved the solution to the problem.

Stark, Peter. *Last Breath: Cautionary Tales from the Limits of Human Endurance.* Ballantine, 2001. OBCB 2004.

Whether the danger is hypothermia, mountain sickness, or cerebral malaria, this blend of adventure and science takes you to the absolute edges of human endurance. Each chapter is a short story, leading the reader step by step through extreme mind and body experiences such as having the bends, being stung by a venomous jellyfish in Australia, or drowning. Some victims survive, some do not.

Strauch, Barbara. *Primal Teen: What the New Discoveries about the Teenage Brain Tell Us about Our Kids.* Doubleday, 2003. OBCB 2004.

Ever wonder what makes teens tick? A tour of the teenage brain reveals startling new research about this pivotal and exciting time of life. Strauch presents research proving that the brain is still developing during adolescence, which could explain changeable teenage behavior. Candid interviews with both teens and parents are included.

Sykes, Bryan. *The Seven Daughters of Eve: The Science That Reveals Our Genetic Ancestry.* Norton, 2001. OBCB 2004.

Fascinating mitochondrial DNA evidence supports the idea that almost all modern Europeans share a common ancestry—that they are descended from just seven women. After sharing the excitement of his scientific discoveries, Sykes conjures up the daily lives of each of the prehistoric women.

Tobin, James. *Great Projects: The Epic Story of the Building of America from the Taming of the Mississippi to the Invention of the Internet.* Free Press, 2001. OBCB 2004.

This generously illustrated story of the milestones of engineering that connected us and moved a nation forward traces the path from personal vision to physical structure that transformed the country. Projects described include the Hoover Dam, the Croton Aqueduct, the Internet, Boston's "big dig," and the bridges of New York City.

· SOCIAL SCIENCES ·

Albom, Mitch. *Tuesdays with Morrie: An Old Man, a Young Man, and Life's Greatest Lesson.* Doubleday, 1997. OBCB 2004, 2009.

Mitch Albom's Tuesday night visits with his dying sociology professor, Morrie, offer valuable lessons about the art of living and dying with dignity. Albom reconnected with his older friend in the final months of his life and took one last class, a class with only one pupil, on the topics of family, money, fear of aging, marriage, love, regrets, and forgiveness.

Best, Joel. *Damned Lies and Statistics: Untangling Numbers from the Media, Politicians, and Activists.* University of California Press, 2001. OBCB 2004, 2009.

Do you know the difference between "good" and "bad" statistics, or how statistics and public policy are connected? Most people naïvely believe reported statistics, which are often mutations of the truth. Best teaches readers to become critical thinkers, and how to evaluate the statistics they encounter.

Conover, Ted. *Newjack: Guarding Sing Sing.* Knopf, 2000. OBCB 2004.

A gripping and sometimes humorous insider's look at Sing Sing prison, through the eyes of a writer who worked for a year as a corrections officer. Unable to obtain access any other way, Conover trained and worked as a guard in order to examine the prison system from the inside. He reveals the tension, frustration, violence, and sadness of life inside, for inmates and officers both.

Corwin, Miles. *And Still We Rise: The Trials and Triumphs of Twelve Gifted Inner-City High School Students.* Morrow, 2000. OBCB 2004.

Twelve seniors from Crenshaw High School's Advanced Placement English class in Los Angeles dream of going to college, but the harsh realities of their lives threaten to derail their plans. Corwin spent the 1996–97 school year observing these gifted students from one of the poorest, most crime- and gang-ridden neighborhoods in America, south-central Los Angeles. Here he tells their stories and argues for affirmative action.

Cuomo, Kerry Kennedy. *Speak Truth to Power: Human Rights Defenders Who Are Changing Our World.* Crown, 2000. OBCB 2004.

A collection of biographical sketches and haunting photographs (by Eddie Adams) of 51 ordinary people from 35 countries who are leading the fight to ensure basic human rights for everyone. From international heroes to complete unknowns, every subject demonstrates moral courage and compassion translated into action, often under appalling circumstances. The book has grown into a nonprofit organization of the same name (www.speaktruth.org).

Davis, Wade. *Light at the Edge of the World: A Journey through the Realm of Vanishing Cultures.* National Geographic, 2001. OBCB 2004.

Through photographs and eloquent text, the author unveils the diversity and unique qualities of human culture around the world. Davis is an ethnobotanist and anthropologist who has traveled the world for over 25 years, studying food, plants, and indigenous cultures in Canada, the Andes, Haiti, Kenya, Borneo, and Tibet, among others. Each chapter begins with an essay followed by photographs. Davis expresses his fears for the decimation of indigenous cultures and the effects of that decimation on our own culture.

Dershowitz, Alan M. *Why Terrorism Works: Understanding the Threat, Responding to the Challenge.* Yale University Press, 2002. OBCB 2004.

Focusing on the idea that terrorism is caused largely by the actions of Western governments, Dershowitz suggests steps to reduce the frequency and severity of these attacks. Terrorism continues as long as it is effective; therefore governments must never give in to terrorist demands. Dershowitz differentiates between tactics that moral governments and amoral governments might consider, including torture, and recommends implementing national identification cards and better coordination among agencies.

Diamond, Jared. *Guns, Germs, and Steel: The Fates of Human Societies.* Norton, 1997. OBCB 1999, 2004.

Why do some societies become rich and powerful while others remain poor and powerless? Diamond, an evolutionary biologist, contends that three elements—guns, germs, and steel—determined the course of history. The rise of human civilizations is explained in terms of geography, ecology, and the development of agriculture.

Doyle, William. *An American Insurrection: The Battle of Oxford, Mississippi, 1962.* Doubleday, 2001. OBCB 2004. (Alex Award)

When James Meredith decided to integrate the University of Mississippi, it caused the worst crisis in American history since the Civil War. Thousands of white civilians rebelled, refusing to allow the federal legal system to change the rules and enroll Meredith in the university. President John F. Kennedy was forced to call in infantry, paratroopers, and the National Guard. Doyle based this account on extensive, original research, including government documents and personal interviews.

Ehrenreich, Barbara. *Nickel and Dimed: On (Not) Getting By in America.* Henry Holt, 2001. OBCB 2004. (Alex Award)

Can you really survive on minimum wage? To find out, the author left her comfortable surroundings for a year to see what life is really like for America's working poor. In jobs from waitress to house cleaner, renting the cheapest accommodations she could find, Ehrenreich discovered that it takes more than hard work to get by in America.

Haddon, Mark. *The Curious Incident of the Dog in the Night-Time.* Doubleday, 2003. OBCB 2004, 2009. (Alex Award, BBYA)

Fifteen-year-old Christopher has two mysteries to solve: who killed Wellington the dog, and what happened to his mother. Christopher has Asperger's syndrome, a form of autism, which causes him to take things very literally and have trouble relating to others. After spending a night in jail accused of Wellington's murder, and inspired by Sherlock Holmes, he determines to investigate.

Hart, Elva Trevino. *The Barefoot Heart: Stories of a Migrant Child.* Bilingual Press, 1999. OBCB 2004. (Alex Award)

This honest and moving memoir follows a Mexican migrant child and her family as they travel from their home in New Mexico to the farms of Minnesota and Wisconsin in search of work in the 1950s and '60s. The toll of poverty and her father's determination to earn enough money for all six children to graduate from high school are clearly portrayed in an account that has continued relevance today.

Hosseini, Khaled. *The Kite Runner.* Putnam, 2003. OBCB 2004, 2009. (Alex Award)

When he was just a young boy, joyfully running kites through the streets of Kabul in the 1970s, Amir betrayed the son of his father's servant, his best friend, Hassan. Years after fleeing Afghanistan, Amir, now an American citizen, returns to his native land (ruled by the Taliban) and attempts to atone for his cowardice and betrayal.

Katz, Jon. *Geeks: How Two Lost Boys Rode the Internet out of Idaho.* Random House, 2000. OBCB 2004. (BBYA)

Eric and Jesse, poor high school students, social outcasts, and online geeks, find their obsession with computers and technology is their ticket to college and success. It all begins when Jesse responds to an online article by Katz, which leads Katz to Idaho to meet them. He encourages their move to Chicago, where they find jobs as part of the new indispensable geek elite. Both a study of geek culture and a moving personal story.

Latifa [pseud.]. *My Forbidden Face: Growing Up under the Taliban; A Young Woman's Story.* Hyperion, 2002. OBCB 2004.

Sixteen-year-old Latifa dreamed of becoming a professional journalist until the Taliban's repression of women changed her life. This first-person account brings home effects of the oppressive laws on the daily lives and psychological well-being of residents of Kabul. Latifa went from loving school, music, and fashion, to being required to wear a chadri and unable to leave home without a male relative.

Martinez, Ruben. *Crossing Over: A Mexican Family on the Migrant Trail.* Henry Holt, 2001. OBCB 2004.

Martinez explores the powerful forces that drive men, women, and even children to risk their lives crossing the border illegally from Mexico to the United States to find work. He traveled to the town of Cheran, west of Mexico City, in order to follow one family who lost three brothers in a border crossing tragedy. Martinez is himself the American son of Mexican émigré parents; his research became a personal journal of discovery of his own roots and cultural identity.

Pipher, Mary. *The Middle of Everywhere: The World's Refugees Come to Our Town.* Harcourt, 2002. OBCB 2004, 2009.

An exploration of the difficulties and struggles of refugees settled by the U.S. government in Lincoln, Nebraska, as they try to adjust and build a life in America. Pipher works as a family therapist in Lincoln, helping families deal with the tragedies of the past and hold onto cultural traditions in the present. She writes about young people from Sudan and Bosnia, and families from Vietnam and Afghanistan.

Salzman, Mark. *True Notebooks.* Knopf, 2003. OBCB 2004. (Alex Award)

When Salzman agreed to teach a writing class at Central Juvenile Hall in Los Angeles, he had no idea how moved he would be by the lives and eloquence of his students, all high-risk violent offenders. Readers meet the young inmates through their own writing, as they wait for trial and conviction and face up to their own lives and actions.

Schlosser, Eric. *Fast Food Nation: The Dark Side of the All-American Meal.* Houghton Mifflin, 2001. OBCB 2004.

The growth of the fast food industry has changed America's eating habits and greatly affected agriculture, the meatpacking industry, the minimum wage, and other aspects of American life. Schlosser investigates the corporate farms, slaughterhouses, and flavor factories, exposing unsanitary conditions and effects on obesity and disease rates.

Senna, Danzy. *Caucasia.* Riverhead, 1998. OBCB 2004. (Alex Award)

Separated when their parents' interracial marriage ends in divorce, light-skinned Birdie and her dark-skinned sister Cole lead very different lives while hoping for a reunion with one another. Both parents leave 1970s Boston on the run; the father and Cole move to Brazil, while Birdie and her mother change their names and move from town to town, eventually settling in New Hampshire, where Birdie is expected to pass as white. Birdie narrates, full of longing for her lost sister and frustration with the effects of racial identity on her life.

Simon, Rachel. *Riding the Bus with My Sister: A True Life Journey.* Houghton Mifflin, 2002. OBCB 2004.

Rachel Simon's sister, who has mental retardation, spends her days riding buses in the Pennsylvania city where she lives. When Rachel begins to accompany her sister on the bus, she learns a lot about her sister and her disability, and about her own limitations. Beth asks Rachel to ride the buses with her for a year. Rachel is surprised to find herself accepting, hoping to become closer to her sister. She finds that Beth has a stronger social network and more fulfilling relationships than Rachel herself, a workaholic with a narrow view of life.

Smith, Zadie. *White Teeth.* Random House, 2000. OBCB 2004.

Archie and Samad, two unlikely friends, are brought together by bizarre twists of fate and near-death experiences in this epic, multiethnic novel of family, culture, love, and loss set in post–World War II London. Archie's much younger, Jamaican second wife, Clara, gives him a new lease on life and a daughter, Irie. Samad marries Alsana late in life and ends up with twin sons, whom he separates, sending one back to Bangladesh for a traditional upbringing.

Steinberg, Jacques. *The Gatekeepers: Inside the Admissions Process of a Premier College.* Viking, 2002. OBCB 2004. (BBYA)

Getting in—who and what drives the college admissions cycle? Find out in a behind-the-scenes look at Wesleyan University through the eyes of an admissions officer, Ralph Figueroa, seeking members for the class of 2004. Steinberg followed Figueroa every step of the way, from initial "marketing" school visits, through the early decision process, reading the applications, and even trying to win over particularly strong candidates. Steinberg also followed several high school seniors, simultaneously recording their thoughts and the progress of their applications through the process.

Turner, Sugar, and Tracy Bachrach Ehlers. *Sugar's Life in the Hood: The Story of a Former Welfare Mother.* University of Texas Press, 2002. OBCB 2004.

An anthropologist who befriends a welfare mother learns about her world and the strategies she uses to get off welfare and into college. Turner is an African American mother of five children who shares her experiences of being a single mother on food stamps, struggling with crack addiction and prostitution. She also shares her determination to improve her life, which landed her a good job, a happy marriage, and education, as well as college education for three of her children. Ehlers and Turner take the reader beyond stereotypes of inner-city life.

Wheelan, Charles. *Naked Economics: Undressing the Dismal Science.* Norton, 2002. OBCB 2004, 2009.

Without using charts, graphs, or jargon, Wheelan makes economics understandable, even interesting, as he demystifies basic concepts and applies them to everyday life. With his informal style and sense of humor, he shares his enthusiasm for the big economic picture.

OUTSTANDING BOOKS FOR THE COLLEGE BOUND AND LIFELONG LEARNERS, 2009

IN AN EFFORT to mirror the college experience, the 2009 list is divided into five academic disciplines: arts and humanities, history and cultures, literature and language arts, science and technology, and social sciences. It is a combination of fiction, nonfiction, poetry, and drama. Titles were selected based on criteria including readability, racial and cultural diversity, balance of viewpoints, variety of formats and genres, and title availability. The committee also attempted to provide balance between modern classic titles and those that are newer or speak to current events.

· ARTS AND HUMANITIES ·

Bernier-Grand, Carmen. *Frida: Viva la Vida! Long Live Life!* Marshall Cavendish, 2007. OBCB 2009.
In 26 original, free-verse poems the author depicts the thoughts, feelings, and life events of Mexican self-portraitist Frida Kahlo. The poems are accompanied by full-color reproductions of Kahlo's paintings. Substantial background materials include a biographical sketch, chronology, and glossary.

Blumenthal, Karen. *Let Me Play: The Story of Title IX; The Law That Changed the Future of Girls in America.* Simon & Schuster/Atheneum, 2005. OBCB 2009. (BBYA)
Passed in 1972, Title IX legislation mandated that schools receiving federal funds could not discriminate on the basis of gender, ensuring equal treatment and opportunity for girls in sports and education. Includes period photos, a time line, "then and now" commentary, extensive source notes, and suggested resources for further reading.

Bowker, John. *World Religions: The Great Faiths Explored and Explained.* DK, 2006. OBCB 2009.

This comprehensive work introduces the reader to faiths of the world through religious artifacts, paintings, architecture, and annotations of sacred texts. Not limiting his survey to the present, Bowker also illustrates ancient Greek, Roman, Egyptian, and Celtic religions. A time line comparing significant events and people is included.

Bryson, Bill. *Shakespeare: The World as Stage.* HarperCollins, 2007. OBCB 2009.

Bryson hits the mark with his characteristic wit as he explores the world of Shakespeare and the mystery surrounding the man and his plays. Seventeenth-century England comes to life as Bryson takes the reader along on his research into what is known and not known about Shakespeare.

Campbell, Joseph, and Bill Moyers. *The Power of Myth.* Doubleday/Broadway Books, 1988. OBCB 2009.

Bill Moyers and Joseph Campbell discuss the role of mythology in the modern world, the journey inward, the hero's adventure, and tales of love and marriage. A companion to the six-part television documentary originally broadcast on PBS.

Diamant, Anita. *The Red Tent: A Novel.* St. Martin's, 1997. OBCB 2009.

This novel re-creates the biblical life of Dinah, daughter of Leah and Jacob, from her birth in Mesopotamia through her death in Egypt. The red tent is where women go during births, menstruation, and illness. There Dinah observes Jacob's four wives, who share their secrets with her as she grows up. After a doomed marriage, Dinah becomes a mother and a midwife.

D'Orso, Michael. *Eagle Blue: A Team, a Tribe, and a High School Basketball Season in Arctic Alaska.* Bloomsbury, 2006. OBCB 2009. (Alex Award)

This true story explores the tiny village of Fort Yukon, Alaska, its vanishing cultural heritage, and its relationship with mainstream American culture through its high school basketball teams. D'Orso lived in the village, following the boys' basketball team through the 2004–5 season, at the end of which they made it to the state championship game. The reader gets to know each player on the team, their coach and families, and the challenges they all face.

Engle, Margarita. Illus. by Sean Qualls. *The Poet Slave of Cuba: A Biography of Juan Francisco Manzano.* Henry Holt, 2006. OBCB 2009. (BBYA)

Written in verse, this is a Pura Belpré Award–winning portrait of Juan Francisco Manzano, the poet who was born a slave in Cuba in 1797. Narrated by Manzano, his mother, his owners, and others, the telling of the child- and young adulthood of the young genius emphasizes the power of stories, which sustained him through horrible experiences.

Follett, Ken. *The Pillars of the Earth.* Morrow, 1989. OBCB 2009.

This best-selling epic tale of ambition, anarchy, and absolute power set against the canvas of 12th-century England depicts fascinating characters and provides a spellbinding introduction to medieval religion, architecture, politics, and daily life. Readers follow the lives of men and women struggling to build a cathedral.

Freedman, Russell. *The Voice That Challenged a Nation: Marian Anderson and the Struggle for Equal Rights.* Houghton Mifflin Harcourt/Clarion, 2004. OBCB 2009. (BBYA)

A Newbery Honor book that recounts the life and musical career of the great African American vocalist Marian Anderson in the context of the history of civil rights in the

United States. Framed by Anderson's historic 1939 concert at the Lincoln Memorial, Freedman's account follows her career through American and European concert tours of the 1920s and '30s, and explores the effect of her career on segregation in the arts.

Greenberg, Jan, ed. *Heart to Heart: New Poems Inspired by Twentieth-Century American Art.* Harry N. Abrams, 2001. OBCB 2004, 2009. (BBYA, Printz Honor)
Can a painting speak? This collection of lyrical responses to famous American works of art will make you a believer. Large, colorful reproductions are paired with the poems they inspired in writers such as Jane Yolen, Ron Koertge, and Marvin Bell. Brief biographies of the contributors round out a lively collection.

Gruen, Sara. *Water for Elephants: A Novel.* Algonquin, 2007. OBCB 2009. (Alex Award)
Gruen creates a no-holds-barred story full of enchanting circus lore, mystery, trains, romance, and danger. Jacob Jankowski drops out of veterinarian school on the day of final exams, when he learns of his parents' tragic deaths. He stumbles upon a traveling circus, barely scraping by during the Great Depression, and works with the animals under an insane animal trainer. Jacob falls in love with the trainer's beautiful wife, Marlena, and with Rosie the elephant.

Hemphill, Stephanie. *Your Own, Sylvia: A Verse Portrait of Sylvia Plath.* Random House/Knopf, 2007. OBCB 2009. (BBYA, Printz Honor)
Hemphill creates a chronological biography in verse format from the viewpoint of others in Plath's life. The poetry is written in the style and forms used by Plath herself, some referencing specific poems. Grounded in primary-source research, this intimate, original fictional account will send readers to Plath's poetry and life.

Howe, Peter. *Shooting under Fire: The World of the War Photographer.* Artisan, 2002. OBCB 2004, 2009.
Ten leading combat photographers share their experiences of horror, humor, bravery, and daring while reporting from Vietnam, Haiti, Chechnya, El Salvador, Sarajevo, and Afghanistan. Over 150 black-and-white and color photographs provide a powerful and moving look at war and those who risk everything to document it.

Jacobs, A. J. *The Year of Living Biblically: One Man's Humble Quest to Follow the Bible as Literally as Possible.* Simon & Schuster, 2007. OBCB 2009.
A nonjudgmental and humorous look at the 12 months Jacobs lived as closely as he could to literal compliance with biblical rules. An agnostic Jew, Jacobs worked to follow both well-known and obscure laws, and visited a variety of groups and individuals to learn how they interpret the rules of the Bible. Jacobs writes in a style that manages to be entertaining without being irreverent.

King, Melissa. *She's Got Next: A Story of Getting In, Staying Open, and Taking a Shot.* Houghton Mifflin Harcourt/Mariner Books, 2005. OBCB 2009.
Through pick-up basketball games and the people she meets on the streets of Chicago, the author learns valuable life lessons. After moving from Arkansas to Chicago, King rediscovered basketball, a game she had enjoyed as a girl. Both humorous and thoughtful, King's story follows her transformation from a player into a coach for a young girls' team.

Landis, Deborah Nadoolman. *Dressed: A Century of Hollywood Costume Design.* HarperCollins, 2007. OBCB 2009.
Landis showcases one hundred years of Hollywood's most memorable costumes and the characters they helped bring to life as she reveals a behind-the-scenes look at the

evolution of the costume designer's art. Organized by decade, this lavish volume includes photographs and costume sketches, as well as personal anecdotes and quotes from the actors, directors, and designers involved. Landis herself is a celebrated costume designer for the movie industry.

Martin, Steve. *Born Standing Up: A Comic's Life.* Scribner, 2007. OBCB 2009.

In a memoir full of humor and candor, Martin shares his personal itinerary as he negotiates the maze of honing his profession and the pitfalls he avoided. Martin portrays the world of stand-up comedy, his peers, and the hard work and persistence that took him from Disneyland and Knott's Berry Farm to fame and fortune.

McGreevey, Tom, and Joanne Yeck. *Our Movie Heritage.* Rutgers University Press, 1997. OBCB 2004, 2009.

This work provides over one hundred beautiful pictures of top stars, directors, and others in the film industry, but the focus is on film preservation and the race against time to salvage what is left of the large number of films that are currently deteriorating in our nation's vaults, theaters, and private collections. Film, and its reflection on American culture, is in peril: 90 percent of silent films, and 50 percent of feature films made before 1950, have vanished.

Partridge, Elizabeth. *John Lennon: All I Want Is the Truth.* Penguin/Viking, 2005. OBCB 2009. (BBYA, Printz Honor)

Partridge provides a wide-open view into the work and life of one of the most influential and complicated persons in the world's musical heritage. From Lennon's own writings and interviews and a wealth of photographs, a clear picture emerges of an often misunderstood man.

Partridge, Elizabeth. *This Land Was Made for You and Me: The Life and Songs of Woody Guthrie.* Penguin/Viking, 2002. OBCB 2009. (BBYA)

Woody Guthrie was a humble figure, while at the same time a major catalyst of social change. This work provides insight into one of our most prolific and talented musicians, and the creation of his music. Partridge based her research on Guthrie's own writings and letters, as well as original interviews with Pete Seeger and Arlo Guthrie. The book is illustrated with Woody Guthrie's own lyrics, photographs, and sketches.

Polly, Matthew. *American Shaolin: Flying Kicks, Buddhist Monks, and the Legend of Iron Crotch; An Odyssey in the New China.* Penguin/Gotham Books, 2007. OBCB 2009. (Alex Award, BBYA)

The author reflects on the childhood dream that led him, as an adult, to take a break from Princeton and travel to China's famed Shaolin Temple to study martial arts for two years. Polly's funny and insightful observations and experiences reveal as much about Chinese culture as they do about his own path toward enlightenment and transformation (into a kung fu master!).

Sandler, Martin. *Photography: An Illustrated History.* Oxford University Press, 2002. OBCB 2004, 2009.

This work looks at photography as it evolved from daguerreotypes in the 1800s to the respected art form that it is today. Numerous compelling black-and-white and color photographs document technological developments, the contributions of pioneers in the field, as well as the impact photography has had upon all aspects of society.

Strickland, Carol. *The Annotated Mona Lisa: A Crash Course in Art History from Prehistoric to Post-Modern.* Andrews McMeel, 2007. OBCB 1999, 2009.

In an accessible format, this unique work provides a basic working knowledge of art and art history through short essays, sidebars, and photographs. Strickland covers it all, from cave paintings to digital media.

Weller, Sheila. *Girls like Us: Carole King, Joni Mitchell, Carly Simon—and the Journey of a Generation.* Simon & Schuster/Atria, 2008. OBCB 2009.

In three interwoven biographies, Weller chronicles the life and times of three tradition-breaking women singer-songwriters who came of age in the late 1960s. King, Mitchell, and Simon broke into what had been a male-dominated field, bringing the women's movement with them. Weller covers their music and its effect on a generation, and follows their careers through the 1980s.

· HISTORY AND CULTURES ·

Ahmad, Dohra, ed. *Rotten English: A Literary Anthology.* Norton, 2007. OBCB 2009.

Language is power, and, for the dizzying array of writers collected here, displaying an authentic voice is a means to reclaim what has been stolen, oppressed, or colonized. *Rotten English* collects the poetry, essays, short stories, and novels of the best in global vernacular writing from Mark Twain to Junot Diaz.

Alexie, Sherman. *The Absolutely True Diary of a Part-Time Indian.* Little, Brown, 2007. OBCB 2009. (BBYA)

Arnold Spirit, aka Junior, was born an outsider with water on his brain, lopsided eyes, and an IQ oppressed by extreme poverty and a mediocre reservation education. After switching to an all-white high school he realizes that though he'll never easily fit in, self-determination and a solid personal identity will give him the chance to both succeed and transcend.

Bagdasarian, Adam. *Forgotten Fire: A Novel.* Random House, 2000. OBCB 2004, 2009. (BBYA)

"Who will remember the Armenians?" Hitler asked, referencing the Armenian genocide as his inspiration for the final solution. This brutal hidden chapter of history is seen through the eyes of 12-year-old survivor Vahan Kendarian, whose world was shattered within a matter of days.

Chandrasekaran, Rajiv. *Imperial Life in the Emerald City: Inside Iraq's Green Zone.* Knopf, 2006. OBCB 2009.

A journalist explores the pristine "Emerald City," the American government's enclave in the middle of war-torn Baghdad. This is an eyewitness account of the failures of the first year of the Coalition Provisional Authority's tenure, 2003–4, depicting both those in charge and low level staffers.

Chang, Iris. *The Rape of Nanking: The Forgotten Holocaust of World War II.* Basic Books, 1997. OBCB 1999, 2009.

Barely a postscript in official Japanese history, the horrific torture and murder of hundreds of thousands of Chinese citizens took place over the course of just seven weeks. The Japanese army invaded Nanking in December 1937 and proceeded to slaughter over 300,000 soldiers and civilians. Chang analyzes the continued Japanese denial of responsibility, then turns to the story of a German businessman who persuaded Hitler to put a stop to the killing.

Chotjewitz, David. *Daniel Half-Human and the Good Nazi.* Translated by Doris Orgel. Simon & Schuster/Atheneum, 2004. OBCB 2009. (BBYA)

From Hitler Youth to hunted "mischling," Daniel sees his world unravel when he discovers his mother's hidden history "taints" him with Jewish blood and marks him for extermination. This young adult novel follows the friendship between Daniel and Amin, who join the Hitler Youth together, through Daniel's discovery and the family's escape from the country after Kristallnacht.

Delisle, Guy. *Pyongyang: A Journey in North Korea.* Drawn and Quarterly, 2005. OBCB 2009.

The secretive world of Communist North Korea remains a mystery to French-Canadian cartoonist Delisle, even after he has spent two months inside its borders. In the country doing animation work for a children's television show, Delisle was monitored by his guide and translator at all times. In this graphic depiction, he shares observations of a sadly cold and sterile society, infused with the dark humor he found in the experience.

Diamond, Jared. *Collapse: How Societies Choose to Fail or Succeed.* Penguin, 2005. OBCB 2009.

What do the lack of Icelandic fisherman, the 2008 Chinese Olympics, and Easter Island tree cutters all have in common? Much more than you might think. *Collapse* explores the political, technological, and ecological decisions that merge in order to sustain or destroy societies. Diamond examines the demise of ancient civilizations in order to warn us about the consequences of modern-day environmental decisions.

Diaz, Junot. *The Brief Wondrous Life of Oscar Wao.* Penguin/Riverhead, 2007. OBCB 2009.

"Ghetto nerd," outcast, and anime-loving Oscar Wao is the latest in a long line of doomed generations to suffer the dreaded fuku curse of his native Dominican Republic. With humor and talent as his weapons, he perseveres, knowing "you can never run away. Not ever. The only way out is in."

Egan, Timothy. *The Worst Hard Time: The Untold Story of Those Who Survived the Great American Dust Bowl.* Houghton Mifflin, 2006. OBCB 2009.

Award-winning *New York Times* reporter Egan tackles the great dust bowl phenomenon of the 1930s and '40s in this multi-tiered account. He shares incredible eye-witness accounts as well as the overwhelming convergences of failed agricultural practices, ill-fated government policies, and the costs of "get rich quick" schemes.

Eggers, Dave. *What Is the What: The Autobiography of Valentino Achak Deng; A Novel.* McSweeney's, 2006. OBCB 2009.

As a young boy Valentino witnessed Arab militia men destroy his Sudanese village; hid from hungry lions; wandered through wasted, desert landscapes; and narrowly escaped fatal disease, capture, starvation, and enlistment. The will to survive displayed here is almost as miraculous as the ability to recount a harrowing genocide of home and people with such thoughtfulness and grace.

Fadiman, Anne. *The Spirit Catches You and You Fall Down: A Hmong Child, Her American Doctors, and the Collision of Two Cultures.* Farrar, Straus, and Giroux, 1997. OBCB 2009.

A Hmong refugee family in California clashes with the American medical system when they attribute their daughter's grand mal seizures to a spiritual rather than physical problem. Lia Lee had her first seizure at three months old. When the family did not comply with their doctor's instructions, the medical community removed her from the home. This balanced account of a tragic misunderstanding captures Hmong history and culture.

Fleming, Anne Marie. *The Magical Life of Long Tack Sam.* Penguin/Riverhead, 2007. OBCB 2009.

Born in 1885 in a small Chinese village, Long Tack Sam was an acrobat, a magician, an entrepreneur, a world traveler, a celebrity, a father, a ladies' man, and a husband. This graphic collage biography presents narrative writing, handbills, photographs, and news clippings along with interviews, comics, and commentary to convey the effects of cultural shifts and global politics on individual lives.

Horwitz, Tony. *A Voyage Long and Strange: Rediscovering the New World.* Henry Holt, 2008. OBCB 2009.

Pulitzer Prize–winning journalist Horwitz uses humor and candor to literally follow in the footsteps of the first American explorers—from the Vikings and French utopians to America's first African American trailblazer—whose discoveries took place hundreds of years *before* the legendary landing on Plymouth Rock.

Jones, Edward P. *The Known World.* HarperCollins/Amistad, 2003. OBCB 2009.

In this Pulitzer Prize–winning novel, Jones approaches a little-explored chapter in ante-bellum history, that of African American slave owners. Set several decades before the beginning of the Civil War, in Manchester County, Virginia, this work skillfully weaves plot, time, and perspective amongst a diverse and powerful cast of characters in order to explore the moral complexities inherent in human freedom (or the lack thereof).

Larson, Erik. *The Devil in the White City: Murder, Magic, and Madness at the Fair That Changed America.* Crown, 2003. OBCB 2009.

The 1893 Chicago World's Fair captured the imagination of the whole world, and also provided a playground for a cunning serial killer. Larson alternates between the activities of Daniel H. Burnham, the architect who coordinated the construction of the fair, and those of H. H. Holmes, who killed scores of people in the vicinity.

Maltman, Thomas. *The Night Birds: A Novel.* Soho Press, 2007. OBCB 2009. (Alex Award)

Three generations of settlers and native Dakota weave a dark tale of family secrets and brutal injustice in Civil War–era America. Asa is 14 years old in 1876 when his aunt Hazel is released from an asylum and comes to live with his family in Minnesota. She tells stories of the tragic events of 1862, when a Dakota uprising in Missouri resulted in terrible violence and the loss of her first love, a Dakota man.

Roberts, Gene, and Hank Klibanoff. *The Race Beat: The Press, the Civil Rights Struggle, and the Awakening of a Nation.* Knopf, 2006. OBCB 2009.

When Harry Reasoner thrust a microphone at an angry mob and yelled "I don't care what you're going to do to me, but the whole world is going to know it!" he spoke for all the reporters and photographers, black and white, North and South, who played a critical role in bringing the reality of the civil rights movement into the living rooms and consciousness of the American public. The authors covered the "race beat" from 1954 to 1965, reporting on the Emmett Till case, as well as events in Selma and Montgomery.

Saenz, Benjamin Alire. *Sammy and Juliana in Hollywood.* Cinco Puntos Press, 2004. OBCB 2009. (BBYA)

This Hollywood is a barrio in 1968 New Mexico, where the students at Las Cruces High School struggle through heartbreak, loss, and an entrenched racial divide to find their place in the world. Sammy Santos is a hard-working, smart teenager who faces the death of his first love, the treatment of gay teens, and issues of the Vietnam era, including the draft.

Satrapi, Marjane. *The Complete Persepolis.* Knopf/Pantheon, 2007. OBCB 2009. (*Persepolis*: Alex Award, BBYA) (*Persepolis 2*: BBYA)

This book includes both *Persepolis* and *Persepolis 2*, Marjane Satrapi's complete memoir in beautifully rendered graphic novel format. Beginning with her childhood in Iran during the Islamic Revolution, then moving through her adolescence spent at school in Vienna, the volume ends with Satrapi's unsuccessful attempt to return to Iran as a young woman and her permanent move to Europe.

Spiegelman, Art. *The Complete Maus: A Survivor's Tale.* Knopf/Pantheon, 1996. OBCB 1999, 2009.

The author portrays his parents' experiences during the Holocaust, their time at Auschwitz, survival, and years in the United States in this seminal graphic novel. Spiegelman also reveals his own struggle to come to terms with the past, the success of *Maus: A Survivor's Tale,* and the effects of his choice to represent the Nazis as cats and the Jews as mice.

Ung, Loung. *First They Killed My Father: A Daughter of Cambodia Remembers.* HarperCollins, 2001. OBCB 2004, 2009. (BBYA)

The perils of life under the brutal Pol Pot regime change a young woman's life forever, as she and her family find themselves fugitives of war, without even their names to remind them of what they lost. Ung tells her story in the present tense, taking the reader from her ideal childhood in the cosmopolitan city of Phnom Penh to work camps and training as a child soldier, through the loss of her parents and her eventual escape to Thailand and the United States.

Weiner, Tim. *Legacy of Ashes: The History of the CIA.* Doubleday, 2007. OBCB 2009.

With considerable research and extensive interviews, Weiner shows the grave miscalculations that have plagued the Central Intelligence Agency since its inception. He presents the CIA as trying to change conditions all over the world without taking time to comprehend the situations at hand. Particulars abound, from the Bay of Pigs to the Iranian Revolution to the Iraq War.

Williams, David. *Bitterly Divided: The South's Inner Civil War.* New Press, 2008. OBCB 2009.

The Civil War was lost long before the first shot was ever fired, thanks to deep and violent divisions of class and political allegiance in the Confederacy that resulted in "a rich man's war and a poor man's fight." Williams exposes the internal war that crippled the confederate cause, including the effects of hundreds of thousands of deserters, southern men who fought for the Union, fugitive slaves, and southerners opposed to secession.

Wolf, Allan. *New Found Land: Lewis and Clark's Voyage of Discovery.* Candlewick, 2004. OBCB 2009. (BBYA)

The epic journey of Lewis and Clark comes alive as each member of the expedition tells an intimately personal story of struggle and discovery in this sweeping poetic rendition. Lewis's dog, Seaman, is the primary narrator whose prose clarifies the events described by a full spectrum of participants including the expedition leaders, a slave, a captured Shoshone girl, and President Jefferson.

· LITERATURE AND LANGUAGE ARTS ·

Allison, Dorothy. *Bastard out of Carolina.* Dutton, 1992. OBCB 1999, 2004, 2009.
Bone confronts illegitimacy, poverty, the troubled marriage of her mother and stepfather, and the stigma of being considered "white trash" as she comes of age in South Carolina. Despite the fact that she lives among a large extended and protective family, Bone's stepfather, Daddy Glen, becomes increasingly abusive; her mother is either unable or unwilling to protect her; and Bone herself is too young or too embarrassed to reveal what is happening to her.

Anderson, M. T. *The Astonishing Life of Octavian Nothing, Traitor to the Nation, Vol. 1: The Pox Party.* Candlewick, 2006. OBCB 2009. (BBYA, Printz Honor)
The Astonishing Life of Octavian Nothing, Traitor to the Nation, Vol. 2: The Kingdom on the Waves. Candlewick, 2008. OBCB 2009. (BBYA, Printz Honor)
During the American Revolution, Octavian is raised as a pampered African prince by a society of Enlightenment philosophers who view him as an experiment. Realizing that his freedom is an illusion, Octavian sets off on a journey to find freedom and a place in the world. These books will challenge everything you have ever learned about the Revolutionary War.

Bond, Jenny, and Chris Sheedy. *Who the Hell Is Pansy O'Hara? The Fascinating Stories behind 50 of the World's Best-Loved Books.* Penguin, 2008. OBCB 2009.
Did you ever wonder what an author was thinking when she wrote her book? Explore the quirky backstories of some of the world's most famous books, both contemporary and classic, nonfiction and fiction.

Cameron, Peter. *Someday This Pain Will Be Useful to You.* Farrar, Straus, and Giroux, 2007. OBCB 2009. (BBYA)
James hates everyone except his grandmother. His mother's third marriage failed to last through the honeymoon, he finds himself attracted to an older man who works in his mother's art gallery, and he cannot decide whether to attend Brown University or buy a house in the Midwest somewhere. Take a look at life through this brilliant and mischievous Manhattan teen's eyes as he tries to figure out life and his place in it.

Cisneros, Sandra. *Caramelo.* Knopf, 2002. OBCB 2004, 2009.
LaLa Reyes learns the stories of her Awful Grandmother and weaves them into a colorful history of her 20th-century Mexican family, taking the reader from Mexico City to Chicago to San Antonio. The "caramelo," a striped shawl begun by her great-grandmother, symbolizes their traditions.

Dunn, Mark. *Ella Minnow Pea: A Novel in Letters.* MacAdam/Cage, 2001. OBCB 2009.
The people of Nollop, an island off South Carolina, are good citizens, but as the use of more and more letters in the alphabet is outlawed, how will its residents communicate? Ella Minnow Pea is just a girl, but she steps forward to save her fellow inhabitants from a totalitarian law banning the use of each letter that falls off the memorial statue of Nevin Nollop (letters which then progressively disappear from the novel).

Foer, Jonathan Safran. *Extremely Loud and Incredibly Close.* Houghton Mifflin, 2005. OBCB 2009.
Oskar Schell, a gifted and precocious nine-year-old, explores the mystery of his father's death during the September 11 attack. Oskar's search for the lock that fits the key left

behind by his father intersects with his grandparents' survival of the firebombing of Dresden. Graphics, wordplay, and humor lighten the narrative.

Gaines, Ernest. *A Lesson before Dying.* Knopf, 1993. OBCB 1999, 2009.

In 1940s Louisiana, Jefferson, a young black man, faces the electric chair for murder. When his attorney states, "I would just as soon put a hog in the electric chair as this," his grandmother persuades disillusioned teacher Grant Wiggins to visit Jefferson in the penitentiary and help him gain a sense of dignity and self-esteem before his execution.

Green, John. *Looking for Alaska.* Dutton, 2005. OBCB 2009. (BBYA, Printz Winner)

Join Miles Halter, who is intrigued by famous last words, as he heads off to an Alabama boarding school in search of the "Great Perhaps." Before, his life was a nonevent, boring and unchallenging. What he finds is a beautiful but troubled girl named Alaska. After, he experiences love and loss, adventure and friendship.

Haddon, Mark. *The Curious Incident of the Dog in the Night-Time.* Doubleday, 2003. OBCB 2004, 2009. (Alex Award, BBYA)

Fifteen-year-old Christopher has two mysteries to solve: who killed Wellington the dog, and what happened to his mother. Christopher has Asperger's syndrome, a form of autism, which causes him to take things very literally and have trouble relating to others. After spending a night in jail accused of Wellington's murder, and inspired by Sherlock Holmes, he determines to investigate.

Hosseini, Khaled. *The Kite Runner.* Putnam, 2003. OBCB 2004, 2009. (Alex Award)

When he was just a young boy, joyfully running kites through the streets of Kabul in the 1970s, Amir betrayed the son of his father's servant, his best friend, Hassan. Years after fleeing Afghanistan, Amir, now an American citizen, returns to his native land (ruled by the Taliban) and attempts to atone for his cowardice and betrayal.

Ishiguro, Kazuo. *Never Let Me Go.* Knopf, 2005. OBCB 2009. (Alex Award)

Only special students are chosen to attend Hailsham, an exclusive boarding school tucked away in the English countryside. The chilling truth of their special nature slowly unfolds as we follow the stories of three former students. Kathy, a 31-year-old alumna, narrates this unsettling examination of loyalty, self-sacrifice, and personal freedoms.

Jones, Lloyd. *Mister Pip.* Dial Press, 2007. OBCB 2009. (Alex Award, BBYA)

Matilda's Pacific Island village has been torn apart by civil war. Against this harsh backdrop, Mr. Watts, a lonely British expatriate, maintains calm by reading Dickens's *Great Expectations* aloud to the village children, transforming their lives. Matilda's religious mother objects to the world that Mr. Watts is sharing with the children, a conflict which leads to tragedy.

Keillor, Garrison, ed. *Good Poems.* Penguin, 2002. OBCB 2009.

An essential and accessible anthology of some of the best contemporary and classic poetry. Keillor chose the selections from poems that have been featured on his early morning show, *The Writer's Almanac.* In his introduction, Keillor makes it clear that he eschewed pretentiousness and sought accessibility.

Kidd, Sue Monk. *The Secret Life of Bees.* Viking, 2002. OBCB 2009. (BBYA)

Searching for the truth about her mother's life and death, a grieving Lily finds the answers, love, and acceptance where she least expects them. In 1960s South Carolina, Lily's nanny, Rosaleen, is forced to flee town after trying to exercise her right to vote. Lily accompanies her to Tiburon, the home of Black Madonna Honey, whose owners take them in and put them to work in the honey house.

Kyle, Aryn. *The God of Animals.* Simon & Schuster/Scribner, 2007. OBCB 2009. (Alex Award)

Twelve-year-old Alice faces issues beyond her years. Her older sister has run off with a rodeo cowboy, her mother won't get out of bed, and the family horse farm is failing. She helps her father with their Colorado ranch after school, and spends nights on the phone with a male teacher who probably had something to do with the disappearance of her classmate Polly, but who at least pays Alice the attention she so desperately needs.

Maguire, Gregory. *Wicked: The Life and Times of the Wicked Witch of the West.* ReganBooks, 1995. OBCB 2009.

The Wizard of Oz retold from the point of view of Elphaba, the Wicked Witch of the West. Elphaba is a serious student, rejected by her popular college roommate, Glinda. Oz is a land of marginalized talking Animals and secret police. Elphaba dares to stand up to the corrupt Wizard and defend the Animals, which earns her the label *wicked*.

McCarthy, Cormac. *The Road.* Knopf/Vintage, 2008. OBCB 2009.

After an apocalyptic catastrophe, a father and his young son embark on a grim and perilous quest to travel south before the weather becomes cold enough to kill them. The father remembers the time before, and tries to keep his son safe from other survivors they meet on the road.

Murakami, Haruki. *Kafka on the Shore.* Knopf, 2005. OBCB 2009.

Reality and fantasy converge in this story of Kafka Tamura, a Japanese teenage runaway, and his quest to find his long-lost sister and mother. Headed in the same direction is Satoru Nakata, an older man whose mysterious WWII experiences left him unable to read or communicate, but able to speak with cats.

Myers, Walter Dean. *Sunrise over Fallujah.* Scholastic, 2008. OBCB 2009.

An 18-year-old growing up in Harlem, Robin always intended to go to college. But after September 11 he decides instead to volunteer for the army. After basic training he is deployed to Iraq as part of a Civil Affairs unit, charged with building good relations with the Iraqi people. Experiencing the horrors of war, Robin learns that fighting for freedom is not always black and white.

Roth, Philip. *The Plot against America.* Houghton Mifflin, 2004. OBCB 2009.

This alternate history takes a hard look at one of America's legendary heroes, Charles Lindbergh, and how bigotry and fear can shape politics. Charles Lindbergh defeats FDR for the presidency in 1940. His anti-Semitic policies affect seven-year-old Philip, as pogroms and relocation severely alter the dynamics of his large New Jersey–based family.

Sebold, Alice. *Lucky: A Memoir.* Scribner, 1999. OBCB 2004, 2009.

"You save yourself or you remain unsaved." With these words, Sebold recounts the brutal rape that she was "lucky" to survive as a college freshman. Tragedy and hope combine as she makes her way through a survivor's maze of emotions, and the arrest and trial of her attacker.

Stoppard, Tom. *Rosencrantz and Guildenstern Are Dead.* Grove Press, 1967. OBCB 1999, 2009.

Two bit players from Shakespeare's *Hamlet* are thrust into a terrifying and surreal new situation. Involved in court intrigue beyond their control, Rosencrantz and Guildenstern find themselves trapped in a futile, fatal situation. This witty, existential play addresses individual freedom, fate, and luck.

Thompson, Craig. *Blankets: An Illustrated Novel.* Top Shelf Productions, 2003. OBCB 2009. (BBYA)

A young man living in rural Wisconsin questions his faith and experiences bittersweet first love in this autobiographical and groundbreaking graphic novel. Thompson depicts his fundamentalist Christian upbringing, the rejection of his talent for drawing by his parents and their religious community, closeness with his younger brother, meeting Raina at a church camp, and falling in love for the first time.

Zusak, Marcus. *The Book Thief.* Knopf, 2006. OBCB 2009. (BBYA, Printz Honor)

Living in Nazi Germany, young Liesel and her family choose to lie and steal to protect a Jewish refugee hiding in their basement. Narrated by Death, this is not your typical World War II story. Liesel steals her first book before she even learns to read and, in the end, it is a book that saves her.

· SCIENCE AND TECHNOLOGY ·

Adams, Scott. *God's Debris: A Thought Experiment.* Andrews McMeel, 2001. OBCB 2009.

Take a metaphysical journey into the search for meaning, as you try to deliver a package to the smartest man in the world who won't take it until you understand. This man is able to explain physics, God, gravity, light, psychic phenomena, and more. Written as a parable, this is also a brain teaser, because elements of these perfectly simple explanations are wrong, and the reader has to figure out which.

Anderson, M. T. *Feed.* Candlewick, 2002. OBCB 2004, 2009. (BBYA)

In this society your brain cyberfeed provides an endless stream of information, entertainment, and advertising. Although teenage Titus can sense something wrong, it isn't until he meets Violet during a spring break trip to the moon that he begins to understand. Violet is homeschooled. She can think for herself. When her feed is disrupted, Titus is forced to examine the power of the feed in his life.

Ayres, Ian. *Super Crunchers: Why Thinking-by-Numbers Is the New Way to Be Smart.* Bantam, 2007. OBCB 2009.

With real-life examples from sports, medicine, online dating, and airline pricing, Ayres describes how data about all of us are collected and "crunched" by statisticians and computers in order to profile consumers and make predictions. This benefits both the consumer and the companies interested in selling to them. An entertaining education in the basics of statistics.

Best, Joel. *Damned Lies and Statistics: Untangling Numbers from the Media, Politicians, and Activists.* University of California Press, 2001. OBCB 2004, 2009.

Do you know the difference between "good" and "bad" statistics, or how statistics and public policy are connected? Most people naïvely believe reported statistics, which are often mutations of the truth. Best teaches readers to become critical thinkers, and how to evaluate the statistics they encounter.

Bryson, Bill. *A Short History of Nearly Everything.* Broadway Books, 2003. OBCB 2004, 2009.

A renowned travel writer brings complex scientific concepts to life by describing how the universe and life as we know it came to be. Bryson focuses his distinctive humor and intelligence on every topic from the Big Bang to Darwin's trip on the *Beagle* to the fate of the dodo, how we know what we know, and the people who figured it out.

Casey, Susan. *The Devil's Teeth: A True Story of Obsession and Survival among America's Great White Sharks.* Henry Holt/Owl Books, 2005. OBCB 2009.

While studying migratory birds on the remote Farallon Islands, 30 miles off the coast of San Francisco, biologists noticed red blotches in the surrounding waters. These sightings evolved into a full-blown scientific study of great white sharks revealing unknown secrets of these prehistoric beasts. Casey also traces the history of the dangerous and spooky islands themselves.

Chen, Joanne. *The Taste of Sweet: Our Complicated Love Affair with Our Favorite Treats.* Crown, 2008. OBCB 2009.

Why does chocolate taste so good while broccoli turns many of us off? The science, history, and social changes behind the American sweet tooth are explored, from the taste buds on our tongues to slaves on the sugar plantations. Chen broadens her topic into the search for the next artificial sweetener, and follows connections with the nutrition, exercise, and diet industries.

Doctorow, Cory. *Little Brother.* Tom Doherty/Tor Teen, 2008. OBCB 2009. (BBYA)

In near-future San Francisco, 17-year-old Marcus, known online as w1n5t0n (or Winston), is detained by the Department of Homeland Security under suspicion of participating in a terrorist attack. After days of harsh questioning, Marcus and his friends are released and begin to use technology to fight against the DHS and its infringement of personal liberties.

Firlik, Katrina. *Another Day in the Frontal Lobe: A Brain Surgeon Exposes Life on the Inside.* Random House, 2006. OBCB 2009.

Firlik is one of the rare female neurosurgeons in the world. She writes an honest appraisal of her work, of day-to-day problem solving and ethical dilemmas. Along the way she removes a nail in a carpenter's head and allows maggots to clean an infected brain in this humorous and candid memoir.

Flannery, Tim. *The Weather Makers: How Man Is Changing the Climate and What It Means for Life on Earth.* Atlantic Monthly Press, 2005. OBCB 2009.

What are melting glaciers, disappearing frogs, and a season of perfect storms trying to tell us about the conditions of the planet we call home, and what can we do to prevent a catastrophe? Flannery traces the history of climate change, makes predictions for the future, and offers recommendations for preventing disaster.

George, Rose. *The Big Necessity: The Unmentionable World of Human Waste and Why It Matters.* Metropolitan Books, 2008. OBCB 2009.

It isn't hidden behind the bathroom door or quietly flushed down the toilet in this book: a look at the dirty details of what happens to human waste around the globe and how it affects our health and sanitation.

Hoose, Phillip M. *The Race to Save the Lord God Bird.* Farrar, Straus, and Giroux, 2004. OBCB 2009. (BBYA)

The ivory-billed woodpecker is thought to be extinct, but some disagree. Hoose documents the scientific and bird-watching communities' attempts to find this lost species and save its habitat in the southern United States. Along the way, Hoose traces the recent evolution of human-bird interaction, from an early ornithologist who killed birds in order to catalogue them, to a kinder scientific approach; from the effect of plumed hats on the bird population, to the Bostonian ladies who started the Audubon Society.

Jones, Chris. *Out of Orbit: The Incredible True Story of Three Astronauts Who Were Hundreds of Miles above Earth When They Lost Their Ride Home.* Broadway Books, 2008. OBCB 2009.

The mission seemed jinxed from the start. The destruction of the shuttle *Columbia* and its crew in 2003 stranded three astronauts in earth's orbit. Their only hope was an outdated, malfunctioning capsule latched to the side of their space station. Making it work was a herculean feat of teamwork on and off the planet.

Leopold, Aldo. *A Sand County Almanac.* Oxford University Press, 2001. OBCB 2009.

This classic of environmental and nature writing, arranged by season, provides a poetic view through the window of the Leopold family farm in the Wisconsin meadows. Even 60 years after this book's original publication, Leopold's closing comments on land ethics (nothing that disturbs the balance of nature can be right) and conservation are surprisingly relevant. Leopold believed that it is a duty of the human race to preserve wild land when possible.

Macaulay, David. *Mosque.* Houghton Mifflin Harcourt/Walter Lorraine, 2003. OBCB 2009.

Enter a community mosque in 16th-century Istanbul and discover the techniques (from brick making to stained-glass window production) used to raise towering minarets and a beautiful prayer hall dome. This book for all ages glorifies these magnificent buildings that served as the center of religion and also housed travelers, stored food, and provided public baths.

Macaulay, David. *The Way We Work: Getting to Know the Amazing Human Body.* Houghton Mifflin Harcourt/Walter Lorraine, 2008. OBCB 2009.

Macaulay takes the reader on a tour of the human body with detailed illustrations and succinct, sometimes humorous explanations of its building blocks (beginning on the cellular level) and systems.

McKibben, Bill, ed. *American Earth: Environmental Writing since Thoreau.* Library of America, 2008. OBCB 2009.

Experience the growth of the environmental movement in poetry, essay, song, and prose from its infancy to the present day through the eyes of its champions. This chronological anthology encompasses both the famed and those less known for their environmental writing, such as P. T. Barnum. Each piece is contextualized by McKibben, and the volume is generously illustrated.

Melville, Greg. *Greasy Rider: Two Dudes, One Fry-Oil-Powered Car, and a Cross-Country Search for a Greener Future.* Algonquin, 2008. OBCB 2009.

Take a humorous, green road trip with the author and his college buddy in a converted 1980s Mercedes from Vermont to California, and learn how to be more eco-friendly. Greg and his friend Iggy visit Fort Knox, a wind turbine field, and the first green Walmart along the way.

Pollan, Michael. *The Botany of Desire: A Plant's-Eye View of the World.* Random House, 2001. OBCB 2009.

Through the sweetness of apples, the beauty of tulips, the intoxication of marijuana, and potato control, Pollan shows how mankind has manipulated plants and they, in turn, have enticed us to do their bidding. The journey of each plant combines history, culture, and science, and in the case of potatoes, modern genetic modifications as well.

Preston, Richard. *The Wild Trees: A Story of Passion and Daring.* Random House, 2007. OBCB 2009.

Three buddies on spring break climb into a California redwood and discover a new ecosystem atop the trees. Join a group of young scientists in the canopy as they learn safe climbing techniques for the oldest and tallest trees of North America, encounter new species of plants, animals who never touch the ground, friendship, and love.

Roach, Mary. *Stiff: The Curious Lives of Human Cadavers.* Norton, 2003. OBCB 2004, 2009. (Alex Award, BBYA)

Discover the amazing life-after-death adventures of human bodies in this examination of how medical and research scientists use cadavers to make our lives better. In an engaging, humorous style, Roach takes the reader along on her investigations into the varied fates of cadavers. She also examines the ways in which remains are disposed of in different cultures.

Schroeder, Gerald. *The Hidden Face of God: How Science Reveals the Ultimate Truth.* Simon & Schuster/Free Press, 2001. OBCB 2009.

This somewhat controversial book investigates the relationship between physics and metaphysics, science and religion, but doesn't provide any specific answers. Schroeder posits that there are two sides to life: the material, which science can prove and understand, as well as a universal wisdom at the heart of existence. Schroeder's writing will evoke a sense of wonder about the cosmos and life itself for those who have an open mind.

Silverstein, Ken. *The Radioactive Boy Scout: The True Story of a Boy and His Backyard Nuclear Reactor.* Random House, 2004. OBCB 2009. (BBYA)

What would you do if you came home to find your neighborhood quarantined? Learn the true story of how David Hahn's work toward an Atomic Energy Boy Scout badge turned into a teenage obsession. Government agents descended on his backyard shed when the radiation reached levels toxic to his entire town.

Smith, Gina. *The Genomics Age: How DNA Technology Is Transforming the Way We Live and Who We Are.* AMACOM, 2004. OBCB 2009. o.p.

From Crick and Watson's discovery of the double helix to "designer" embryos, learn the history and truth behind the controversies in today's news, including genetic testing, increased lifespans, a cure for cancer, stem cell research, cloning, gene therapy, and eugenics. Smith, a former network news technology consultant, presents hard scientific facts in an enjoyable, easy-to-read manner.

Teresi, Dick. *Lost Discoveries: The Ancient Roots of Modern Science—From the Babylonians to the Maya.* Simon & Schuster, 2002. OBCB 2009.

Teresi demonstrates that modern science is much older than we think, and shows how scientific and mathematical concepts developed by ancient cultures around the world are the foundations of today's technology.

· SOCIAL SCIENCES ·

Albom, Mitch. *Tuesdays with Morrie: An Old Man, a Young Man, and Life's Greatest Lesson.* Doubleday, 1997. OBCB 2004, 2009.

Mitch Albom's Tuesday night visits with his dying sociology professor, Morrie, offer valuable lessons about the art of living and dying with dignity. Albom reconnected with his older friend in the final months of his life and took one last class, a class with only one pupil, on the topics of family, money, fear of aging, marriage, love, regrets, and forgiveness.

Beah, Ishmael. *A Long Way Gone: Memoirs of a Boy Soldier.* Farrar, Straus, and Giroux, 2007. OBCB 2009. (Alex Award, BBYA)

A Long Way Gone is the riveting, firsthand account of Ishmael Beah, a 12-year-old child soldier, hopped up on drugs and wielding an AK-47, who gets swept up in the horrors of civil war in his homeland of Sierra Leone. Rescued at 15, he spends time at a UNICEF rehabilitation center before coming to the United States to speak to the United Nations.

Bolles, Richard Nelson. *What Color Is Your Parachute? 2009: A Practical Manual for Job-Hunters and Career-Changers.* Ten Speed Press, 2008. OBCB 2009.

With a proven track record of more than thirty years in publication, this top-selling career guide has been updated and revised to help first-time job seekers discover and get the right work for them. This "Job Hunting in Hard Times edition" includes a new chapter on rejection shock for the laid off, and another titled "Think," which provides innovative ways to find an open position, even where one might not be advertised.

Casnocha, Ben. *My Start-Up Life: What a (Very) Young CEO Learned on His Journey through Silicon Valley.* Wiley, 2007. OBCB 2009.

Casnocha, a 19-year-old entrepreneur, tells his own story about the ups and downs of making a business idea work and inspires readers to find their own way to make a difference. Casnocha started at 12. By 16 he had been nominated for an Entrepreneur of the Year award and was chairman of his second company, Comcate, which facilitates web communication between city governments and citizens.

George, Mary W. *The Elements of Library Research: What Every Student Needs to Know.* Princeton University Press, 2008. OBCB 2009.

Succinct and practical, this guide provides students with the tactics, tools, and confidence they need to successfully conduct college-level research, both in print and online.

Gladwell, Malcolm. *The Tipping Point: How Little Things Can Make a Big Difference.* Little, Brown, 2000. OBCB 2009.

Through entertaining anecdotes Gladwell explains the phenomenon of fads, or how little actions can ripple outward until a "tipping point" is reached that results in a dramatic change. He reveals how ideas spread and how societal changes can happen quickly given the right context, the "stickiness" of an idea, and the involvement of key people.

Juette, Melvin, and Ronald J. Berger. *Wheelchair Warrior: Gangs, Disability, and Basketball.* Temple University Press, 2008. OBCB 2009.

This inspiring story follows the transformation of a 16-year-old African American gang member destined for prison or death into a wheelchair athlete playing for the U.S. National Wheelchair Basketball Team. Paralyzed in a gang-related shooting, Juette turned from crime to attend college and become a star athlete. Berger's introduction and conclusion place Juette's affecting, dramatic memoir in a sociological context.

Keen, Lisa. *Out Law: What LGBT Youth Should Know about Their Legal Rights.* Beacon Press, 2007. OBCB 2009.

Keen introduces LGBT youth to their legal rights, encourages them to defend those rights, and provides examples of young people empowered to stand up for themselves. Keen provides the history and evolution of relevant laws, a time line of legal landmarks, and a list of organizations available to help LGBT youth.

Kohl, Jana. *A Rare Breed of Love: The True Story of Baby and the Mission She Inspired to Help Dogs Everywhere.* Simon & Schuster/Fireside, 2008. OBCB 2009. o.p.

The shocking cruelty of legal animal abuse is exposed through the story of Baby, a poodle who lost a leg after years of mistreatment at a puppy mill. Rescued by Jana Kohl, Baby now works together with politicians and Jana's celebrity friends to raise awareness about animal rights.

McCormick, Patricia. *Sold.* Hyperion, 2006. OBCB 2009. (BBYA)

When 13-year-old Lakshmi is sold into prostitution by her gambling stepfather, she is taken from her village in the mountains of Nepal to a brothel in the slums of Calcutta. Her life becomes a nightmare from which she cannot escape. Some hope leavens the horrifying situation when Lakshmi learns to read, and an American arrives to rescue the girls in the brothel. This novel in free verse reflects a situation that many girls around the world endure today.

Menzel, Peter, and Faith D'Aluisio. *Hungry Planet: What the World Eats.* Material World/Ten Speed Press, 2005. OBCB 2009.

Hungry Planet is a photo-chronicle of families around the world, the food they eat, and how uncontrollable forces like poverty, conflict, and globalization affect our most elemental human need—food. Portraits of families (taken with a week's supply of food) from 24 different countries are presented. Recipes and essays complete the package, giving the reader a clear picture of how global changes are affecting daily life and health.

Mortenson, Greg, and David Oliver Relin. *Three Cups of Tea: One Man's Mission to Promote Peace One School at a Time.* Viking, 2006. OBCB 2009.

Lost and near death following an unsuccessful attempt to climb K2, Mortenson is sheltered and nursed in a remote mountain village. Out of gratitude, he vows to return to build a school there. That vow grows into the Central Asia Institute and the creation of over 50 schools in Pakistan and Afghanistan. *Three Cups of Tea* gives the reader a clear picture of life on the ground in both countries and an understanding of how the United States might help villagers in their struggle against extremists by fighting poverty and providing education, particularly for girls.

Picoult, Jodi. *Nineteen Minutes.* Atria, 2007. OBCB 2009.

Seventeen-year-old Peter Houghton wakes up one day, loads his backpack with four guns, walks into the school cafeteria, and kills nine students and one teacher in the span of nineteen minutes. Peter had been bullied relentlessly since kindergarten. Picoult tells the story from several points of view, including those of a detective investigating the incident; Peter's mother; Peter's former friend Josie, who witnessed the shooting; and Josie's mother, the judge hearing Peter's case.

Pipher, Mary. *The Middle of Everywhere: The World's Refugees Come to Our Town.* Harcourt, 2002. OBCB 2004, 2009.

An exploration of the difficulties and struggles of refugees settled by the U.S. government in Lincoln, Nebraska, as they try to adjust and build a life in America. Pipher works as a family therapist in Lincoln, helping families deal with the tragedies of the past and hold onto cultural traditions in the present. She writes about young people from Sudan and Bosnia, and families from Vietnam and Afghanistan.

Pope, Loren. *Colleges That Change Lives: 40 Schools That Will Change the Way You Think about Colleges.* Penguin, 2006. OBCB 2009.

Prospective college students can rely on Pope's indispensable guide to 41 colleges where education rivals that of Ivy League universities in producing outstanding graduates. Pope helps students to understand the personality of each school, and find a school that will help them to aim high, achieve their potential, and feel empowered. Includes information for the homeschooled and those with learning disabilities.

Rogers, Elizabeth, and Thomas Kostigen. *The Green Book: The Everyday Guide to Saving the Planet One Simple Step at a Time.* Crown/Three Rivers Press, 2007. OBCB 2009.

Celebrities Ellen DeGeneres, Jennifer Aniston, Tim McGraw, Dale Earnhardt Jr., and others contribute suggestions of small, everyday changes that will have a positive impact on the health of our planet. Suggestions are divided into sections for home, school, work, shopping, entertainment, travel, health and beauty, and sports.

Sheff, David. *Beautiful Boy: A Father's Journey through His Son's Addiction.* Houghton Mifflin Harcourt, 2008. OBCB 2009.

A father's anguished account of his promising son's meth addiction and its painful impact on the entire family is honest, raw, and full of information about the realities of drug addiction. Nic was a bright, athletic 17-year-old when he began experimenting with drugs. Within months he was an addict. David Sheff writes about attempts at rehab and being the parent of an addict.

Sheff, Nic. *Tweak: Growing Up on Methamphetamines.* Simon & Schuster/Atheneum, 2008. OBCB 2009.

Nic Sheff was destined for a rich life and career until he is derailed by drugs. Dabbling in his early teens turned into serious addiction. This wrenchingly honest account of life as a teenage meth addict is the companion book to *Beautiful Boy* by David Sheff, Nic's father. It ends on a hopeful note as Nic finds the road to recovery.

Smith, Jodi R. R. *From Clueless to Class Act: Manners for the Modern Man.* Sterling, 2006. OBCB 2009.

This unstuffy, witty guide to good behavior will help young men develop the style and panache to make a good impression in social and professional circles. Etiquette advice encompasses dining, dating, the workplace, attending the theater, and e-mail and cell-phone conduct.

Stern, Jessica. *Terror in the Name of God: Why Religious Militants Kill.* Ecco, 2003. OBCB 2009.

Seeking to understand how religious ardor leads to violence, Stern recounts her dramatic encounters with Christians, Jews, and Muslims who use terrorism in the name of God. Stern studied militants in Palestine, Israel, Indonesia, and America, their recruitment techniques, as well as the best nonviolent strategies for defeating and disarming them.

Urrea, Luis Alberto. *The Devil's Highway: A True Story.* Little, Brown, 2004. OBCB 2009.

Thousands of illegal immigrants yearly scramble across the U.S.-Mexican border and into an area of the Arizona desert known as the Devil's Highway. Many do not make it out alive. Urrea details the 2001 attempt of 26 men to cross into the United States, which only 12 survived. This is the human story of illegal immigration told with facts, anger, and poetry.

Wallis, David, ed. *Killed Cartoons: Casualties from the War on Free Expression.* Norton, 2007. OBCB 2009.

Wallis's book is full of political cartoons killed before publication. Each cartoon is accompanied by a brief narrative explaining why it was considered too controversial for publication. Both contemporary and historical cartoons are included, making this a history of political cartooning.

Walls, Jeannette. *The Glass Castle: A Memoir.* Simon & Schuster/Scribner, 2005. OBCB 2009. (Alex Award)

This is Jeannette Walls's memoir of growing up in chaos and poverty with a family that prized freedom and unconventionality over comfort and safety, eventually making them homeless. Despite their negligence, Walls has a clear affection for her eccentric parents, who continued to be homeless after she and her siblings found ways to lead more conventional lives.

Wheelan, Charles. *Naked Economics: Undressing the Dismal Science.* Norton, 2002. OBCB 2004, 2009.

Without using charts, graphs, or jargon, Wheelan makes economics understandable, even interesting, as he demystifies basic concepts and applies them to everyday life. With his informal style and sense of humor, he shares his enthusiasm for the big economic picture.

9
....

OUTSTANDING BOOKS FOR THE COLLEGE BOUND AND LIFELONG LEARNERS, BY GENRE, 1999–2009

IN THIS SECTION, the 1999, 2004, and 2009 lists are grouped into the following genre lists: arts and humanities, history and cultures, literature and language arts, science and technology, and social sciences. These are the categories used by the most recent committee (2009) in order to mirror the college curriculum experience.

In combining the 1999, 2004, and 2009 OBCB lists by genre, it quickly became clear that the placement of fiction has been inconsistent over the years. Most fiction is assigned to the literature and language arts category, but many titles are assigned to another category.

Because of this, and in order to stay true to the original lists, some books appear in more than one genre list. For example, *The Kite Runner* by Khaled Hosseini appears under both literature and language arts (2009) and social sciences (2004). M. T. Anderson's *Feed* appears under both literature and language arts (2004) and science and technology (2009).

The 1999 list was originally separated into different categories entirely: fiction, nonfiction, biography, poetry, and drama. In placing these titles into subject areas, every attempt was made to follow the lead of the 2004 and 2009 lists. It was also logical to simplify: Fiction titles are listed under literature and language arts; drama titles are listed under arts and humanities; poetry titles are listed under literature and language arts.

· ARTS AND HUMANITIES ·

Adler, Sabine. *Lovers in Art.* Prestel USA, 2002. OBCB 2004.
Romance and art are natural companions in this gorgeous book that spans five centuries of Western European art.

Albee, Edward. *Three Tall Women.* Dramatists Play Service, 1994. OBCB 1999.
A frustrated 92-year-old reveals three arduous and painful stages of her life, embodied by three versions of the same woman (one in her 20s, one at 52, and one at 92).

Aronson, Marc. *Art Attack: A Short Cultural History of the Avant-Garde.* Clarion, 1998. OBCB 1999.
Discover everything you ever wanted to know about bohemians, hipsters, and the development of the world's most radical art. In this social history of art in the 20th century, the visual is accompanied by the musical and literary, from Stravinsky and Nijinsky to Warhol to rock and roll.

Asinof, Eliot. *Eight Men Out: The Black Sox and the 1919 World Series.* Holt, Rinehart, and Winston, 1963. OBCB 1999.
It's all here: the players, the scandal, the shame, and the damage the 1919 World Series caused America's national pastime.

Beckett, Samuel. *Waiting for Godot.* Grove Press, 1954. OBCB 1999.
Two tramps wait eternally for the elusive Godot in this first success of the Theater of the Absurd.

Belloli, Andrea P. *Exploring World Art.* Getty Publications, 1999. OBCB 2004.
Divided into chapters titled "Time and Space," "Other Worlds," "Daily Life," "History and Myth," and "The World of Nature," Belloli's book gives young readers a fresh look at Western European art in a global context.

Bernier-Grand, Carmen. *Frida: Viva la Vida! Long Live Life!* Marshall Cavendish, 2007. OBCB 2009.
In 26 original, free-verse poems the author depicts the thoughts, feelings, and life events of Mexican self-portraitist Frida Kahlo.

Bernstein, Leonard. *The Joy of Music.* Simon & Schuster, 1959. OBCB 1999.
Bernstein describes all aspects of classical music in a passionate, accessible narrative, even while admitting the impossibility of fully explaining organized sound with words.

Bernstein, Leonard, Arthur Laurents, and Stephen Sondheim. *West Side Story.* Random House, 1958. OBCB 1999.
The "American" Jets and Puerto Rican Sharks, rival gangs on the west side of New York City, battle it out in song and dance as Tony and Maria fall in love in this musical based on Shakespeare's *Romeo and Juliet.*

Bissinger, H. G. *Friday Night Lights: A Town, a Team, and a Dream.* Perseus Books, 1990. OBCB 2004.
Bissinger, an investigative journalist, portrays individual team members and townspeople, exploring racial attitudes and favoritism shown to the athletes, representing both the flaws and the attraction of the football craze in Texas.

Blackstone, Harry, Jr. *The Blackstone Book of Magic and Illusion.* Newmarket Press, 1985. OBCB 1999, 2004.
The classic of legerdemain describes the rich history of modern magic from ancient times to the present, including vaudeville, Broadway, Vegas, and television.

Blais, Madeleine. *In These Girls, Hope Is a Muscle.* Atlantic Monthly Press, 1995. OBCB 1999. (BBYA)

Learn about the year of heart, sweat, and muscle that transformed the Amherst Lady Hurricanes basketball team into state champions.

Blumenthal, Karen. *Let Me Play: The Story of Title IX; The Law That Changed the Future of Girls in America.* Simon & Schuster/Atheneum, 2005. OBCB 2009. (BBYA)

Passed in 1972, Title IX legislation mandated that schools receiving federal funds could not discriminate on the basis of gender, ensuring equal treatment and opportunity for girls in sports and education.

Boorstin, Jon. *Making Movies Work: Thinking like a Filmmaker.* Silman-James Press, 1996. OBCB 1999.

Boorstin posits that movies must work on three levels: voyeur, vicarious, and visceral. Successful films make the audience feel, and Boorstin writes about the craft necessary to create that success.

Bowker, John. *World Religions: The Great Faiths Explored and Explained.* DK, 2006. OBCB 2009.

This comprehensive work introduces the reader to faiths of the world through religious artifacts, paintings, architecture, and annotations of sacred texts, including ancient Greek, Roman, Egyptian, and Celtic religions.

Brassaï. *Brassaï: Letters to My Parents.* University of Chicago Press, 1997. OBCB 2004.

European photographer Brassaï (1899–1984) details his life's experiences in letters home, describing both his own development as an artist and the fascinating world of Paris from 1920 to 1940.

Bryson, Bill. *Shakespeare: The World as Stage.* HarperCollins, 2007. OBCB 2009.

Bryson hits the mark with his characteristic wit as he explores the world of Shakespeare and the mystery surrounding the man and his plays.

Campbell, Joseph, and Bill Moyers. *The Power of Myth.* Doubleday/Broadway Books, 1988. OBCB 2009.

Bill Moyers and Joseph Campbell discuss the role of mythology in the modern world, the journey inward, the hero's adventure, and tales of love and marriage.

Card, Orson Scott. *Sarah.* Forge, 2001. OBCB 2004.

The character of Sarah, Abraham's beloved wife, illuminates this rendering of a pivotal story from the Old Testament.

Chevalier, Tracy. *Girl with a Pearl Earring.* Dutton, 1999. OBCB 2004. (Alex Award, BBYA)

Sixteen-year-old Griet tells the story of her time as a maid in the busy 17th-century household of Delft painter Johannes Vermeer. Griet has an artistic eye and eventually becomes assistant and muse to the famous artist. But she is confined by the class system of her time.

Christie, Agatha. *Mousetrap.* Samuel French, 1954. OBCB 1999.

A group of guests is stranded at an inn by a snowstorm. The next day, a police sergeant arrives to tell them that a woman was murdered in London, and that her murderer is likely among their group.

Cooke, Mervyn. *The Chronicle of Jazz.* Abbeville Press, 1998. OBCB 1999. o.p.

Cooke provides a comprehensive guide to this uniquely American musical form. This is a chronological, year-by-year history of jazz from the turn of the century to the early

1990s, including discographies, biographies, and photographs, which takes into account the roots of the form as well as its interaction with other musical styles.

Copland, Aaron. *What to Listen For in Music.* McGraw-Hill, 1939. OBCB 1999.

The composer provides a basic introduction to the mysteries of musical composition and music appreciation, moving from fundamentals to texture, classical forms, and contexts.

Corio, David, and Vivian Goldman. *The Black Chord.* Universe Books, 1999. OBCB 2004. o.p.

The often-painful evolution of African American music is explored with a funky text by Vivian Goldman and lively, original photographs by David Corio.

Coulton, Larry. *Counting Coup: A True Story of Basketball and Honor on the Little Big Horn.* Warner, 2000. OBCB 2004. (Alex Award, BBYA)

Working through racism, alcoholism, and domestic violence, the players on Hardin High School's girls' basketball team struggle to win in life as well as on the court.

Coward, Noel. *Blithe Spirit.* Doubleday, Doran, 1941. OBCB 1999.

A drawing-room farce in which a novelist's second marriage is disturbed by the ghost of his first wife.

Crutcher, Chris. *Whale Talk.* Greenwillow, 2001. OBCB 2004. (BBYA)

What does a guy do when he has all the talents to be a star athlete, but hates his high school athletic program? T.J. Jones is black, Japanese, and white in a town with little diversity, and he hates injustice.

Cumming, Robert. *Annotated Art.* Dorling Kindersley, 1995. OBCB 1999. o.p.

Art masterpieces from the 14th century to the present are made understandable through the exploration of some of the world's greatest paintings.

Diamant, Anita. *The Red Tent: A Novel.* St. Martin's, 1997. OBCB 2009.

This novel re-creates the biblical life of Dinah, daughter of Leah and Jacob, from her birth in Mesopotamia through her death in Egypt.

D'Orso, Michael. *Eagle Blue: A Team, a Tribe, and a High School Basketball Season in Arctic Alaska.* Bloomsbury, 2006. OBCB 2009. (Alex Award)

This true story explores the tiny village of Fort Yukon, Alaska, its vanishing cultural heritage, and its relationship with mainstream American culture through its high school basketball teams.

Engle, Margarita. Illus. by Sean Qualls. *The Poet Slave of Cuba: A Biography of Juan Francisco Manzano.* Henry Holt, 2006. OBCB 2009. (BBYA)

Written in verse, this is a Pura Belpré Award–winning portrait of Juan Francisco Manzano, the poet who was born a slave in Cuba in 1797.

Finn, David. *How to Look at Sculpture: Text and Photographs.* Harry N. Abrams, 1989. OBCB 1999. o.p.

Finn teaches the reader how to fully experience and appreciate sculpture: the importance of viewing from multiple angles, placement of the sculpture, light, touch, texture, form, and materials.

Follett, Ken. *The Pillars of the Earth.* Morrow, 1989. OBCB 2009.

This best-selling epic tale of ambition, anarchy, and absolute power set against the canvas of 12th-century England depicts fascinating characters and provides a spellbinding introduction to medieval religion, architecture, politics, and daily life.

Franck, Frederick, ed. *What Does It Mean to Be Human? Reverence for Life Reaffirmed by Responses from Around the World.* St. Martin's, 2000. OBCB 2004.

Social activists, artists, and spiritual leaders reflect on being human in a changing society. Contributors range from Wilma Mankiller to James Earl Jones, Joan Chittister to Cornel West, Jimmy Carter to the Dalai Lama.

Freedman, Russell. *The Voice That Challenged a Nation: Marian Anderson and the Struggle for Equal Rights.* Houghton Mifflin Harcourt/Clarion, 2004. OBCB 2009. (BBYA)

A Newbery Honor book that recounts the life and musical career of the great African American vocalist Marian Anderson in the context of the history of civil rights in the United States.

Fugard, Athol. *"Master Harold" . . . and the Boys.* Knopf, 1982. OBCB 1999.

In this one-act play set in South Africa, Hally, a precocious white teenager and son of a tea room owner, lashes out at two older black friends, substitute figures for his alcoholic father who is returning home from the hospital later that day.

Garfunkel, Trudy. *On Wings of Joy: The Story of Ballet from the 16th Century to Today.* Little, Brown, 1994. OBCB 1999, 2004.

Immerse yourself in the world of ballet, from its earliest choreography to the life of a modern ballerina.

Goldberg, Myla. *Bee Season.* Doubleday, 2000. OBCB 2004.

Eliza's extraordinary gift for spelling leads her to understand the sounds of the alphabet in a way that echoes the teachings of the mystical Kabbalah.

Goldberg, Vicki. *The Power of Photographs: How Photography Changed Our Lives.* Abbeville Press, 1991. OBCB 1999.

The history of the photograph is traced from the daguerreotype to the present, and specific, famous photographs are reproduced and studied for their influence on larger events such as the Vietnam War and the civil rights movement.

Gombrich, E. H. *The Story of Art.* Phaidon, 1995 (original: Phaidon, 1950). OBCB 1999.

Everything from cave paintings to the experimental art of today is covered, in words and pictures, in one of the most famous and popular art books ever published.

Greenberg, Jan, ed. *Heart to Heart: New Poems Inspired by Twentieth-Century American Art.* Harry N. Abrams, 2001. OBCB 2004, 2009. (BBYA, Printz Honor)

Can a painting speak? This collection of lyrical responses to famous American works of art will make you a believer.

Gruen, Sara. *Water for Elephants: A Novel.* Algonquin, 2007. OBCB 2009. (Alex Award)

Gruen creates a no-holds-barred story full of enchanting circus lore, mystery, trains, romance, and danger.

Hamilton, Edith. *Mythology.* Little, Brown, 1942. OBCB 1999.

Gods and heroes, their clashes and adventures, come alive in this splendid retelling of the Greek, Roman, and Norse myths.

Hansberry, Lorraine. *A Raisin in the Sun.* Random House, 1959. OBCB 1999.

The sudden appearance of money tears a 1950s African American family apart.

Hedges, Chris. *War Is a Force That Gives Us Meaning.* Public Affairs, 2002. OBCB 2004.

A Pulitzer Prize–winning author presents a passionate, thought-provoking look at war through the ages, and exposes the myths of the culture of combat.

Hellman, Lillian. *The Little Foxes.* Random House, 1939. OBCB 1999.

Members of the greedy and treacherous Hubbard family compete with each other for control of the mill that will bring them riches in the post–Civil War South in a play resembling a Greek tragedy.

Hemphill, Stephanie. *Your Own, Sylvia: A Verse Portrait of Sylvia Plath.* Random House/Knopf, 2007. OBCB 2009. (BBYA, Printz Honor)

Hemphill creates a chronological biography in verse format from the viewpoint of others in Plath's life. The poetry is written in the style and forms used by Plath herself, some referencing specific poems.

Holy Bible: New Revised Standard Version. Collins, 1973. OBCB 1999.

Biblical scholars revise text and modernize terms to bring one version of the Bible up-to-date.

Howe, Peter. *Shooting under Fire: The World of the War Photographer.* Artisan, 2002. OBCB 2004, 2009.

Ten leading combat photographers share their experiences of horror, humor, bravery, and daring while reporting from Vietnam, Haiti, Chechnya, El Salvador, Sarajevo, and Afghanistan.

Ibsen, Henrik. *A Doll's House.* Joshua James Press, 1879. OBCB 1999.

In this 19th-century Scandinavian play, Nora, one of feminism's great heroines, steps off her pedestal and encounters the real world.

Ionesco, Eugene. *Rhinoceros.* Grove Press, 1959. OBCB 1999.

The subject is conformity; the treatment is comedy and terror. As everyone in his town turns into a rhinoceros, Berenger rejects his former alienation, alcohol abuse, and laziness to become a man willing to resist conformity, even if he is the only one left.

Jacobs, A. J. *The Year of Living Biblically: One Man's Humble Quest to Follow the Bible as Literally as Possible.* Simon & Schuster, 2007. OBCB 2009.

A nonjudgmental and humorous look at the 12 months Jacobs lived as closely as he could to literal compliance with biblical rules.

Jonas, Gerald. *Dancing: The Pleasure, Power, and Art of Movement.* Harry N. Abrams, 1992. OBCB 1999.

This international survey explores dance as social, cultural, and religious expression, including both Western and non-Western, traditional and modern, and points out similarities in the way dance is used in various societies.

Jones, K. Maurice. *Say It Loud! The Story of Rap Music.* Millbrook Press, 1994. OBCB 1999. o.p.

Jones traces rap music from its birth thousands of years ago, to its dissemination via the slave trade, through its effects on young people today.

Karnos, David D., and Robert G. Shoemaker, eds. *Falling in Love with Wisdom: American Philosophers Talk about Their Calling.* Oxford University Press, 1993. OBCB 1999.

Contemporary philosophers share their contemplations and epiphanies.

Kendall, Elizabeth. *Where She Danced.* Knopf, 1979. OBCB 1999. o.p.

Kendall studies the ancestors of modern art dance in America, from spectacle-extravaganzas to the revival of ballet as an art form, Ruth St. Denis, Martha Graham, musical theater, and Hollywood.

Kerner, Mary. *Barefoot to Balanchine: How to Watch Dance.* Anchor Books, 1990. OBCB 1999. o.p.

Understand dance by reading about its history, choreography, and backstage action. Kerner teaches readers to evaluate dance by outlining the elements (basic steps, techniques, and types of movement), and what to watch for in a performance.

King, Melissa. *She's Got Next: A Story of Getting In, Staying Open, and Taking a Shot.* Houghton Mifflin Harcourt/Mariner Books, 2005. OBCB 2009.

Through pick-up basketball games and the people she meets on the streets of Chicago, the author learns valuable life lessons.

King, Ross. *Brunelleschi's Dome: How a Renaissance Genius Reinvented Architecture.* Walker, 2000. OBCB 2004.

In this vivid re-creation of the political and artistic milieu of 15th-century Florence, the audacious and secretive Filippo Brunelleschi achieves the impossible and makes possible modern building.

Krakauer, John. *Into Thin Air: A Personal Account of the Mount Everest Disaster.* Villard, 1997. OBCB 1999. (Alex Award, BBYA)

Krakauer went to Nepal in 1996 to report on the commercialization of climbing to Everest's peak, and came away with a tragic narrative of survivor's guilt, questions about the presence of amateur climbers in such a setting, and the responsibilities of the relationship between guides and clients.

Kushner, Tony. *Angels in America: A Gay Fantasia on National Themes. Pt. 1, Millennium Approaches (1992); Pt. 2, Perestroika (1993).* Theatre Communications Group. OBCB 1999.

Kushner chronicles AIDS in America during the Reagan era, through the lives of two couples.

Landis, Deborah Nadoolman. *Dressed: A Century of Hollywood Costume Design.* HarperCollins, 2007. OBCB 2009.

Landis showcases one hundred years of Hollywood's most memorable costumes and the characters they helped bring to life as she reveals a behind-the-scenes look at the evolution of the costume designer's art.

Larson, Jonathan. *Rent.* Morrow, 1996. OBCB 1999.

This award-winning musical depicts life, death, passion, drug addiction, and loyalty among AIDS-stricken artists in New York's East Village. Loosely based on Giacomo Puccini's 19th-century opera, *La Bohème.*

Light, Alan, ed. *The Vibe History of Hip Hop.* Three Rivers Press, 1999. OBCB 2004.

The editors of *Vibe* magazine look at the music, dance, and fashion that have evolved into hip-hop culture.

Livingstone, Lili Cockerville. *American Indian Ballerinas.* University of Oklahoma Press, 1999. OBCB 2004.

Four Native American women from Oklahoma share the struggles and triumphs of their dance careers and personal lives in stories that inspire with courage and beauty.

Martin, Steve. *Born Standing Up: A Comic's Life.* Scribner, 2007. OBCB 2009.
In a memoir full of humor and candor, Martin shares his personal itinerary as he negotiates the maze of honing his profession and the pitfalls he avoided.

McCloud, Scott. *Understanding Comics: The Invisible Art.* Kitchen Sink Press, 1993. OBCB 1999.
McCloud tells the history of using pictures to tell stories and explains how comics are created and how they should be read.

McGreevey, Tom, and Joanne Yeck. *Our Movie Heritage.* Rutgers University Press, 1997. OBCB 2004, 2009.
This work provides over one hundred beautiful pictures of top stars, directors, and others in the film industry, but the focus is on film preservation and the race against time to salvage what is left of the large number of films that are currently deteriorating in our nation's vaults, theaters, and private collections.

Miller, Arthur. *Death of a Salesman.* Viking, 1949. OBCB 1999.
After years on the road as a traveling salesman, Willy Loman faces his failure as husband, father, and human being.

Murray, Albert. *Stomping the Blues.* McGraw-Hill, 1976. OBCB 1999.
An aficionado gives the lowdown on what the blues are, what they are not, and their origins. Murray also finds the connections between blues and both art music and popular music today.

Occhiogrosso, Peter. *The Joy of Sects: A Spirited Guide to the World's Religious Traditions.* Doubleday, 1994. OBCB 1999.
This lively, easy-to-understand guidebook to world religions is for everyone from the faithful believer to the curious doubter.

O'Gorman, James F. *ABC of Architecture.* University of Pennsylvania Press, 1998. OBCB 1999.
Writing for the beginner, O'Gorman provides a concise introduction to both the history and theory of architecture.

O'Neill, Eugene. *Long Day's Journey into Night.* Yale University Press, 1956. OBCB 1999.
This painful autobiographical play set in 1912 Connecticut reveals the illusions and delusions of the Tyrone family.

Partridge, Elizabeth. *John Lennon: All I Want Is the Truth.* Penguin/Viking, 2005. OBCB 2009. (BBYA, Printz Honor)
Partridge provides a wide-open view into the work and life of one of the most influential and complicated persons in the world's musical heritage.

Partridge, Elizabeth. *This Land Was Made for You and Me: The Life and Songs of Woody Guthrie.* Penguin/Viking, 2002. OBCB 2009. (BBYA)
Woody Guthrie was a humble figure, while at the same time a major catalyst of social change. This work provides insight into one of our most prolific and talented musicians and the creation of his music.

Penn, W. S., ed. *The Telling of the World: Native American Stories and Art.* Stewart, Tabori, & Chang, 1996. OBCB 1999. o.p.
Traditional and contemporary legends, stories, and art from many North American tribes explain our world. The book is organized according to the life cycle, from birth through adolescence, marriage, family, old age, death, and renewal.

Perry, John. *Encyclopedia of Acting Techniques: Illustrated Instruction, Examples, and Advice for Improving Acting Techniques and Stage Presence—from Tragedy to Comedy, Epic to Farce.* Quarto, 1997. OBCB 2004.

See how it's done by the pros in this extravagantly color illustrated primer on dramatic performance.

Polly, Matthew. *American Shaolin: Flying Kicks, Buddhist Monks, and the Legend of Iron Crotch; An Odyssey in the New China.* Penguin/Gotham Books, 2007. OBCB 2009. (Alex Award, BBYA)

The author reflects on the childhood dream that led him, as an adult, to take a break from Princeton and travel to China's famed Shaolin Temple to study martial arts for two years.

Rybczynski, Witold. *The Most Beautiful House in the World.* Viking, 1989. OBCB 1999.

The author's dream of building a boat evolves into the expansion of a boathouse into a full-scale home, a process he uses to explain complex architectural ideas. Rybczynski meditates on the meaning of a house and the nature of an architect's work.

Sandler, Martin. *Photography: An Illustrated History.* Oxford University Press, 2002. OBCB 2004, 2009.

This work looks at photography as it evolved from daguerreotypes in the 1800s to the respected art form that it is today. Numerous compelling black-and-white and color photographs document technological developments and the impact photography has had upon all aspects of society.

Sartre, Jean Paul. *No Exit.* Knopf, 1946. OBCB 1999.

In this existential drama, three people are trapped in a drawing room together, an experience which constitutes their punishment in hell.

Shakespeare, William. *King Lear.* 1605. OBCB 1999.

King Lear decides to divide his kingdom among his daughters, according to how well they express their love for him. The one daughter who sincerely loves him refuses to make a speech, and is disinherited. When the other two fail to support him, Lear goes mad. Political deception and romantic jealousy cause tragic ends for all.

Shaw, George Bernard. *Pygmalion.* Dodd, Mead, 1914. OBCB 1999.

Professor Higgins bets a friend he can turn common Eliza Doolittle into a duchess.

Sherman, Robert, and Philip Seldon. *The Complete Idiot's Guide to Classical Music.* Alpha Books, 1997. OBCB 1999. o.p.

This practical guide will help the reader to understand and enjoy classical music. The authors cover all the basics, including a history of classical music, composers, performers, instrumental and vocal music including opera, identifying the sound of particular instruments, concert hall etiquette, starting a listening collection, and even buying a sound system.

Smith, Huston. *Illustrated World Religions: A Guide to Our Wisdom Traditions.* Harper, 1995. OBCB 2004.

The interconnectivity of the world's great religious movements, with their parallel and disparate beliefs, is lyrically explored. The author intersperses his own text with excerpts from the sacred texts and important images from each religion in this introduction to Hinduism, Buddhism, Confucianism, Taoism, Islam, Judaism, Christianity, and the primal religions. This edition places the emphasis on religious art.

Stoppard, Tom. *Rosencrantz and Guildenstern Are Dead.* Grove Press, 1967. OBCB 1999, 2009.
Two bit players from Shakespeare's *Hamlet* are thrust into a terrifying and surreal new situation.

Strickland, Carol. *The Annotated Mona Lisa: A Crash Course in Art History from Prehistoric to Post-Modern.* Andrews McMeel, 2007. OBCB 1999, 2009.
In an accessible format, this unique work provides a basic working knowledge of art and art history through short essays, sidebars, and photographs. Strickland covers it all, from cave paintings to digital media.

Uhry, Alfred. *Driving Miss Daisy.* Theatre Communications Group, 1988. OBCB 1999.
At the beginning of the play, 72-year-old Daisy crashes her car backing out of her garage. Her son hires a black chauffeur, Hoke. Over the next 25 years, Hoke and Daisy develop a deep and abiding friendship, even as they fight to maintain their dignity as they age.

Vogel, Paula. *How I Learned to Drive.* Theatre Communications Group, 1998. OBCB 1999.
The friendship between Li'l Bit and her uncle Peck turns toward alcohol and seduction over the course of Li'l's adolescence.

Vreeland, Susan. *The Passion of Artemisia.* Viking, 2002. OBCB 2004.
This eloquent rendering of the story of Italian painter Artemisia Gentileschi (1593–1653) evokes appreciation of both her magnificent art and her struggles to succeed as an artist.

Weller, Sheila. *Girls like Us: Carole King, Joni Mitchell, Carly Simon—and the Journey of a Generation.* Simon & Schuster/Atria, 2008. OBCB 2009.
In three interwoven biographies, Weller chronicles the life and times of three tradition-breaking women singer-songwriters who came of age in the late 1960s.

Wilde, Oscar. *The Importance of Being Earnest.* Joshua James Press, 1895. OBCB 1999.
Can a baby, abandoned at Victoria Station, grow up to find love, romance, identity, and the importance of being earnest? In this satirical play, two couples create and endure much identity confusion before living happily ever after.

Wilder, Thornton. *Our Town.* Coward McCann, 1938. OBCB 1999.
Love and death in a typical American small town are seen through the eyes of the Stage Manager. Neighbors George and Emily happily court and marry. When Emily dies in childbirth she is given the chance to experience one day over again.

Williams, Tennessee. *The Glass Menagerie.* Random House, 1945. OBCB 1999.
A brother is haunted by the memory of his teenage sister, who took refuge from the world in her collection of glass animal figurines.

Wilson, August. *Fences: A Play.* New American Library, 1986. OBCB 1999.
Troy, a garbageman and ex-convict, recalls his career as a Negro League baseball star. He admits to his wife, Rose, that he has fathered a child with another woman. When the other woman dies in childbirth, Troy and Rose take responsibility for the baby, even as their grown son leaves home for good.

· HISTORY AND CULTURES ·

Ahmad, Dohra, ed. *Rotten English: A Literary Anthology.* Norton, 2007. OBCB 2009.
Rotten English collects the poetry, essays, short stories, and novels of the best in global vernacular writing from Mark Twain to Junot Diaz.

Alexander, Caroline. *The Endurance: Shackleton's Legendary Antarctic Expedition.* Knopf, 1998. OBCB 2004. (Alex Award, BBYA)

It's man against nature at the dawn of World War I, as the lure of the last unclaimed land on earth dazzles with its beauty and danger in this adventure of discovery and survival.

Alexie, Sherman. *The Absolutely True Diary of a Part-Time Indian.* Little, Brown, 2007. OBCB 2009. (BBYA)

Arnold Spirit, aka Junior, was born an outsider with water on his brain, lopsided eyes, and an IQ oppressed by extreme poverty and a mediocre reservation education. After switching to an all-white high school he realizes that though he'll never easily fit in, self-determination and a solid personal identity will give him the chance to both succeed and transcend.

Ambrose, Stephen E. *Undaunted Courage: Meriwether Lewis, Thomas Jefferson, and the Opening of the American West.* Simon & Schuster, 1996. OBCB 1999.

Lewis and Clark brave the wilds of North America in a vivid account of exploration and adventure. This biography of Meriwether Lewis relies on the journals of both Lewis and Clark, as well as the author's own travels along their route.

Aronson, Marc. *Witch Hunt: Mysteries of the Salem Witch Trials.* Simon & Schuster, 2003. OBCB 2004.

Revisit a time of nightmare, fear, hysteria—beyond *The Crucible*, sift through the myths, half-truths, and misinformation to make up your own mind about what really happened in Salem Village and why.

Bagdasarian, Adam. *Forgotten Fire: A Novel.* Random House, 2000. OBCB 2004, 2009. (BBYA)

"Who will remember the Armenians?" Hitler asked, referencing the Armenian genocide as his inspiration for the final solution. This brutal hidden chapter of history is seen through the eyes of 12-year-old survivor Vahan Kendarian.

Berg, A. Scott. *Lindbergh.* Putnam, 1998. OBCB 2004.

Daring, mysterious, and one of the 20th century's first superstars—who was the man behind the myth, and how did his historic flight across the Atlantic remake the world?

Brown, Dee. *Bury My Heart at Wounded Knee: An Indian History of the American West.* Holt, Rinehart, and Winston, 1970. OBCB 1999.

Brown tells how American Indians lost their land to white settlers from 1860 to 1890, tracing history from the Long Walk to Wounded Knee, and the brutal results of resistance.

Chandrasekaran, Rajiv. *Imperial Life in the Emerald City: Inside Iraq's Green Zone.* Knopf, 2006. OBCB 2009.

A journalist explores the pristine "Emerald City," the American government's enclave in the middle of war-torn Baghdad. This is an eyewitness account of the failures of the first year of the Coalition Provisional Authority's tenure.

Chang, Iris. *The Rape of Nanking: The Forgotten Holocaust of World War II.* Basic Books, 1997. OBCB 1999, 2009.

Barely a postscript in official Japanese history, the horrific torture and murder of hundreds of thousands of Chinese citizens took place over the course of just seven weeks. The Japanese army invaded Nanking in December 1937 and proceeded to slaughter over 300,000 soldiers and civilians.

Chotjewitz, David. *Daniel Half-Human and the Good Nazi.* Translated by Doris Orgel. Simon & Schuster/Atheneum, 2004. OBCB 2009. (BBYA)

From Hitler Youth to hunted "mischling," Daniel sees his world unravel when he discovers his mother's hidden history "taints" him with Jewish blood and marks him for extermination.

Clark, Kenneth. *Civilisation: A Personal View.* Harper & Row, 1969. OBCB 1999. o.p.

Clark explores history through the works, impulses, and beliefs of the great creative individuals of Western civilization.

Cook, Blanche Wiesen. *Eleanor Roosevelt: Vol. 1, 1884–1933.* Viking, 1992. OBCB 1999.

After a difficult childhood, Eleanor was orphaned at age 12 and taken in by relatives, fell in love with and married her cousin, then found an agenda of her own, supporting the rights of women, children, and workers.

Danticat, Edwidge. *The Farming of Bones.* Soho Press, 1998. OBCB 2004.

During a time when nationalist madness and ethnic hatred turn island neighbors into executioners, Haitian immigrants Amabelle and Sebastien hold on to love, to dignity— and struggle to survive.

Day, David. *The Search for King Arthur.* Facts on File, 1995. OBCB 1999. o.p.

Discover through magnificent illustrations and romantic retellings what is fact and what is legend about this fifth-century hero, Artorius Dux Bellorum.

Delisle, Guy. *Pyongyang: A Journey in North Korea.* Drawn and Quarterly, 2005. OBCB 2009.

In North Korea doing animation work for a children's television show, Delisle was monitored by his guide and translator at all times. In this graphic depiction, he shares observations of a sadly cold and sterile society, infused with the dark humor he found in the experience.

Diamond, Jared. *Collapse: How Societies Choose to Fail or Succeed.* Penguin, 2005. OBCB 2009.

What do the lack of Icelandic fisherman, the 2008 Chinese Olympics, and Easter Island tree cutters all have in common? Much more than you might think. *Collapse* explores the political, technological, and ecological decisions that merge in order to sustain or destroy societies.

Diaz, Junot. *The Brief Wondrous Life of Oscar Wao.* Penguin/Riverhead, 2007. OBCB 2009.

"Ghetto nerd," outcast, and anime-loving Oscar Wao is the latest in a long line of doomed generations to suffer the dreaded fuku curse of his native Dominican Republic.

Douglass, Frederick. *Narrative of the Life of Frederick Douglass, an American Slave, Written by Himself.* Anti-Slavery Office, 1845. OBCB 1999.

Former slave and famed abolitionist Frederick Douglass describes the horrors of his enslavement and eventual escape.

Edelman, Bernard, ed. *Dear America: Letters Home from Vietnam.* Norton, 1985. OBCB 1999.

Letters from those who made it back and from those who did not return provide a glimpse into the lives of the men and women who served during the Vietnam War.

Egan, Timothy. *The Worst Hard Time: The Untold Story of Those Who Survived the Great American Dust Bowl.* Houghton Mifflin, 2006. OBCB 2009.

Award-winning *New York Times* reporter Egan tackles the great dust bowl phenomenon of the 1930s and '40s in this multi-tiered account.

Eggers, Dave. *What Is the What: The Autobiography of Valentino Achak Deng; A Novel.* McSweeney's, 2006. OBCB 2009.

As a young boy Valentino witnessed Arab militia men destroy his Sudanese village; hid from hungry lions; wandered through wasted, desert landscapes; and narrowly escaped fatal disease, capture, starvation, and enlistment.

Ellis, Joseph E. *Founding Brothers: The Revolutionary Generation.* Knopf, 2000. OBCB 2004.

Six dramatic vignettes reveal the men behind the events of the most decisive decade in American history, covering the Burr/Hamilton rivalry, negotiations for the location of the capital, the future of slavery, Washington's farewell address, John and Abigail Adams during his presidency, and the correspondence between Adams and Jefferson late in their lives.

Epictetus and Sharon Lebell. *The Art of Living: The Classic Manual on Virtue, Happiness, and Effectiveness.* HarperCollins, 1995. OBCB 1999.

A modern interpretation of the Stoic philosopher (Epictetus was born in 55 A.D.) answers the timeless questions of how to be a good person and live a good life. Lebell updates his advice, which is based on knowing the difference between what we can and cannot control and responding to life accordingly.

Fadiman, Anne. *The Spirit Catches You and You Fall Down: A Hmong Child, Her American Doctors, and the Collision of Two Cultures.* Farrar, Straus, and Giroux, 1997. OBCB 2009.

A Hmong refugee family in California clashes with the American medical system when they attribute their daughter's grand mal seizures to a spiritual rather than physical problem. This balanced account of a tragic misunderstanding captures Hmong history and culture.

Fleming, Anne Marie. *The Magical Life of Long Tack Sam.* Penguin/Riverhead, 2007. OBCB 2009.

Born in 1885 in a small Chinese village, Long Tack Sam was an acrobat, a magician, an entrepreneur, a world traveler, a celebrity, a father, a ladies' man, and a husband.

Frank, Anne. *Anne Frank: The Diary of a Young Girl.* Doubleday, 1952. OBCB 1999. (BBYA)

In 1942 Amsterdam, Anne and her sister and parents went into hiding in an attempt to escape deportment to a concentration camp. Through the diary she kept, 13-year-old Anne Frank puts a human face on the Holocaust experience.

Frank, Mitch. *Understanding September 11: Answering Questions about the Attacks on America.* Penguin, 2002. OBCB 2004.

These events are burned into images we can never forget—but after the pain of September 11 we ask why and learn about the historical, religious, and cultural issues that led to the attacks.

Geras, Adele. *Troy.* Scholastic, 2001. OBCB 2004. (BBYA)

A city under siege, epic battles and heroes, powerful supernatural forces—it's the story of the Trojan War seen through the eyes of its women in one of our oldest stories of the cruelty of war.

Glancy, Diane. *Stone Heart: A Novel of Sacajawea.* Overlook Press, 2003. OBCB 2004.

You are there on the epic journey of Lewis and Clark that opened the West to the call of manifest destiny. Sacajawea narrates through fictional diary entries revealing her mystical experience of the journey.

Gould, Stephen Jay. *The Mismeasure of Man.* Norton, 1981. OBCB 1999.

Gould's history of the attempt to quantify intelligence could be called the "misuse of science." He demonstrates that those who insisted on finding ways to measure intelligence throughout history did so in order to maintain their own position as the most worthy, in particular white European men.

Hansen, Drew D. *The Dream: Martin Luther King Jr. and the Speech That Inspired a Nation.* HarperCollins, 2003. OBCB 2004.

This great humanitarian and leader did indeed have a dream, and it has resonated through the years to expand all of our hopes for a future built on tolerance.

Harper, Kenn. *Give Me My Father's Body: The Life of Minik, the New York Eskimo.* Steerforth Press, 2000. OBCB 2004.

Imagine the horror as Minik, orphaned and abandoned by explorer Robert Peary, visits the Museum of Natural History and learns the true fate of his father. This is Minik's story, focusing on his efforts to recover his father's body from the museum and give him a traditional burial.

Hersey, John. *Hiroshima.* Knopf, 1946. OBCB 1999.

Six Hiroshima survivors reflect on the aftermath of the first atomic bomb. Hersey begins with what each person was doing when the bomb was dropped, then follows them through the aftermath.

Horwitz, Tony. *A Voyage Long and Strange: Rediscovering the New World.* Henry Holt, 2008. OBCB 2009.

Pulitzer Prize–winning journalist Horwitz uses humor and candor to literally follow in the footsteps of the first American explorers—from the Vikings and French utopians to America's first African American trailblazer—whose discoveries took place hundreds of years *before* the legendary landing on Plymouth Rock.

Jiang, Ji-li. *Red Scarf Girl: A Memoir of the Cultural Revolution.* HarperCollins, 1997. OBCB 1999. (BBYA)

A young Chinese girl must make difficult choices when the government urges her to repudiate her ancestors and inform on her own parents. Over time Jiang transforms from a follower to a young adult who questions those in power.

Jones, Edward P. *The Known World.* HarperCollins/Amistad, 2003. OBCB 2009.

In this Pulitzer Prize–winning novel, Jones approaches a little-explored chapter in antebellum history, that of African American slave owners. Set several decades before the beginning of the Civil War in Manchester County, Virginia, this work skillfully weaves plot, time, and perspective among a diverse and powerful cast of characters in order to explore the moral complexities inherent in human freedom (or the lack thereof).

Junger, Sebastian. *The Perfect Storm: A True Story of Men against the Sea.* Norton, 1997. OBCB 1999. (Alex Award)

Haunting premonitions didn't save seven fisherman from the ferocious and deadly power of the sea, in this adventure narrative about the doomed swordfish boat and crew that perished in October 1991 off the coast of Nova Scotia.

Lanier, Shannon. *Jefferson's Children: The Story of One American Family.* Random House, 2000. OBCB 2004. (BBYA)

Thomas Jefferson fathered two families—one black, one white. Lanier, a descendant of Jefferson and Sally Hemings, traveled the country with photographer Jane Feldman talking with and photographing other descendants of Thomas Jefferson.

Larson, Erik. *The Devil in the White City: Murder, Magic, and Madness at the Fair That Changed America.* Crown, 2003. OBCB 2009.

The 1893 Chicago World's Fair captured the imagination of the whole world, and also provided a playground for a cunning serial killer.

Least Heat-Moon, William. *Columbus in the Americas.* Wiley, 2002. OBCB 2004.

Was he a visionary and daring explorer, or a ruthless conquistador with dreams of riches and glory? Discover the truth behind the myth of a man whose impact still resonates through the continents he stumbled across.

Maltman, Thomas. *The Night Birds: A Novel.* Soho Press, 2007. OBCB 2009. (Alex Award)

Three generations of settlers and native Dakota weave a dark tale of family secrets and brutal injustice in Civil War–era America.

Marrin, Albert. *Terror of the Spanish Main: Sir Henry Morgan and His Buccaneers.* Dutton, 1999. OBCB 2004.

What lies behind the dark and romantic image of the pirate, and what is the legacy of this brutal and bloody time?

Massie, Robert K. *Nicholas and Alexandra.* Atheneum, 1967. OBCB 1999.

On the brink of revolution, the last tsar of Russia and his family become victims of their own mismanagement and personal problems. While the royal family is Massie's focus, he presents a clear picture of Russia as a whole during the time period.

McCourt, Frank. *Angela's Ashes: A Memoir.* Scribner, 1996. OBCB 1999.

Illness, hunger, alcoholism, and death plagued McCourt's childhood in Ireland, but somehow he survived with his spirit and humor intact.

McCullough, David G. *John Adams.* Simon & Schuster, 2001. OBCB 2004.

He was a man of his times who transcended his times, and one of the least understood of the Founding Fathers.

McCullough, David G. *Truman.* Simon & Schuster, 1992. OBCB 1999.

This notable president earned America's respect by helping to end World War II and reshape the world for postwar peace. McCullough evaluates Truman's presidency and praises him for being an ordinary American with solid values.

Poets of World War II. Library of America, 2003. OBCB 2004.

They have been called the Greatest Generation, and in their own voices they reveal the true price of their call to arms. Edited by Harvey Shapiro, whose own work is included.

Roberts, Gene, and Hank Klibanoff. *The Race Beat: The Press, the Civil Rights Struggle, and the Awakening of a Nation.* Knopf, 2006. OBCB 2009.

When Harry Reasoner thrust a microphone at an angry mob and yelled "I don't care what you're going to do to me, but the whole world is going to know it!" he spoke for all the reporters and photographers, black and white, North and South, who played a critical role in bringing the reality of the civil rights movement into the living rooms and consciousness of the American public.

Robertson, James I. *Stonewall Jackson: The Man, the Soldier, the Legend.* Macmillan, 1997. OBCB 1999.

Both the genius and the failings of the confederate Civil War general are chronicled in this meticulous account, which emphasizes Jackson's religious faith and military career.

Rogasky, Barbara. *Smoke and Ashes: The Story of the Holocaust.* Holiday House, 2002 (revised, expanded edition). OBCB 2004. o.p.

Some of history's darkest days are examined in this even-handed yet moving look at the horror and humanity of the Holocaust and its aftermath.

Saenz, Benjamin Alire. *Sammy and Juliana in Hollywood.* Cinco Puntos Press, 2004. OBCB 2009. (BBYA)

This Hollywood is a barrio in 1968 New Mexico, where the students at Las Cruces High School struggle through heartbreak, loss, and an entrenched racial divide to find their place in the world.

Sagas of Icelanders: A Selection. Penguin, 2001. OBCB 2004.

Nordic epics open up a world of wonder and power, a Viking world of heroic adventure and discovery at the turn of the first millennium. This collection includes the Vinland Sagas, which tell the story of Leif Eriksson's voyage to North America.

Satrapi, Marjane. *The Complete Persepolis.* Knopf/Pantheon, 2007. OBCB 2009. (*Persepolis*: Alex Award, BBYA) (*Persepolis 2*: BBYA)

This book includes both *Persepolis* and *Persepolis 2,* Marjane Satrapi's complete graphic memoir. Beginning with her childhood in Iran during the Islamic Revolution, then moving through her adolescence spent at school in Vienna, the volume ends with Satrapi's unsuccessful attempt to return to Iran as a young woman and her permanent move to Europe.

Sheehan, Neil. *A Bright Shining Lie: John Paul Vann and America in Vietnam.* Random House, 1988. OBCB 1999.

Lt. Col. John Paul Vann was an army field adviser who became disillusioned with the way the war was being fought and run. He shared his pessimism with the press in Saigon, including Sheehan.

Spiegelman, Art. *The Complete Maus: A Survivor's Tale.* Knopf/Pantheon, 1996. OBCB 1999, 2009.

The author portrays his parents' experiences during the Holocaust and their time at Auschwitz, survival, and years in the United States, along with his own struggle to come to terms with the past in this seminal, two-part graphic novel.

Starkey, David. *Six Wives: The Queens of Henry VIII.* HarperCollins, 2003. OBCB 2004.

How one man's matrimonial woes elevated a very disparate group of women to temporary positions of power, changed the way a nation was ruled, and shook the foundations of the Catholic Church.

Tuchman, Barbara. *A Distant Mirror: The Calamitous 14th Century.* Knopf, 1978 (reissue). OBCB 2004.

Castles and crusades, plague and famine, the glittering excitement of new ideas and discoveries, and the agony and displacement of war—the 14th century was a time not unlike our own in its rhythms and dimension.

Ung, Loung. *First They Killed My Father: A Daughter of Cambodia Remembers.* HarperCollins, 2001. OBCB 2004, 2009. (BBYA)

The perils of life under the brutal Pol Pot regime change a young woman's life forever, as she and her family find themselves fugitives of war, without even their names to remind them of what they lost.

Von Drehle, David. *Triangle: The Fire That Changed America.* Atlantic Monthly Press, 2003. OBCB 2004.

On March 25, 1911, in New York City, 146 people, most teenagers or women in their early 20s, were killed in a fire in the Triangle Shirtwaist factory. Von Drehle recounts the events with an emphasis on the people involved, social justice, and labor history.

War Letters: Extraordinary Correspondence from American Wars. Scribner, 2001. OBCB 2004.

The Legacy Project preserves the voices of soldiers and statesmen who lived through violent times that changed the course of nations. Listen to their stories in their words—they will inform and inspire you.

Watson, Peter. *The Modern Mind: An Intellectual History of the 20th Century.* HarperCollins, 2001. OBCB 2004.

Explore the thoughts of the major players from Freud to Einstein, and events from Kitty Hawk to the distant reaches of the universe.

Weatherford, Jack. *Indian Givers: How the Indians of the Americas Transformed the World.* Crown, 1988. OBCB 2004.

Discover how profoundly the native peoples of North and South America influenced what we eat, how we trade, and our system of government.

Weiner, Tim. *Legacy of Ashes: The History of the CIA.* Doubleday, 2007. OBCB 2009.

With considerable research and extensive interviews, Weiner shows the grave miscalculations that have plagued the Central Intelligence Agency since its inception.

Williams, David. *Bitterly Divided: The South's Inner Civil War.* New Press, 2008. OBCB 2009.

The Civil War was lost long before the first shot was ever fired, thanks to deep and violent divisions of class and political allegiance in the Confederacy that resulted in "a rich man's war and a poor man's fight."

Winchester, Simon. *Krakatoa: The Day the World Exploded; August 27, 1883.* HarperCollins, 2003. OBCB 2004.

When the earth's most dangerous volcano exploded off the coast of Java, hundred-foot waves flung ships inland, a rain of hot ash made temperatures plummet, the shock wave traveled around the world seven times, and 40,000 people died.

Wolf, Allan. *New Found Land: Lewis and Clark's Voyage of Discovery.* Candlewick, 2004. OBCB 2009. (BBYA)

The epic journey of Lewis and Clark comes alive as each member of the expedition tells an intimately personal story of struggle and discovery in this sweeping poetic rendition.

· LITERATURE AND LANGUAGE ARTS ·

Abelove, Joan. *Go and Come Back.* Puffin, 2000. OBCB 2004. (BBYA)
In a story of mutual culture shock, Alicia, a young Isabo girl in a remote area of Peru, is just as fascinated by the American anthropologists, Joanna and Margarita, as they are with the ways of her people.

Agee, James. *A Death in the Family.* McDowell Oblensky, 1957. OBCB 1999.
The enchanted childhood summer of 1915 becomes a baffling experience for six-year-old Rufus Follet when his father dies suddenly in a car accident.

Allende, Isabel. *Paula.* HarperCollins, 1995. OBCB 1999.
At the bedside of her dying daughter, Allende spins tales of childhood, of ancestors, and of becoming a novelist.

Allison, Dorothy. *Bastard out of Carolina.* Dutton, 1992. OBCB 1999, 2004, 2009.
Bone confronts illegitimacy, poverty, the troubled marriage of her mother and stepfather, and the stigma of being considered "white trash" as she comes of age in South Carolina.

Alvarez, Julia. *In the Time of Butterflies.* Algonquin, 1994. OBCB 1999, 2004.
Alvarez brings the four Mirabel sisters to life by having them tell their own story, beginning in childhood, through involvement with the resistance, culminating in murder and martyrdom.

Anaya, Rudolfo. *Bless Me, Ultima.* Warner, 1972. OBCB 1999.
In rural New Mexico shortly after World War II, Ultima, a wise old mystic, helps Antonio, a young Hispanic boy, resolve personal dilemmas caused by the differing backgrounds and aspirations of his parents and society.

Anderson, Laurie Halse. *Speak.* Farrar, Straus, and Giroux, 1999. OBCB 2004. (BBYA, Printz Honor)
Calling the police to a party is a tough choice, but what made Melinda call is the devastating secret that keeps her locked in silence.

Anderson, M. T. *The Astonishing Life of Octavian Nothing, Traitor to the Nation, Vol. 1: The Pox Party.* Candlewick, 2006. OBCB 2009. (BBYA, Printz Honor);
The Astonishing Life of Octavian Nothing, Traitor to the Nation, Vol. 2: The Kingdom on the Waves. Candlewick, 2008. OBCB 2009. (BBYA, Printz Honor)
During the American Revolution, Octavian is raised as a pampered African prince by a society of Enlightenment philosophers who view him as an experiment.

Anderson, M. T. *Feed.* Candlewick, 2002. OBCB 2004, 2009. (BBYA)
In this society your brain cyberfeed provides an endless stream of information, entertainment, and advertising. When Violet's feed is disrupted, she's cast adrift, and everyone is forced to examine the power of the feed in his or her life.

Angelou, Maya. *I Know Why the Caged Bird Sings.* Random House, 1970. OBCB 1999.
In the first of her five autobiographies, the African American writer, poet, and actress traces her coming of age in 1930s and '40s America.

Atwood, Margaret. *The Handmaid's Tale.* Houghton Mifflin Harcourt, 1986. OBCB 1999.
In Gilead, a Christian fundamentalist dystopia, fertile lower-class women serve as birth-mothers for the upper class.

Bagdasarian, Adam. *Forgotten Fire: A Novel.* Random House, 2000. OBCB 2004, 2009. (BBYA)

"Who will remember the Armenians?" Hitler asked, referencing the Armenian genocide as his inspiration for the final solution. This brutal hidden chapter of history is seen through the eyes of 12-year-old survivor Vahan Kendarian.

Baker, Russell. *Growing Up.* Congdon & Weed, 1982. OBCB 1999.

A columnist with a sense of humor takes a gentle look at his childhood in Virginia, New Jersey, and Baltimore during the Depression.

Blum, Joshua, et al., eds. *The United States of Poetry.* Harry N. Abrams, 1996. OBCB 1999. (BBYA)

Contemporary poems enhanced by outstanding photographs and other illustrations highlight poets ranging from Nobel laureates to rappers.

Bond, Jenny, and Chris Sheedy. *Who the Hell Is Pansy O'Hara? The Fascinating Stories behind 50 of the World's Best-Loved Books.* Penguin, 2008. OBCB 2009.

Did you ever wonder what an author was thinking when she wrote her book? Explore the quirky backstories of some of the world's most famous books, both contemporary and classic, nonfiction and fiction.

Butler, Octavia. *Parable of the Sower.* Four Walls Eight Windows, 1993. OBCB 1999.

Lauren Olamina begins her story in 2024, at the age of 15, living outside Los Angeles in a gated community that barely protects its inhabitants from the crime and poverty outside.

Carlson, Lori M., ed. *Cool Salsa: Bilingual Poems on Growing Up Latino in the United States.* Henry Holt, 1994. OBCB 1999.

Party times, hard times, memories, and dreams come to life in these English, Spanish, and Spanglish poems.

Cameron, Peter. *Someday This Pain Will Be Useful to You.* Farrar, Straus, and Giroux, 2007. OBCB 2009. (BBYA)

James hates everyone except his grandmother. Take a look at life through this brilliant and mischievous Manhattan teen's eyes as he tries to figure out life and his place in it.

Card, Orson Scott. *Ender's Game.* Tor, 1985. OBCB 1999.

In a world decimated by alien attacks, the government trains young geniuses like Ender Wiggin in military strategy with increasingly complex computer games.

Chambers, Aidan. *Postcards from No Man's Land.* Dutton, 2002. OBCB 2004. (BBYA, Printz Winner)

At 17, Jacob has gone to Amsterdam to explore his life. His quest strangely parallels discoveries about his grandfather's life there during World War II.

Chopin, Kate. *The Awakening.* H. S. Stone & Co., 1899. OBCB 1999.

Edna Pontellier, an unhappy wife and mother, discovers new qualities in herself when she visits Grand Isle, a resort for the Creole elite of New Orleans. Her restlessness increases when she meets and falls in love with Robert Lebrun at the resort. When he leaves her abruptly she never fully recovers, eventually leaving her family and refusing to follow convention.

Ciardi, John, and Miller Williams. *How Does a Poem Mean?* Houghton Mifflin, 1960. OBCB 1999. o.p.

A poet and a critic discuss the value and nature of poetry, using selections from six centuries of American and English poems. A poem is more than its subject matter; it is about form, imagery, rhythm, sound.

Cisneros, Sandra. *Caramelo.* Knopf, 2002. OBCB 2004, 2009.

LaLa Reyes learns the stories of her Awful Grandmother and weaves them into a colorful history of her 20th-century Mexican family, taking the reader from Mexico City to Chicago to San Antonio.

Cisneros, Sandra. *The House on Mango Street.* Vintage, 1991. OBCB 1999.

In short, poetic stories, Esperanza describes life in a low-income, predominantly Hispanic neighborhood in Chicago.

Dickinson, Emily. *Dickinson: Poems.* Everyman's Library Pocket Poets. Everyman's Library, 1993. OBCB 1999.

A compact collection of the best known works of an eminent American poet proves that good things do come in small packages.

Dostoyevsky, Fyodor. *Crime and Punishment.* J. M. Dent, 1866. OBCB 1999.

A sensitive intellectual is driven by poverty to believe himself exempt from moral law.

Dunn, Mark. *Ella Minnow Pea: A Novel in Letters.* MacAdam/Cage, 2001. OBCB 2009.

The people of Nollop, an island off South Carolina, are good citizens, but as the use of more and more letters in the alphabet is outlawed, how will its residents communicate?

Dunning, Stephen, Edward Lueders, Naomi Shihab, Deith Gilyard, and Demetrice Q. Worldy, comps. *Reflections on a Gift of Watermelon Pickle . . . and Other Modern Verse.* Scott Foresman, 1995. OBCB 1999.

Photographs complement or illustrate 114 poems chosen for their appeal to young people. The poems range from sharp and biting to easygoing and optimistic; poets from the recognized to the relatively unknown.

Ellison, Ralph. *Invisible Man.* Random House, 1952. OBCB 1999.

A young African American seeking identity during his high school and college days, and later in New York's Harlem, relates his terrifying experiences.

Emecheta, Buchi. *The Bride Price.* G. Braziller, 1976. OBCB 1999.

Aku-nna, a very young Nigerian (Ibo) girl, and Chike, her teacher, fall in love despite tribal custom forbidding their romance.

Faulkner, William. *The Bear.* Vintage, 1931. OBCB 1999.

Ike McCaslin's hunting trips for the legendary bear, Old Ben, are played out against opposing ideas of corruption and innocence. Ike's story is told in past and present narratives, laying out the hunting trips in which he participated from ages 10 to 16, in the late 1870s and early 1880s, ending with a final glimpse of the Mississippi woods in the present, about to fall to a lumber company.

Foer, Jonathan Safran. *Extremely Loud and Incredibly Close.* Houghton Mifflin, 2005. OBCB 2009.

Oskar Schell, a gifted and precocious nine-year-old, explores the mystery of his father's death during the September 11 attack.

Foster, Thomas. *How to Read Literature like a Professor: A Lively and Entertaining Guide to Reading between the Lines.* HarperCollins, 2003. OBCB 2004.

All authors leave clues to lead readers deeper into the inner meanings of their writings. Learn how to follow literary breadcrumbs in any story with this practical and entertaining guide.

Frank, E. R. *Life Is Funny.* DK, 2000. OBCB 2004.

Growing up in New York can be agonizing, humorous, and always a challenge for the Brooklyn teens who tell their stories in rich hip-hop language.

Frazier, Charles. *Cold Mountain.* Atlantic Monthly Press, 1997. OBCB 1999.

Inman, a wounded Civil War soldier, escapes the hospital to endure the elements, The Guard, and his own weakness and infirmity in a journey, an odyssey, to return to his sweetheart, Ada, who is fighting her own battle to survive while farming the mountainous North Carolina terrain.

Freymann-Weyr, Garret. *My Heartbeat.* Houghton Mifflin, 2002. OBCB 2004. (BBYA, Printz Honor)

Ellen loves her older brother, Link, and has a crush on his best friend, James. When she turns 14 and starts high school, Ellen begins to suspect a special relationship between them, even as she becomes closer to James.

Gaines, Ernest. *A Lesson before Dying.* Knopf, 1993. OBCB 1999, 2009.

In 1940s Louisiana, Jefferson, a young black man, faces the electric chair for murder. When his attorney states, "I would just as soon put a hog in the electric chair as this," his grandmother persuades disillusioned teacher Grant Wiggins to visit Jefferson in the penitentiary and help him gain a sense of dignity and self-esteem before his execution.

Gardner, John. *Grendel.* Knopf, 1971. OBCB 1999.

In a unique interpretation of the Beowulf legend, the monster Grendel relates his struggle to understand the ugliness in himself and mankind in the brutal world of 14th-century Denmark.

Gibbons, Kaye. *Ellen Foster.* Algonquin, 1987. OBCB 1999.

Casting an unflinching yet humorous eye on her situation, 11-year-old Ellen tells the story of surviving her mother's death, an abusive father, and uncaring relatives to find a loving home and a new mama.

Giddings, Robert. *The War Poets.* Orion Books, 1988. OBCB 1999. o.p.

The work of a variety of World War I poets, many of whom died in the conflict, is reinforced with biographical notes and a brief history of "the war to end all wars."

Gillan, Maria Mazziotti, and Jennifer Gillan, eds. *Unsettling America: An Anthology of Contemporary Multicultural Poetry.* Penguin, 1994. OBCB 1999.

This poetry feast challenges stereotypes about who or what is American.

Gordon, Ruth, ed. *Pierced by a Ray of Sun: Poems about the Times We Feel Alone.* HarperCollins, 1995. OBCB 1999. o.p. (BBYA)

Poets from around the world and across time reflect on solitude and loneliness. The poems in this collection chosen for young readers reflect both hope and despair.

Green, John. *Looking for Alaska.* Dutton, 2005. OBCB 2009. (BBYA, Printz Winner)

Join Miles Halter, who is intrigued by famous last words, as he heads off to an Alabama boarding school in search of the "Great Perhaps."

Haddon, Mark. *The Curious Incident of the Dog in the Night-Time.* Doubleday, 2003. OBCB 2004, 2009. (Alex Award, BBYA)

Fifteen-year-old Christopher, who has Asperger's syndrome, has two mysteries to solve: who killed Wellington the dog, and what happened to his mother.

Heaney, Seamus, and Ted Hughes, eds. *The Rattle Bag.* Faber and Faber, 1982. OBCB 1999.

This hefty compilation includes poems from the oral tradition. The two editors, famous poets themselves, simply present their favorite poetry arranged alphabetically, in hopes that each poem will communicate on its own terms.

Heller, Joseph. *Catch-22.* Simon & Schuster, 1961. OBCB 1999.
In this satirical novel, Captain Yossarian confronts the hypocrisy and absurdity of war and bureaucracy as he frantically attempts to outwit the army and survive.

Hemingway, Ernest. *A Farewell to Arms.* Scribner, 1929. OBCB 1999.
World War I is the setting for this love story of an English nurse and a wounded American ambulance officer.

Hesse, Hermann. *Siddhartha.* New Directions, 1951. OBCB 1999.
Emerging from a kaleidoscope of experiences and tasted pleasures, Siddhartha transcends to a state of peace and mystic holiness in this strangely simple story.

Homer. *Odyssey.* Translated by Robert Fagles. Viking, 1996. OBCB 1999.
Smell the salt air and experience Odysseus's temptations as the ancient world and his journey come alive again through this fresh poetic translation.

Hosseini, Khaled. *The Kite Runner.* Putnam, 2003. OBCB 2004, 2009. (Alex Award)
When he was just a young boy, joyfully running kites through the streets of Kabul in the 1970s, Amir betrayed the son of his father's servant, his best friend, Hassan. Years after fleeing Afghanistan, Amir, now an American citizen, returns to his native land.

Huxley, Aldous. *Brave New World.* Chatto & Windus, 1932. OBCB 1999.
In a chilling vision of the future, babies are produced in bottles and exist in a mechanized world without soul. Individuality is not allowed by the state; stability is everything.

Ishiguro, Kazuo. *Never Let Me Go.* Knopf, 2005. OBCB 2009. (Alex Award)
Only special students are chosen to attend Hailsham, an exclusive boarding school tucked away in the English countryside. The chilling truth of their special nature slowly unfolds as we follow the stories of three former students.

Jones, Lloyd. *Mister Pip.* Dial Press, 2007. OBCB 2009. (Alex Award, BBYA)
Matilda's Pacific Island village has been torn apart by civil war. Against this harsh backdrop, Mr. Watts, a lonely British expatriate, maintains calm by reading Dickens's *Great Expectations* aloud to the village children.

Kaplow, Robert. *Me and Orson Welles.* MacAdam/Cage, 2003. OBCB 2004.
What would it be like to spend a week with the great Orson Welles, even sleeping in his pajamas? Richard Samuels, a budding teenage actor, gets the opportunity to see what life on stage, and backstage, is really like on Broadway in 1937.

Karr, Mary. *The Liars' Club: A Memoir.* Viking, 1995. OBCB 1999.
Growing up in "a family of liars and drunks" is never easy, and yet, despite alcoholism, rape, and other dark secrets, the author makes childhood in an east Texas refinery town sound as funny as it was painful.

Keillor, Garrison, ed. *Good Poems.* Penguin, 2002. OBCB 2009.
An essential and accessible anthology of some of the best contemporary and classic poetry.

Keneally, Thomas. *Schindler's List.* Simon & Schuster, 1982. OBCB 1999.
Oskar Schindler, a rich German factory owner, risks his life and spends his personal fortune to save Jews listed as his workers during World War II.

Kidd, Sue Monk. *The Secret Life of Bees.* Viking, 2002. OBCB 2009. (BBYA)
Searching for the truth about her mother's life and death, a grieving Lily finds the answers, love, and acceptance where she least expects them.

King, Laurie R. *The Beekeeper's Apprentice; or, On the Segregation of the Queen.* St. Martin's, 1994. OBCB 1999.

In 1915, retired Sherlock Holmes meets his intellectual match in 15-year-old orphan Mary Russell, who collaborates with him to investigate the kidnapping of an American senator's daughter.

Kingsolver, Barbara. *The Bean Trees.* Harper & Row, 1988. OBCB 2004.

In Kingsolver's debut novel, Taylor Greer leaves Kentucky after high school and heads west to find a new life.

Kosinski, Jerzy. *The Painted Bird.* Houghton Mifflin, 1965. OBCB 1999.

An abandoned dark-haired child wanders alone through isolated villages of Eastern Europe in World War II, struggling to survive.

Kyle, Aryn. *The God of Animals.* Simon & Schuster/Scribner, 2007. OBCB 2009. (Alex Award)

Twelve-year-old Alice faces issues beyond her years. Her older sister has run off with a rodeo cowboy, her mother won't get out of bed, and the family horse farm is failing.

Lamott, Anne. *Bird by Bird: Some Instructions on Writing and Life.* Anchor Books, 1995. OBCB 2004.

Advice to the fledgling writer: "Just take it bird by bird." A gentle, anecdotal guide for beginning authors about both the writing process and the writer's life.

Lee, Harper. *To Kill a Mockingbird.* Lippincott, 1960. OBCB 1999.

Scout, a young girl, tells of life in a small Alabama town in the 1930s, and how she and her brother, Jem, learn to fight prejudice by watching their father's defense in court of an African American man falsely accused of raping a white woman.

LeGuin, Ursula. *The Left Hand of Darkness.* Walker, 1969. OBCB 1999.

First envoy to the technologically primitive world of Gethen (Winter), Genly Ai is sent to persuade the planet to join Ekumen, an organization of planets promoting cooperation and harmony.

Maguire, Gregory. *Wicked: The Life and Times of the Wicked Witch of the West.* ReganBooks, 1995. OBCB 2009.

The Wizard of Oz retold from the point of view of Elphaba, the Wicked Witch of the West.

Mah, Adeline. *Chinese Cinderella: The True Story of an Unwanted Daughter.* Delacorte, 1999. OBCB 2004. (BBYA)

Wu Mei, also called Adeline, is the Fifth Younger Sister of her family, and the one who bears the blame for all their bad fortune.

Malamud, Bernard. *The Fixer.* Farrar, Straus, and Giroux, 1966. OBCB 1999.

Victim of a vicious anti-Semitic conspiracy, Yakov Bok is in a Russian prison for years, waiting for a trial, with only his indomitable will to sustain him through solitary confinement.

Markandaya, Kamala. *Nectar in a Sieve.* J. Day Co., 1954. OBCB 1999.

Natural disasters, arranged marriage, and industrialization of her village are the challenges educated Rukmani must face as the bride of a peasant farmer in southern India in the early 1950s.

Mason, Bobbi Ann. *In Country.* Harper & Row, 1985. OBCB 1999.

After her father is killed in the Vietnam War, teenager Samantha Hughes lives with her uncle Emmett, whom she suspects suffers from the effects of Agent Orange.

McCarthy, Cormac. *The Road.* Knopf/Vintage, 2008. OBCB 2009.

After an apocalyptic catastrophe, a father and his young son embark on a grim and peril-ous quest to travel south before the weather becomes cold enough to kill them.

McCullers, Carson. *The Member of the Wedding.* Houghton Mifflin, 1946. OBCB 1999.

Twelve-year-old tomboy Frankie Adams is determined to be the third party on her brother's honeymoon, despite all advice.

McKinley, Robin. *Beauty.* Harper & Row, 1978. OBCB 1999.

Ironically, Beauty's sisters are the ones who grow up to be lovely, while she must be content with intelligence. The family is forced to abandon their comfortable life in the city and move to a country house on the edge of a dense forest.

Miller, E. Ethelbert, ed. *In Search of Color Everywhere: A Collection of African-American Poetry.* Stewart, Tabori, & Chang, 1994. OBCB 1999. o.p. (BBYA)

From spirituals to rap to classic works by famous poets, this presentation delights the senses. Recent and past poetry, by the renowned and the up-and-coming, unite in an anthology with range.

Mori, Kyoko. *Shizuko's Daughter.* Henry Holt, 1993. OBCB 1999.

In the years following her mother's suicide, Japanese teenager Yuki develops the inner strength to cope with her distant father, her resentful stepmother, and her haunting, pain-ful memories.

Morrison, Toni. *Beloved.* Knopf, 1987. OBCB 1999.

Preferring death over slavery for her children, Sethe murders her infant daughter who later mysteriously returns and almost destroys the lives of her mother and sister.

Murakami, Haruki. *Kafka on the Shore.* Knopf, 2005. OBCB 2009.

Reality and fantasy converge in this story of Kafka Tamura, a Japanese teenage runaway, and his quest to find his long-lost sister and mother.

Myers, Walter Dean. *Monster.* HarperCollins, 1999. OBCB 2004. (BBYA, Printz Winner)

Sixteen-year-old Steve Harmon is accused of being an accomplice to murder in the shooting of a Harlem convenience store owner. Is Steve guilty, or was he simply in the wrong place at the wrong time?

Myers, Walter Dean. *Sunrise over Fallujah.* Scholastic, 2008. OBCB 2009.

An 18-year-old growing up in Harlem, Robin always intended to go to college. But after September 11 he decides instead to volunteer for the army.

Neil, Philip, ed. *Singing America.* Viking, 1995. OBCB 1999. o.p.

Experience American poetic heritage through dramatic black-and-white drawings that illustrate a wealth of poetry from Walt Whitman to spirituals, songs of the Sioux, the national anthem, and Woody Guthrie.

Niatum, Duane, ed. *Harper's Anthology of 20th Century Native American Poetry.* Harper & Row, 1988. OBCB 1999.

The century's best Native American poets capture their cultural heritage through powerful poetry. Niatum has gathered work by 36 poets from 30 different tribes. The collection ends with a brief biography of each poet.

Nye, Naomi Shihab. *Nineteen Varieties of Gazelle: Poems of the Middle East.* HarperCollins/Greenwillow, 2002. OBCB 2004. (BBYA)

Another world, another culture—poems that personalize the conflicts and people, deep-ening understanding of the impact of September 11.

Nye, Naomi Shihab, sel. *The Tree Is Older Than You Are: A Bilingual Gathering of Poems and Stories from Mexico with Paintings by Mexican Artists.* Simon & Schuster Books for Young Readers, 1995. OBCB 1999. (BBYA)

Modern and ancient Mexican poetry, prose, and paintings from all regions come alive in this lavish anthology. English translations are laid out next to the original folktales, stories, and poems.

Nye, Naomi Shihab, and Paul B. Janeczko, eds. *I Feel a Little Jumpy around You: A Book of Her Poems and His Poems Collected in Pairs.* Simon & Schuster Books for Young Readers, 1996. OBCB 1999. (BBYA)

In this anthology of thought-provoking modern poems, male and female writers view life from gender perspectives. The grouping of nearly 200 poems in pairs by topic reveals as many similarities as differences.

O'Brien, Tim. *The Things They Carried: A Work of Fiction.* Houghton Mifflin, 1990. OBCB 1999.

Interrelated short stories follow Tim O'Brien's platoon of American soldiers through a variety of personal and military encounters during the Vietnam War.

O'Connor, Flannery. *Everything That Rises Must Converge.* Farrar, Straus, and Giroux, 1965. OBCB 1999.

A collection of nine short stories about misfits in small southern towns that force the reader to confront hypocrisy, prejudice, and complacency.

O'Connor, Patricia. *Woe Is I: The Grammarphobe's Guide to Better English in Plain English.* Putnam, 1996. OBCB 2004.

When there's something important to say, how you say it counts. O'Connor makes pronouns, antecedents and more grammar-ology fun and painless for both novices and experts, including many examples.

Oliver, Mary. *New and Selected Poems.* Beacon Press, 1992. OBCB 1999.

The Pulitzer–Prize–winning poet presents a smorgasbord of her poems, composed and published over the last three decades, about life, death, and humanity's relationship to the natural world.

Potok, Chaim. *The Chosen.* Simon & Schuster, 1967. OBCB 1999.

A baseball injury brings two Jewish boys together in World War II-era Brooklyn. When they enter college, both boys study to be rabbis, one by choice, the other out of obligation.

Power, Susan. *The Grass Dancer.* Putnam, 1994. OBCB 1999.

Ending in the 1980s with the love story of Charlene Thunder and grass dancer Harley Wind Soldier, this multigenerational tale of a Sioux family is told in the voices of the living and the dead, reaching back to 1864.

Pullman, Philip. *The Golden Compass.* Knopf, 1996. OBCB 2004. (BBYA)

Lyra Belacqua, a young girl living in an alternate Oxford, and her animal daemon, Pantalaimon, save her uncle from an assassination attempt, then set out to find her kidnapped playmate and uncover a sinister plot involving disappearing children and mysterious Dust.

Reynolds, Sheri. *A Gracious Plenty.* Harmony Books, 1997. OBCB 2004.

Finch Nobles was only four when she pulled a pot of boiling water down on herself, resulting in horrible scars. Now she is a recluse, a cemetery keeper in a small southern town who can talk to the dead, helping them examine what keeps them tied to the earth and resolve their tragedies.

Rosenberg, Liz, ed. *Earth-Shattering Poems.* Henry Holt, 1998. OBCB 1999. o.p.

Poets from around the world and through the centuries, encompassing many different cultures, express the emotional intensity of life's experiences. The poems are presented in chronological order, beginning with Sappho.

Roth, Philip. *The Plot against America.* Houghton Mifflin, 2004. OBCB 2009.

This alternate history takes a hard look at one of America's legendary heroes, Charles Lindbergh, and how bigotry and fear can shape politics.

Rubin, Robert Alden, ed. *Poetry Out Loud.* Algonquin, 1993. OBCB 1999.

Poems from the world's greatest poets, including raps, ballads, and other lyrics, are annotated and followed by suggestions for reading aloud.

Sapphire. *Push.* Knopf, 1996. OBCB 2004.

Precious Jones had her father's baby at 12 and now, at 16, she is pregnant by him again and abused by her mother. But an alternative school, a dedicated teacher, and classmates who understand help her fight back.

Satrapi, Marjane. *Persepolis.* Pantheon, 2003. OBCB 2004. (Alex Award, BBYA)

Marjane Satrapi grew up in revolutionary Iran, experiencing the overthrow of the Shah and the establishment of a new regime that abolished personal freedoms, especially for women.

Sebold, Alice. *Lucky: A Memoir.* Scribner, 1999. OBCB 2004, 2009.

"You save yourself or you remain unsaved." With these words, Sebold recounts the brutal rape that she was "lucky" to survive as a college freshman.

Shaara, Michael. *The Killer Angels.* McKay, 1974. OBCB 1999.

Officers and foot soldiers from both the Union and Confederacy approach and then fight the bloody Battle of Gettysburg.

Shakur, Tupac. *A Rose That Grew from Concrete.* Simon & Schuster, 1999. OBCB 2004.

Written when Tupac was 19 and not yet a star, these poems bring emotion, power, and passion to the experience of becoming yourself.

Smith, Anna Deveare. *Fires in the Mirror: Crown Heights and Other Identities.* Dramatists Play Service, 1999. OBCB 2004.

A dramatic look at the Crown Heights riots and race in the United States through the voices of 23 fascinating and unique characters, based on interviews with real people.

Smith, Philip, ed. *100 Best-Loved Poems.* Dover, 1995. OBCB 1999.

Shakespeare, English and American ballads, and the classics most of us remember and love are part of the treasure found in this collection of traditional poetry.

Stallworthy, Jon, ed. *A Book of Love Poetry.* Oxford University Press, 1986. OBCB 1999.

You can experience love throughout the ages, as expressed in the past 2,000 years of poetry from around the world.

Steinbeck, John. *The Grapes of Wrath.* Viking, 1939. OBCB 1999.

An Oklahoma farmer and his family leave the Dust Bowl during the Great Depression to go to the promised land of California. The Joads endure a difficult journey only to encounter the hard life of migrant workers.

Stoppard, Tom. *Rosencrantz and Guildenstern Are Dead.* Grove Press, 1967. OBCB 1999, 2009.

Two bit players from Shakespeare's *Hamlet* are thrust into a terrifying and surreal new situation.

Thompson, Craig. *Blankets: An Illustrated Novel.* Top Shelf Productions, 2003. OBCB 2009. (BBYA)

A young man living in rural Wisconsin questions his faith and experiences bittersweet first love in this autobiographical and groundbreaking graphic novel.

Uchida, Yoshiko. *Picture Bride.* Northland, 1987. OBCB 1999.

In the early 1900s, Hana Omiya journeys from her small village in Japan to the promised land of America to marry a man she has never met.

Watson, Larry. *Montana 1948.* Milkweed, 1993. OBCB 1999.

The summer he is 12, David watches as his family and small town are shattered by scandal and tragedy.

Wolff, Tobias. *This Boy's Life: A Memoir.* Atlantic Monthly Press, 1989. OBCB 1999.

In and out of trouble in his youth, this charter member of the "Bad Boys' Club" survives boyhood in this coming-of-age memoir.

Wright, Richard. *Native Son.* Harper, 1940. OBCB 1999.

For Bigger Thomas, an African American man accused of a crime in the white man's world, there could be no extenuating circumstances, no explanations—only death.

Yolen, Jane. *Briar Rose.* Tom Doherty, 1992. OBCB 1999.

Disturbed by her grandmother Gemma's unique version of "Sleeping Beauty," Rebecca seeks the truth behind the fairy tale.

Yolen, Jane, ed. *Favorite Folktales from Around the World.* Pantheon, 1986. OBCB 1999.

This collection of international folktales provides an understanding of the roots of diverse cultures.

Zusak, Marcus. *The Book Thief.* Knopf, 2006. OBCB 2009. (BBYA, Printz Honor)

Living in Nazi Germany, young Liesel and her family choose to lie and steal to protect a Jewish refugee hiding in their basement. Narrated by Death, this is not your typical World War II story.

· SCIENCE AND TECHNOLOGY ·

Adams, Scott. *God's Debris: A Thought Experiment.* Andrews McMeel, 2001. OBCB 2009.

Take a metaphysical journey into the search for meaning, as you try to deliver a package to the smartest man in the world who won't take it until you understand.

Alvarez, Walter. *T. Rex and the Crater of Doom.* Princeton University Press, 1997. OBCB 1999.

Geologist Alvarez presents the development of the impact theory of dinosaur extinction as the adventure/mystery it was.

Anderson, M. T. *Feed.* Candlewick, 2002. OBCB 2004, 2009. (BBYA)

In this society your brain cyberfeed provides an endless stream of information, entertainment, and advertising. When Violet's feed is disrupted, she's cast adrift, and everyone is forced to examine the power of the feed in his or her life.

Ayres, Ian. *Super Crunchers: Why Thinking-by-Numbers Is the New Way to Be Smart.* Bantam, 2007. OBCB 2009.

With real-life examples from sports, medicine, online dating, and airline pricing, Ayres describes how data about all of us are collected and "crunched" by statisticians and computers in order to profile consumers and make predictions.

Best, Joel. *Damned Lies and Statistics: Untangling Numbers from the Media, Politicians, and Activists.* University of California Press, 2001. OBCB 2004, 2009.
Most people naïvely believe reported statistics, which are often mutations of the truth. Best teaches readers to evaluate the statistics they encounter.

Bodanis, David. *The Secret Family: Twenty-four Hours Inside the Mysterious World of Our Minds and Bodies.* Simon & Schuster, 1997. OBCB 1999. o.p. (Alex Award)
The unseen world around us and within our bodies is shown in vivid detail as we follow a typical family through their day.

Bradshaw, Gillian. *The Sand-Reckoner.* Forge, 2000. OBCB 2004. (Alex Award)
A youthful Archimedes comes into his own as a mathematician, an engineer, and a fascinating human being in this engaging novel.

Brown, David. *Inventing Modern America: From the Microwave to the Mouse.* MIT Press, 2001. OBCB 2004.
Brown reveals the human stories and faces behind American scientific and technological innovations and achievements from the computer mouse to the pacemaker.

Bryson, Bill. *A Short History of Nearly Everything.* Broadway Books, 2003. OBCB 2004, 2009.
Bryson brings complex scientific concepts to life by describing how the universe and life as we know it came to be.

Carson, Rachel. *Silent Spring.* Houghton Mifflin, 1962. OBCB 1999.
This landmark book about pesticides and other chemicals gave birth to the environmental movement and is still chillingly relevant today.

Casey, Susan. *The Devil's Teeth: A True Story of Obsession and Survival among America's Great White Sharks.* Henry Holt/Owl Books, 2005. OBCB 2009.
A scientific study of great white sharks off the Farallon Islands, near San Francisco, reveals unknown secrets of the prehistoric beasts.

Chen, Joanne. *The Taste of Sweet: Our Complicated Love Affair with Our Favorite Treats.* Crown, 2008. OBCB 2009.
The science, history, and social changes behind the American sweet tooth are explored, from the taste buds on our tongues to slaves on sugar plantations.

Curie, Eve. *Madam Curie: A Biography.* Doubleday, 1937. OBCB 1999.
In sharing personal papers and her own memories, a daughter pays tribute to her unique and generous mother, a scientific genius.

Doctorow, Cory. *Little Brother.* Tom Doherty/Tor Teen, 2008. OBCB 2009. (BBYA)
In near-future San Franciso, 17-year-old Marcus, known online as w1n5t0n (or Winston), is detained by the Department of Homeland Security under suspicion of participating in a terrorist attack.

Enzensberger, Hans. *The Number Devil: A Mathematical Adventure.* Henry Holt, 1998. OBCB 2004.
A boy who hates math in school dreams of a devil who guides him through a colorful, Alice in Wonderland–like world of mathematical concepts.

Fagan, Brian. *The Little Ice Age: How Climate Made History, 1300–1850.* Basic Books, 2000. OBCB 2004.
Fagan provides a fascinating look at how climate change influenced the course of the last thousand years of Western history.

Feynman, Richard. *What Do You Care What Other People Think? Further Adventures of a Curious Character.* Norton, 1998. OBCB 2004.

Quirky, hilarious, and fascinating essays from one of the 20th century's greatest physicists cover everything from his early childhood to his work on the atomic bomb.

Feynman, Richard P., as told to Ralph Leighton. *Surely You're Joking, Mr. Feynman: Adventures of a Curious Character.* Norton, 1985. OBCB 1999.

This Nobel Prize–winning physicist's autobiography is a series of anecdotes based on conversations with Ralph Leighton.

Firlik, Katrina. *Another Day in the Frontal Lobe: A Brain Surgeon Exposes Life on the Inside.* Random House, 2006. OBCB 2009.

One of the few female neurosurgeons in the world writes an honest appraisal of her work, of day-to-day problem solving and ethical dilemmas.

Flannery, Sarah, with David Flannery. *In Code: A Mathematical Journey.* Workman Publishing, 2001. OBCB 2004. o.p.

In this mixture of memoir and mathematical puzzle book, one 16-year-old's discoveries in the science of cryptography dramatically impact the modern world.

Flannery, Tim. *The Weather Makers: How Man Is Changing the Climate and What It Means for Life on Earth.* Atlantic Monthly Press, 2005. OBCB 2009.

What are melting glaciers, disappearing frogs, and a season of perfect storms trying to tell us about the conditions of the planet we call home, and what can we do to prevent a catastrophe?

Fouts, Roger. *Next of Kin: What Chimpanzees Have Taught Me about Who We Are.* Morrow, 1997. OBCB 1999.

Describing his career of communicating with chimpanzees, Fouts explains evolutionary, genetic, and emotional bonds with our next of kin.

George, Rose. *The Big Necessity: The Unmentionable World of Human Waste and Why It Matters.* Metropolitan Books, 2008. OBCB 2009.

A look at the dirty details of what happens to human waste around the globe and how it affects our health and sanitation.

Green, Bill. *Water, Ice, and Stone: Science and Memory on the Antarctic Lakes.* Harmony Books, 1995. OBCB 1999.

A chemist investigates Antarctica's ice-covered lakes and discovers beauty and poetry.

Hafner, Katie, and Matthew Lyon. *Where Wizards Stay Up Late: The Origins of the Internet.* Simon & Schuster, 1996. OBCB 1999.

The origins of the world's first computer network are explained, with tales of the motivations, breakthroughs, and personalities that created it.

Hawking, Stephen. *A Brief History of Time: From the Big Bang to Black Holes.* Bantam, 1988. OBCB 1999.

Cosmology becomes understandable as the author discusses the origin, evolution, and fate of our universe.

Hawking, Stephen. *The Universe in a Nutshell.* Bantam, 2001. OBCB 2004.

The physics guru illuminates startling new theories about our world in a lavishly illustrated sequel to *A Brief History of Time.*

Hoose, Phillip M. *The Race to Save the Lord God Bird.* Farrar, Straus, and Giroux, 2004. OBCB 2009. (BBYA)

The ivory-billed woodpecker is thought to be extinct, but some disagree. Hoose documents the scientific and bird-watching communities' attempts to find this lost species and save its habitat in the southern United States.

Horvitz, Leslie A. *Eureka! Scientific Breakthroughs That Changed the World.* Wiley, 2002. OBCB 2004.

Horvitz explores the dramatic events and thought processes of 12 great minds that led to profound scientific discoveries, including television and the double helix.

Hoyt, Erich, and Ted Schultz, eds. *Insect Lives: Stories of Mystery and Romance from a Hidden World.* Wiley, 1999. OBCB 2004.

A diverse collection of brief essays and illustrations that entice readers to explore the fascinating and mysterious world of insects.

Hubbell, Sue. *A Country Year: Living the Questions.* Random House, 1986. OBCB 1999.

A former wife and librarian observes her natural surroundings during a year spent as a beekeeper on a beautiful Ozark farm.

Jones, Chris. *Out of Orbit: The Incredible True Story of Three Astronauts Who Were Hundreds of Miles above Earth When They Lost Their Ride Home.* Broadway Books, 2008. OBCB 2009.

The 2003 destruction of the shuttle *Columbia* and its crew stranded three astronauts in earth's orbit.

Judson, Olivia. *Dr. Tatiana's Sex Advice to All Creation: The Definitive Guide to the Evolutionary Biology of Sex.* Metropolitan Books, 2002. OBCB 2004.

A "Dear Abby"–style science column that answers the who, what, when, where, why, and how of a fascinating variety of sexual activity for all creatures great and small.

Kolb, Rocky. *Blind Watchers of the Sky: The People and Ideas That Shaped Our View of the Universe.* Addison-Wesley, 1996. OBCB 1999.

Kolb delivers a witty, lively history of astronomy and cosmology over the last 400 years.

Krauss, Lawrence. *Atom: An Odyssey from the Big Bang to Life on the Earth . . . and Beyond.* Little, Brown, 2001. OBCB 2004.

Follow a single oxygen atom on a fantastic voyage from the beginning of the universe to far into the future.

Lambrecht, Bill. *Dinner at the New Gene Café: How Genetic Engineering Is Changing What We Eat, How We Live, and the Global Politics of Food.* St. Martin's, 2001. OBCB 2004.

Lambrecht traces the scientific and political controversies surrounding the use of genetically modified organisms and the food we eat.

Leopold, Aldo. *A Sand County Almanac.* Oxford University Press, 2001. OBCB 2009.

This classic of environmental and nature writing, arranged by season, provides a poetic view through the window of the Leopold family farm in the Wisconsin meadows.

Livio, Mario. *The Golden Ratio: The Story of Phi, the World's Most Astonishing Number.* Broadway Books, 2002. OBCB 2004.

A captivating journey through art and architecture, botany and biology, physics and mathematics. This ratio, 1.6180339887 . . . has fascinated us through the ages.

Macaulay, David. *Mosque.* Houghton Mifflin Harcourt/Walter Lorraine, 2003. OBCB 2009.

Enter a community mosque in 16th-century Istanbul and discover the techniques (from brick making to window production) used to raise towering minarets and a prayer hall dome.

Macaulay, David. *The Way We Work: Getting to Know the Amazing Human Body.* Houghton Mifflin Harcourt/Walter Lorraine, 2008. OBCB 2009.

Macaulay takes the reader on a tour of the human body with detailed illustrations and succinct, sometimes humorous explanations of its building blocks and systems.

McKibben, Bill, ed. *American Earth: Environmental Writing since Thoreau.* Library of America, 2008. OBCB 2009.

Experience the growth of the environmental movement in poetry, essay, song, and prose from its infancy to the present day through the eyes of its champions.

McPhee, John. *In Suspect Terrain.* Farrar, Straus, and Giroux, 1982. OBCB 1999.

Traveling along I-80 from New York City to Chicago with geologist Anita Harris, McPhee describes the geologic features that reveal the history of the Appalachians.

Melville, Greg. *Greasy Rider: Two Dudes, One Fry-Oil-Powered Car, and a Cross-Country Search for a Greener Future.* Algonquin, 2008. OBCB 2009.

Take a humorous, green road trip with the author and his college buddy in a converted 1980s Mercedes from Vermont to California, and learn how to be more eco-friendly.

Nash, Madeline. *El Niño: Unlocking the Secrets of the Master Weather-Maker.* Warner, 2002. OBCB 2004.

Hard work and chance led to the discovery of El Niño and La Niña, powerful climatic systems that we still struggle to understand.

Nolen, Stephanie. *Promised the Moon: The Untold Story of the First Women in the Space Race.* Four Walls Eight Windows, 2002. OBCB 2004.

The story of Dr. Randy Lovelace and Jerri Cobb and the other female pilots tested for their abilities to become NASA astronauts during the 1960s.

Paulos, John Allen. *Innumeracy: Mathematical Illiteracy and Its Consequences.* Hill and Wang, 1988. OBCB 1999.

Paulos illustrates the importance of understanding (and the consequences of misunderstanding) mathematical concepts in everyday life.

Petroski, Henry. *Invention by Design: How Engineers Get from Thought to Thing.* Harvard University Press, 1996. OBCB 1999.

Presenting case studies from paper clips to monumental bridges, Petroski shows how engineers work.

Pollan, Michael. *The Botany of Desire: A Plant's-Eye View of the World.* Random House, 2001. OBCB 2009.

Through the sweetness of apples, the beauty of tulips, the intoxication of marijuana, and potato control, Pollan shows how mankind has manipulated plants and they, in turn, have enticed us to do their bidding.

Porter, Roy. *Madness: A Brief History.* Oxford University Press, 2002. OBCB 2004.

Porter addresses the causes and treatments of mental illness in every period of history.

Preston, Richard. *The Demon in the Freezer: A True Story.* Random House, 2002. OBCB 2004.

A striking portrait of smallpox makes readers uncomfortably aware that it could rise again as a biological weapon of mass destruction.

Preston, Richard. *The Wild Trees: A Story of Passion and Daring.* Random House, 2007. OBCB 2009.

Three buddies on spring break climb into a California redwood and discover a new ecosystem atop the trees.

Regis, Ed. *Virus Ground Zero: Stalking the Killer Viruses with the Centers for Disease Control.* Pocket Books, 1996. OBCB 1999.

The history of the CDC is told through the handling of the 1995 Ebola outbreak in Zaire.

Rigden, John S. *Hydrogen: The Essential Element.* Harvard University Press, 2002. OBCB 2004.

Rigden tells the stories of the many scientists absorbed in the study of hydrogen since its discovery in the 18th century.

Roach, Mary. *Stiff: The Curious Lives of Human Cadavers.* Norton, 2003. OBCB 2004, 2009. (Alex Award, BBYA)

Discover the amazing life-after-death adventures of human bodies in this examination of how medical and research scientists use cadavers to improve our lives.

Schroeder, Gerald. *The Hidden Face of God: How Science Reveals the Ultimate Truth.* Simon & Schuster/Free Press, 2001. OBCB 2009.

Schroeder investigates the relationship between physics and metaphysics, science and religion.

Silverstein, Ken. *The Radioactive Boy Scout: The True Story of a Boy and His Backyard Nuclear Reactor.* Random House, 2004. OBCB 2009. (BBYA)

Learn the true story of how David Hahn's work toward an Atomic Energy Boy Scout badge turned into an obsession.

Singh, Simon. *Fermat's Enigma: The Epic Quest to Solve the World's Greatest Mathematical Problem.* Walker, 1997. OBCB 1999.

Singh follows the story of Andrew Wiles, a Princeton professor who worked in solitude for seven years before presenting a solution for Fermat's theorem in 1993.

Smith, Gina. *The Genomics Age: How DNA Technology Is Transforming the Way We Live and Who We Are.* AMACOM, 2004. OBCB 2009. o.p.

From Crick and Watson's discovery of the double helix to "designer" embryos, learn the history and truth behind the controversies in today's news.

Sobel, Dava. *Longitude: The True Story of a Lone Genius Who Solved the Greatest Scientific Problem of His Time.* Walker, 1995. OBCB 1999, 2004.

The little-known story behind the greatest innovation in navigational science: the chronometer, an 18th-century GPS.

Stark, Peter. *Last Breath: Cautionary Tales from the Limits of Human Endurance.* Ballantine, 2001. OBCB 2004.

Whether the danger is hypothermia, mountain sickness, or cerebral malaria, this blend of adventure and science takes you to the absolute edges of human endurance.

Strauch, Barbara. *Primal Teen: What the New Discoveries about the Teenage Brain Tell Us about Our Kids.* Doubleday, 2003. OBCB 2004.

A tour of the teenage brain reveals startling new research about this pivotal and exciting time of life.

Stringer, Christopher, and Robin McKie. *African Exodus: The Origins of Modern Humanity.* Henry Holt, 1997. OBCB 1999. o.p.

The authors support the theory of a single origin of modern humanity with paleoanthropological, archaeological, and DNA evidence.

Sykes, Bryan. *The Seven Daughters of Eve: The Science That Reveals Our Genetic Ancestry.* Norton, 2001. OBCB 2004.

Fascinating mitochondrial DNA evidence supports the idea that almost all modern Europeans are descended from just seven women.

Teresi, Dick. *Lost Discoveries: The Ancient Roots of Modern Science—From the Babylonians to the Maya.* Simon & Schuster, 2002. OBCB 2009.

Teresi shows how scientific and mathematical concepts developed by ancient cultures around the world are the foundations of today's technology.

Thomas, Lewis. *The Lives of a Cell: Notes of a Biology Watcher.* Viking, 1974. OBCB 1999.

Twenty-nine short essays offer an optimistic scientist's view of a wide variety of subjects.

Tobin, James. *Great Projects: The Epic Story of the Building of America from the Taming of the Mississippi to the Invention of the Internet.* Free Press, 2001. OBCB 2004.

The generously illustrated story of the milestones of engineering that connected us and moved a nation forward.

Watson, James D. *The Double Helix: A Personal Account of the Discovery and Structure of DNA.* Atheneum, 1968. OBCB 1999.

The author re-creates the excitement of co-discovering the structure of DNA with Francis Crick and winning the Nobel Prize.

· SOCIAL SCIENCES ·

Albom, Mitch. *Tuesdays with Morrie: An Old Man, a Young Man, and Life's Greatest Lesson.* Doubleday, 1997. OBCB 2004, 2009.

Mitch Albom's Tuesday night visits with his dying sociology professor, Morrie, offer valuable lessons about the art of living and dying with dignity.

Atkin, S. Beth. *Voices from the Streets: Young Former Gang Members Tell Their Stories.* Little, Brown, 1996. OBCB 1999. o.p. (BBYA)

Gang members from all races and backgrounds describe why they joined, and why—and how—they left.

Beah, Ishmael. *A Long Way Gone: Memoirs of a Boy Soldier.* Farrar, Straus, and Giroux, 2007. OBCB 2009. (Alex Award, BBYA)

Ishmael Beah was a 12-year-old child soldier, hopped up on drugs and wielding an AK-47, swept up in the horrors of civil war in his homeland of Sierra Leone.

Best, Joel. *Damned Lies and Statistics: Untangling Numbers from the Media, Politicians, and Activists.* University of California Press, 2001. OBCB 2004, 2009.

Most people naïvely believe reported statistics, which are often mutations of the truth. Best teaches readers to evaluate the statistics they encounter.

Bolles, Richard Nelson. *What Color Is Your Parachute? 2009: A Practical Manual for Job-Hunters and Career-Changers.* Ten Speed Press, 2008. OBCB 2009.

This "Job Hunting in Hard Times edition" of the top-selling career guide serves those laid off in the recent recession as well as first-time job seekers.

Brumberg, Joan Jacobs. *The Body Project: An Intimate History of American Girls.* Random House, 1997. OBCB 1999.

The evolution of body perception turned the value system of American girls inside out in the 19th and 20th centuries.

Casnocha, Ben. *My Start-Up Life: What a (Very) Young CEO Learned on His Journey through Silicon Valley.* Wiley, 2007. OBCB 2009.

Casnocha, a 19-year-old entrepreneur, tells his own story about the ups and downs of making a business idea work and inspires readers to find their own way to make a difference.

Conover, Ted. *Newjack: Guarding Sing Sing.* Knopf, 2000. OBCB 2004.

An insider's look at Sing Sing prison, through the eyes of a writer who worked for a year as a corrections officer.

Corwin, Miles. *And Still We Rise: The Trials and Triumphs of Twelve Gifted Inner-City High School Students.* Morrow, 2000. OBCB 2004.

Twelve seniors from Crenshaw High School's Advanced Placement English class in south-central Los Angeles dream of going to college, but the harsh realities of their lives threaten to derail their plans.

Cuomo, Kerry Kennedy. *Speak Truth to Power: Human Rights Defenders Who Are Changing Our World.* Crown, 2000. OBCB 2004.

A collection of biographical sketches and haunting photographs of ordinary people from 35 countries who are leading the fight to ensure basic human rights for everyone.

Davis, Wade. *Light at the Edge of the World: A Journey through the Realm of Vanishing Cultures.* National Geographic, 2001. OBCB 2004.

Through photographs and eloquent text, the author unveils the diversity and unique qualities of indigenous human cultures around the world.

Dershowitz, Alan M. *Why Terrorism Works: Understanding the Threat, Responding to the Challenge.* Yale University Press, 2002. OBCB 2004.

Believing that terrorism is caused largely by the actions of Western governments, Dershowitz suggests steps to reduce the frequency and severity of attacks.

Diamond, Jared. *Guns, Germs, and Steel: The Fates of Human Societies.* Norton, 1997. OBCB 1999, 2004.

The rise of human civilizations is explained in terms of geography, ecology, and the development of agriculture.

Dorris, Michael. *The Broken Cord.* Harper & Row, 1989. OBCB 1999.

Dorris, part Native American, was 26 and single when he decided to adopt a child, who suffered from Fetal Alcohol Syndrome.

Doyle, William. *An American Insurrection: The Battle of Oxford, Mississippi, 1962.* Doubleday, 2001. OBCB 2004. (Alex Award)

When James Meredith decided to integrate the University of Mississippi, it caused the worst crisis in American history since the Civil War.

Du Bois, W. E. B. *The Souls of Black Folk: Essays and Sketches.* A. C. McClurg, 1903. OBCB 1999.

In this collection of 14 essays, Du Bois illuminates the injustices of being an African American at the turn of the 20th century.

Due, Linnea. *Joining the Tribe: Growing Up Gay and Lesbian in the '90s.* Anchor Books, 1995. OBCB 1999.

Being young and gay in America means surviving cruelty, abuse, and isolation, as these individual stories from teens around the country attest.

Edelman, Marion Wright. *The Measure of Our Success: A Letter to My Children and Yours.* Beacon Press, 1992. OBCB 1999.

A child advocate shares her thoughts on values, raising families, service, and the future of our country.

Ehrenreich, Barbara. *Nickel and Dimed: On (Not) Getting By in America.* Henry Holt, 2001. OBCB 2004. (Alex Award)

Can you really survive on minimum wage? To find out, the author left her comfortable surroundings for a year to see what life is really like for America's working poor.

Faludi, Susan. *Backlash: The Undeclared War against American Women.* Crown, 1991. OBCB 1999.

Faludi posits that the achievements of feminism unleashed a backlash against women in the 1980s and finds evidence in TV, film, advertising, fashion, politics, and popular psychology.

Ford, Michael Thomas. *The Voices of AIDS: Twelve Unforgettable People Talk about How AIDS Has Changed Their Lives.* Morrow Junior Books, 1995. OBCB 1999. o.p. (BBYA)

Individuals whose AIDS experiences have been catalysts for making a difference share their poignant and personal stories.

Freedman, Samuel G. *Small Victories: The Real World of a Teacher, Her Students, and Their High School.* Harper & Row, 1989. OBCB 1999.

How does New York's Seward Park, an overcrowded, underfunded inner-city high school, send 92 percent of its graduates to college?

Fremon, Celeste. *Father Greg and the Homeboys: The Extraordinary Journey of Father Greg Boyle and His Work with the Latino Gangs of East L.A.* Hyperion, 1995. OBCB 1999. o.p. (BBYA)

Conscience, parent, motivator, drill sergeant: Father Greg helps the gangbangers who call his barrio parish community home to change their lives.

George, Mary W. *The Elements of Library Research: What Every Student Needs to Know.* Princeton University Press, 2008. OBCB 2009.

Succinct and practical, this guide provides students with the tactics, tools, and confidence they need to successfully conduct college-level research, both in print and online.

Gladwell, Malcolm. *The Tipping Point: How Little Things Can Make a Big Difference.* Little, Brown, 2000. OBCB 2009.

Gladwell explains the phenomenon of fads, or how little actions can ripple outward until a "tipping point" is reached that results in a dramatic change.

Haddon, Mark. *The Curious Incident of the Dog in the Night-Time.* Doubleday, 2003. OBCB 2004, 2009. (Alex Award, BBYA)

Fifteen-year-old Christopher, who has Asperger's syndrome, has two mysteries to solve: who killed Wellington the dog, and what happened to his mother.

Hart, Elva Trevino. *The Barefoot Heart: Stories of a Migrant Child.* Bilingual Press, 1999. OBCB 2004. (Alex Award)

This memoir follows a Mexican migrant child and her family as they travel from their home in New Mexico to the farms of Minnesota and Wisconsin in search of work in the 1950s and '60s.

Hersch, Patricia. *A Tribe Apart: A Journey into the Heart of American Adolescence.* Fawcett Columbine, 1998. OBCB 1999.

Three years spent with eight "typical" teens in Reston, Virginia, reveal a separate culture spawned not from personal choice, but rather from adult alienation and abandonment.

Hockenberry, John. *Moving Violations: War Zones, Wheelchairs, and Declarations of Independence.* Hyperion, 1995. OBCB 1999. (BBYA)

Journalist Hockenberry relates the personal and professional experiences he encounters from his wheelchair.

Hosseini, Khaled. *The Kite Runner.* Putnam, 2003. OBCB 2004, 2009. (Alex Award)

When he was just a young boy, joyfully running kites through the streets of Kabul in the 1970s, Amir betrayed the son of his father's servant, his best friend, Hassan. Years after fleeing Afghanistan, Amir, now an American citizen, returns to his native land.

Humes, Edward. *No Matter How Loud I Shout: A Year in the Life of Juvenile Court.* Simon & Schuster, 1996. OBCB 1999.

Humes follows the cases of seven young people, painting a tragic portrait of the chaos characterizing America's juvenile justice system.

Juette, Melvin, and Ronald J. Berger. *Wheelchair Warrior: Gangs, Disability, and Basketball.* Temple University Press, 2008. OBCB 2009.

This story follows the transformation of a 16-year-old African American gang member destined for prison into an athlete playing for the U.S. National Wheelchair Basketball Team.

Katz, Jon. *Geeks: How Two Lost Boys Rode the Internet out of Idaho.* Random House, 2000. OBCB 2004. (BBYA)

Eric and Jesse, poor high school students, social outcasts, and online geeks, find that an obsession with computers and technology is their ticket to college and success.

Keen, Lisa. *Out Law: What LGBT Youth Should Know about Their Legal Rights.* Beacon Press, 2007. OBCB 2009.

Keen introduces LGBT youth to their legal rights and provides examples of young people empowered to stand up for themselves.

Keller, Helen. *The Story of My Life.* Grosset & Dunlap, 1902. OBCB 1999.

Helen Keller writes about the illness that left her disabled; learning to read, write, and speak; and her relationship with her teacher, Annie Sullivan.

Khanga, Yelena, and Susan Jacoby. *Soul to Soul: A Black Russian American Family, 1865–1992.* Norton, 1992. OBCB 1999. o.p.

A young Russian journalist of African American and Jewish heritage analyzes and compares attitudes on race, religion, and sexism in Russia and America.

Kincaid, Jamaica. *My Brother.* Farrar, Straus, and Giroux, 1997. OBCB 1999.

The author returns to the Caribbean island of her birth to help care for her younger brother who is dying of AIDS.

Kohl, Jana. *A Rare Breed of Love: The True Story of Baby and the Mission She Inspired to Help Dogs Everywhere.* Simon & Schuster/Fireside, 2008. OBCB 2009. o.p.

The shocking cruelty of legal animal abuse is exposed through the story of Baby, a poodle who lost a leg after years of mistreatment at a puppy mill.

Kotlowitz, Alex. *The Other Side of the River: A Story of Two Towns, a Death, and America's Dilemma.* Nan A. Talese, 1998. OBCB 1999.

Geographically, only a river separates two neighboring Michigan towns, but the murder of a young black man exposes a deeply rooted racial divide.

Kozol, Jonathan. *Savage Inequalities: Children in America's Schools.* Crown, 1991. OBCB 1999.

Kozol's stinging indictment of America's public school system advocates an equal distribution of per pupil funding to right the gross inequities in our current system.

Latifa [pseud.]. *My Forbidden Face: Growing Up under the Taliban; A Young Woman's Story.* Hyperion, 2002. OBCB 2004.

Sixteen-year-old Latifa dreamed of becoming a professional journalist until the Taliban's repression of women changed her life.

Martinez, Ruben. *Crossing Over: A Mexican Family on the Migrant Trail.* Henry Holt, 2001. OBCB 2004.

Martinez explores the powerful forces that drive men, women, and even children to risk their lives crossing the border illegally from Mexico to the United States to find work.

Mathabane, Mark. *Kaffir Boy: The True Story of a Black Youth's Coming of Age in Apartheid South Africa.* Macmillan, 1986. OBCB 1999.

Mathabane describes growing up under the brutalities of apartheid South Africa and his escape to America.

McBride, James. *The Color of Water: A Black Man's Tribute to His White Mother.* Riverhead, 1996. OBCB 1999.

McBride blends his own story with that of his white mother, who battled poverty and racism to raise 12 children in Queens.

McCormick, Patricia. *Sold.* Hyperion, 2006. OBCB 2009. (BBYA)

When 13-year-old Lakshmi is sold into prostitution by her gambling stepfather, she is taken from her village in the mountains of Nepal to a brothel in the slums of Calcutta.

Mehta, Ved. *Sound-Shadows of the New World.* Norton, 1985. OBCB 1999.

Leaving his family, country, and culture behind, a blind Indian 15-year-old boy travels to Arkansas in 1949 to attend a special school where he learns to walk without a cane, using the school's system of sounds and shadows.

Menzel, Peter, and Faith D'Aluisio. *Hungry Planet: What the World Eats.* Material World/Ten Speed Press, 2005. OBCB 2009.

Hungry Planet is a photo-chronicle of families around the world, the food they eat, and how uncontrollable forces like poverty, conflict, and globalization affect our most elemental human need—food.

Moody, Ann. *Coming of Age in Mississippi.* Dial Press, 1968. OBCB 1999.

Moody grew up in the rural South in the 1940s and '50s and became a heroine of the civil rights movement.

Mora, Pat. *House of Houses.* Beacon Press, 1997. OBCB 1999.
> With magic and imagination, author Pat Mora weaves the voices of her ancestors into her own personal account of growing up in a Mexican American family in El Paso, Texas.

Mortenson, Greg, and David Oliver Relin. *Three Cups of Tea: One Man's Mission to Promote Peace One School at a Time.* Viking, 2006. OBCB 2009.
> Lost and near death following an unsuccessful attempt to climb K2, Mortenson is nursed in a remote mountain village. Out of gratitude, he returns to build a school there. That project grew into the Central Asia Institute and the creation of over 50 schools in Pakistan and Afghanistan.

Picoult, Jodi. *Nineteen Minutes.* Atria, 2007. OBCB 2009.
> Seventeen-year-old Peter Houghton wakes up one day, loads his backpack with four guns, walks into the school cafeteria, and kills nine students and one teacher in the span of nineteen minutes.

Pipher, Mary. *The Middle of Everywhere: The World's Refugees Come to Our Town.* Harcourt, 2002. OBCB 2004, 2009.
> An exploration of the difficulties and struggles of refugees settled by the U.S. government in Lincoln, Nebraska, as they try to adjust and build a life in America.

Pipher, Mary. *Reviving Ophelia: Saving the Selves of Adolescent Girls.* Putnam, 1994. OBCB 1999.
> Pipher looks at societal "girl poisoning" and the emotional and psychological havoc it wreaks on the lives of young women.

Pope, Loren. *Colleges That Change Lives: 40 Schools That Will Change the Way You Think about Colleges.* Penguin, 2006. OBCB 2009.
> Pope portrays 41 colleges where the education rivals that of Ivy League universities in producing outstanding graduates.

Rodriguez, Luis. *Always Running: La Vida Loca, Gang Days in L.A.* Curbstone Press, 1993. OBCB 1999.
> Hoping to dissuade his son from the life, Rodriguez tells the story of his youth in a Los Angeles gang in the 1960s and '70s.

Rodriguez, Richard. *Hunger of Memory: The Education of Richard Rodriguez; An Autobiography.* D. R. Godine, 1982. OBCB 1999.
> Rodriguez is the son of Mexican immigrants whose journey through the educational system convinced him that family, culture, and language must be left behind to succeed in mainstream America.

Rogers, Elizabeth, and Thomas Kostigen. *The Green Book: The Everyday Guide to Saving the Planet One Simple Step at a Time.* Crown/Three Rivers Press, 2007. OBCB 2009.
> Celebrities contribute suggestions of small, everyday changes that will have a positive impact on the health of our planet.

Salzman, Mark. *True Notebooks.* Knopf, 2003. OBCB 2004. (Alex Award)
> When Salzman agreed to teach a writing class at Central Juvenile Hall in Los Angeles, he had no idea how moved he would be by the lives and eloquence of his students, all high-risk violent offenders.

Schlosser, Eric. *Fast Food Nation: The Dark Side of the All-American Meal.* Houghton Mifflin, 2001. OBCB 2004.

The growth of the fast food industry has changed America's eating habits and affected agriculture, the meatpacking industry, the minimum wage, and other aspects of American life.

Senna, Danzy. *Caucasia.* Riverhead, 1998. OBCB 2004. (Alex Award)

Separated when their parents' interracial marriage ends in divorce, light-skinned Birdie and her dark-skinned sister Cole lead very different lives while hoping for a reunion with one another.

Sheff, David. *Beautiful Boy: A Father's Journey through His Son's Addiction.* Houghton Mifflin Harcourt, 2008. OBCB 2009.

A father's anguished account of his 17-year-old son's meth addiction and its impact on the entire family is honest, raw, and full of information about the realities of drug addiction.

Sheff, Nic. *Tweak: Growing Up on Methamphetamines.* Simon & Schuster/Atheneum, 2008. OBCB 2009.

A wrenchingly honest account of life as a teenage meth addict, the companion book to *Beautiful Boy* by David Sheff, Nic's father.

Simon, David, and Edward Burns. *The Corner: A Year in the Life of an Inner-City Neighborhood.* Broadway Books, 1997. OBCB 1999.

Simon and Burns follow the McCullough family for a year, exposing life on the drug-filled streets of Baltimore.

Simon, Rachel. *Riding the Bus with My Sister: A True Life Journey.* Houghton Mifflin, 2002. OBCB 2004.

Rachel Simon begins to accompany her sister, who has mental retardation, on her days spent riding buses in the Pennsylvania city where she lives.

Smith, Jodi R. R. *From Clueless to Class Act: Manners for the Modern Man.* Sterling, 2006. OBCB 2009.

This witty guide to good behavior will help young men develop the style and panache to make a good impression in social and professional circles.

Smith, Zadie. *White Teeth.* Random House, 2000. OBCB 2004.

Archie and Samad, two unlikely friends, are brought together by bizarre twists of fate and near-death experiences in this epic, multiethnic novel of family, culture, love, and loss set in post–World War II London.

Steinberg, Jacques. *The Gatekeepers: Inside the Admissions Process of a Premier College.* Viking, 2002. OBCB 2004. (BBYA)

Who and what drives the college admissions cycle? Find out in a behind-the-scenes look at Wesleyan University through the eyes of an admissions officer, Ralph Figueroa, seeking members for the class of 2004.

Stern, Jessica. *Terror in the Name of God: Why Religious Militants Kill.* Ecco, 2003. OBCB 2009.

Seeking to understand how religious ardor leads to violence, Stern recounts her dramatic encounters with Christians, Jews, and Muslims who use terrorism in the name of God.

Turner, Sugar, and Tracy Bachrach Ehlers. *Sugar's Life in the Hood: The Story of a Former Welfare Mother.* University of Texas Press, 2002. OBCB 2004.

An anthropologist befriends a welfare mother and learns about her world and the strategies she uses to get off welfare and into college.

Urrea, Luis Alberto. *The Devil's Highway: A True Story.* Little, Brown, 2004. OBCB 2009.

Urrea details the 2001 attempt of 26 men to cross into the United States from Mexico, which only 12 survived. This is the human story of illegal immigration told with facts, anger, and poetry.

Wallis, David, ed. *Killed Cartoons: Casualties from the War on Free Expression.* Norton, 2007. OBCB 2009.

Wallis's book is full of political cartoons killed before publication, each accompanied by a brief narrative explaining why it was considered too controversial for publication.

Walls, Jeannette. *The Glass Castle: A Memoir.* Simon & Schuster/Scribner, 2005. OBCB 2009. (Alex Award)

Walls grew up in chaos and poverty with a family that prized freedom and unconventionality over comfort and safety, eventually making them homeless.

Wheelan, Charles. *Naked Economics: Undressing the Dismal Science.* Norton, 2002. OBCB 2004, 2009.

Without using charts, graphs, or jargon, Wheelan makes economics understandable, even interesting, as he demystifies basic concepts and applies them to everyday life.

Williams, Juan. *Eyes on the Prize: America's Civil Rights Years, 1954–1965.* Viking, 1987. OBCB 1999.

From *Brown v. Board of Education* to the Voting Rights Act, Williams outlines the social and political gains of African Americans, detailing the events of the civil rights movement.

Wright, Richard. *Black Boy: A Record of Childhood and Youth.* Harper, 1945. OBCB 1999.

Wright writes his autobiography as a novel, recalling his pre–World War II youth in the Jim Crow South, when racial and personal obstacles seemed insurmountable.

X, Malcolm with the assistance of Alex Haley. *The Autobiography of Malcolm X.* Grove Press, 1965. OBCB 1999.

A great and controversial Black Muslim figure relates his transformation from street hustler to religious and national leader.

APPENDIX

POLICIES AND PROCEDURES

CHARGE

To prepare a revised and updated edition of the Outstanding Books for the College Bound booklists every five years.

PURPOSE

To provide reading recommendations to students of all ages who plan to continue their education beyond high school.

AUDIENCE

The lists are primarily intended for students in grades 9–12 who wish to enrich and strengthen their knowledge of various subject areas in both classic and contemporary literature.

The lists can be used both by students wishing to round out their reading before entering college and by those taking college entrance examinations such as the ACT and SAT.

The lists can also be used by young adults and adults who are lifelong learners wishing to increase or update their knowledge of literature in areas covered by the lists.

COMMITTEE MEMBERS

The committee will consist of 15 members who are appointed by the YALSA Vice President/President-Elect for a two-year term beginning immediately after the conclusion of one Midwinter Meeting and ending at the conclusion of Midwinter two years later.

Ten members are required to attend both the Annual Conferences and the Midwinter Meetings during their term on this committee. As many as five members may be "virtual" members. The virtual members will be encouraged to attend the Annual Conferences and the Midwinter Meetings during their term of office, but are not required to do so. However, they must participate, along with the other committee members, electronically throughout their two-year term on a special electronic list. Therefore, access to the Internet is a requirement for all committee members.

CHAIR

The Chair will be appointed for a two-year term by the Vice President/President-Elect. While the primary role of the Chair is to facilitate the work of the committee, the Chair will have the right to participate in all committee activities. Access to the Internet and a willingness to communicate continuously and electronically with committee members are requirements for chairing the committee.

LIAISON

The Association of College and Research Libraries (ACRL) will appoint a liaison to serve as a consultant to work with this committee. The liaison will advise the committee on the reading of college students today, and will be available to comment on and react to selections of categories and titles.

COMMITTEE ORGANIZATION

The Chair will organize the committee in a way that will get the work done in the most efficient manner. The committee may operate as a committee of the whole or in subcommittees according to categories.

SELECTION CRITERIA

- Standard selection criteria consonant with the ALA Library Bill of Rights shall be applied.
- Although copyright is not a consideration, all titles should be widely available.
- Each category may have a special set of criteria.
- Books can be in print or out of print, in hardcover or paperback.
- Books that have appeared on earlier Outstanding Books lists or are available in revised editions are eligible.

CATEGORIES

The committee may select up to five (5) categories. The traditional categories for Outstanding Books are: The Arts, Biography, Fiction, and Nonfiction. Poetry has sometimes been a separate category, sometimes not. A Now/Current category was used for a time. Plays have been a subcategory of The Arts. There may be some variance in selected categories depending on the trends in society and in publishing. There may be subcategories, as well.

SUGGESTED SELECTION PROCEDURES

- Determine categories.
- Determine criteria, if needed, for selection in each category.
- Review titles in Outstanding Books for the College Bound: Choices for a Generation, ALA, 1996 to determine which titles should be reconsidered.
- Survey other lists of recommended books and look for titles that are recommended in several sources. The following sources may be helpful:

  Good Reading: A Guide for Serious Readers, Bowker, 1990.
  Books for You, latest ed., NCTE.
  Senior High School Library Catalog, latest ed., H. W. Wilson.
  Best Books for Young Adults: The Selection, the History, the Romance, ALA, 1994.
  Best Books for Young Adults, second edition, ALA, 2000.
  Fifty Years of Notable Books, Booklist Publications, 1996.
  Reading Lists for College Bound Students, third edition, Prentice-Hall, 2000.
  Recommended Reading: 5000 Classics Reviewed, Salem Press, 1995.
  New Lifetime Reading Plan, by Clifton Fadiman, HarperCollins, 1999.
  Bibliographies from specific subject areas.
  Current reviews and retrospective reviews.
  Annual lists of outstanding and notable books.

- Construct a working list of possible titles for study and reading.
- Select up to twenty-five (25) titles for each category.

VOTING PROCEDURES

The committee will determine its own voting procedure, however, most committees use a simple or a two-thirds majority for their final vote.

ANNOTATIONS

- Using "Procedures for Writing and Publishing Annotations" (YALSA Handbook, VII-4), determine bibliographic information needed and style required for annotations.
- Locate essential bibliographic information according to the "Procedures for Writing and Publishing Annotations" and verify author, title, and publisher's name.
- Write annotations that will appeal to young adults.

- The Chair must turn in to the YALSA staff by the end of the Midwinter Meeting a completed list of "Outstanding Books" by category, arranged alphabetically by author within each category in an electronic format.

TITLE AND AUTHOR INDEX

Page numbers in bold indicate annotated bibliographies.

You may also be interested in

YOUNG ADULTS DESERVE THE BEST
YALSA'S COMPETENCIES IN ACTION
Sarah Flowers for YALSA

As high school enrollment continues to rise, the need for effective librarianship serving young adults is greater than ever before. YALSA's Competencies outline areas of focus for providing quality library service in collaboration with teenagers. In this book, Flowers identifies and expands on these competency areas with success stories, how-tos, and additional resources.

PRINT ISBN: 978-0-8389-3587-3
eBOOK: 7400-5873
PRINT/eBOOK BUNDLE: 7700-5873
136 PAGES / 6" X 9"

QUICK AND POPULAR READS FOR TEENS
EDITED BY PAM SPENCER HOLLEY FOR YALSA
ISBN: 978-0-8389-3577-4

RISKY BUSINESS
LINDA W. BRAUN, HILLIAS J. MARTIN, AND CONNIE URQUHART FOR YALSA
ISBN: 978-0-8389-3596-5

MULTICULTURAL PROGRAMS FOR TWEENS AND TEENS
EDITED BY LINDA B. ALEXANDER AND NAHYUN KWON FOR YALSA
ISBN: 978-0-8389-3582-8

YOUNG ADULT LITERATURE: FROM ROMANCE TO REALISM
MICHAEL CART
ISBN: 978-0-8389-1045-0

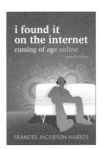

I FOUND IT ON THE INTERNET, 2E
FRANCES JACOBSON HARRIS
ISBN: 978-0-8389-1066-5

URBAN TEENS IN THE LIBRARY
EDITED BY DENISE E. AGOSTO AND SANDRA HUGHES-HASSELL
ISBN: 978-0-8389-1015-3